Ephraim Chamiel

To Know Torah

Dedicated to the memory of my father and teacher
Haim Yitzchak Chamiel z"l
And in Honor of my mother and teacher
Hava Chamiel (Hertz)

Table of Contents

Introduction   10
Preface   19

The Book of Genesis

Part one - The Beginning of the World and of Mankind

Parashat Bereshit

The Narratives of the Torah – Historical Truth, Myth or Message? 29; The Creation Narrative 34; The Garden of Eden Narrative – Historical Truth or Lesson? 38; The Cain and Abel Narrative – the First Murder and its Significance 47; The Second Failure 52

Parashat Noah

Noah, a Righteous Man 54; The Ark and the Deluge – the Destruction of Mankind and Noah's Salvation 58; After the Deluge – A New beginning 62; The Descendants of Noah – Archetypes of the New Mankind 64; The Generation of the Divide – the Danger of Uniformity and the Third Failure 68

Part two - Abraham

Parashat Lekh Lekha

The Divine Plan – Why was Abraham Chosen and What was his Mission? 71; Abraham in the Land of Israel 76; Abraham – the Man 78; Abraham and His Neighbors – Respect Him and Suspect Him 83; The Covenant between the Pieces – the Fear and the Hope 85; Our Brother Ishmael 87; The Circumcision and the Tidings 89

Parashat Vayera

Ethical Monotheism 91; Divine Conduct towards Man 96; Abraham and Abimelech – An Encounter between Cultures 101; Two 'Bindings' 104; The Binding – Attempts to Understand It 111

Parashat Hayyei Sarah

Acquiring land in the land of Israel – with humility or by force? 116; A Wife from the Family of Abraham – Ethical Purity 121; After Sarah's Death 128

Part three - Isaac
Parashat Toldot
The Blessing of Isaac – A Guided Drama 130; Before God – Rebecca's Mistake 138; The Blessing and the Flight 143; Isaac and Abimelech – Cultural Encounters in the Second Generation 146

Part four - Jacob
Parashat Vayetze
The Dream of the Ladder – The Dream and its Meaning 149; Jacob Raises a Family – Birth Pains of the Nation 156; The Clash between Jacob and Laban – Transformation from Naiveté 163

Parashat Vayishlah
Encountering Esau – the Characteristic of Faith and the Return of the Blessing 170; Lethal Zealotry 178; Balancing between Subservience and Zealotry 183

Part five – Joseph and his Brothers
Parashat Vayeshev
Do Dreams, in fact, Speak Lies? 187; The Selling of Joseph – Clashes of Leadership and Domination 192; Selected for Primogeniture 197; Joseph's Servitude in Egypt – a Spark Amongst the Shells 203

Parashat Miketz
Pharaoh's Dreams – Joseph's Opportunity 209; Joseph and his Brothers – Spy Stories 214; Joseph's Treatment of his Father and Brothers – the Psychological Aspect 221

Parsahat Vayigash
The Speech of Judah's Life 229; Salvation and Confession 233; Descent to Egypt and Settling there – a Symptom of the Exile 234; The Strengthening of Joseph 241

Parashat Vayehi
Jacob's Departure from Joseph – the Actualization of the Primogeniture 243; Jacob's Blessing to his Sons – Integration of Abilities 251; After Jacob's Death 254

List of Commentators 257

Introduction to the English Version

This book was originally published by Mendele in Hebrew in 2013. Ever since then, I have aspired to translate it into English. With the help of Academic Language Experts, in partnership with the CEO of the company, Avi Staiman, the idea began to take shape. They began translating the manuscript about a year ago, and have now completed it, in the most professional manner. It was proofread, but any remaining errors are, of course, my responsibility, and I would appreciate it if you would point them out to me. The production of the book was once again assigned to Mendele, under the dedicated leadership of Yaron Goldstein, thereby providing an edition for those wishing to read and study it in English. I hope that presenting this book to the English-speaking public will help increase its circulation and the transmission of the monotheistic ethical-educational message of the Torah, the greatest treasure of Jewish culture.

Ephraim Chamiel

July 2017, Jerusalem

Introduction

Commentary and homiletical exposition of the weekly Torah portion has always been a popular endeavor. Every Torah scholar, indeed every literate individual, reads the Bible in the spirit of his time, place and propensities; and all of these readings are appropriate and worthwhile, in the sense that there are seventy facets to the Torah. Personally, I am not a Bible scholar, my field of expertise is Jewish thought. Therefore, this book is not the product of academic research, but rather one of personal expression, which strives to reveal the intended meaning of the texts from the perspective of a modern scholar who believes in the sanctity of the Torah and is an observant Jew.

Toward this end, I adopted peshat (the plain sense) when interpreting the text- i.e. the primary interpretation of the text, along the lines of its meaning - and its ideas which are inherent to the text. In my reading of the text, I made every effort to avoid speculative interpretation; whether of a mystical-kabbalistic, philosophical-esoteric or midrashic nature. In my opinion, these do not represent the intent of the text, but rather the meaning which the person expounding it wishes to convey to those listening to or reading his commentary.

My reading relies on the modern and post-modern commentary, as well as that of the layers which preceded them. I selected from among all of these interpretations, those which I felt were consistent with the text's primary meaning, and wove them together to form one fabric. In the course of this research, it became clear to me the degree to which modern commentary is based on its predecessors throughout the generations. I came to understand that the Midrash sometimes presents us with that which contemporary commentators see as the primary meaning of the text; and consequently as the Torah's view regarding theology and ethics. Nonetheless, I want to emphasize that I view the rabbinical exegesis as but one legitimate interpretation of the Bible. In my opinion, the Sages did not generally intend to offer their opinion as to the primary meaning of the text. Rather, they wished to express their views with respect to fundamental issues or concerns relevant to their era or to institute new enactments or laws; and they interpreted the text in a manner that achieves these goals. Midrash aggadah has its own messages, which often have little in common with those of the Bible. Midrash Halakhah also altered the primary meaning of the text; whether in order to reconcile it with traditions that they had, or whether-based on an opposite impulse, one of innovation - for the worthy goal of changing values to conform to the cultural circumstances of the time. I accept the opinion of Ben Saruq, Maimonides and Luzzatto, that most of the halakhot in the Mishna and Talmud are not of Sinaitic origin, but rather are the invention of the Sages. According to Luzzatto, the Ibn Ezra also was of this opinion, but hid his real opinion behind a veil of apologetics. In the final analysis, a contemporary commentator, who observes the commandments and believes in the sanctity of the Bible, cannot evade the tension between the claims of scholarship and the literalists concerning the primary meaning of certain verses, and the meaning the Sages ascribed to those verses, upon which they established the Halakhah, which is sacrosanct in the eyes of that very commentator.[1]

This has been the difficulty facing observant, Jewish interpreters of the Bible in the modern age. Their exegesis, with its wide range

---

1. See Rashbam Genesis 37:2; Maimonides, Introduction to the Mishna, *Sefer Hamitzvot,* Shoresh one and two; Luzzatto, Introduction to *Hamishtadel* and the Introduction to his Commentary on the Torah.

of directions and ideologies, was guided by Moses Mendelsohn, in his *Bi'ur*, Yitzchak Samuel Reggio, S. D. Luzzatto, S. R. Hirsch, Yaakov Tzvi Mecklenburg, (Haketav Vehaqabbala), Malbim (Meir Leibush Malbim, Hatorah Vehamitzvah), Netziv (Naphtali Tzvi Berlin, Haamek Davar), M. D. Cassuto, M. Buber, A. J. Heschel, N. Leibowitz, Y. Leibowitz, Haim Yitzchak Chamiel, and others. They strove to understand both the primary meaning of the text and its implications for their era. They incorporated new scientific knowledge from the fields of archeology, history, psychology, literature, philology, grammar and hermeneutics in their commentaries. At the same time, it is inevitable that their personal perspectives also influenced their interpretations, whether consciously or not. Many medieval commentators, defined as literalists (being more or less minimalists), already trod this path: Saadia Gaon, Rashi, Rashbam, Ibn Ezra, Rivash (Yosef Bechor-Shor), David Kimhi, Hizkuni, Nahmanides, Ibn Caspi, Abravanel, and Sforno. Modern commentary is based on their interpretations, merely presenting them in more familiar language and context. It is rare to find actual innovation in contemporary interpretation of the peshat. Therefore, the uniqueness of this work is not to be found in the occasional innovative interpretations which it contains; but rather in its forging of a unified, easy to read and clear commentary out of selected interpretations spanning the generations, in the path of my predecessors, the modern observant commentators, and 'like a dwarf on the shoulder of giants.'

Similarly, I do not ignore Bible criticism's demonstrations that the Bible is composed of four main documents, and only received its current unified form in the fifth century BCE. I am also cognizant of the opinions of Bible critics (such as Yisrael Knohl and Alexander Rofe), and of contemporary archeologists who differ as to the historicity of the biblical narrative. I am aware of the possibility

Introduction

that the various biblical texts which were assembled by an editor are from different periods, and were brought to Canaan by various groups who migrated from sundry geographic locations, who had varying religious beliefs and cultic practices. I am also aware of the alternative approach, which holds that the Jewish people came from Haran and fought against Egypt in the Golan Heights; and that the narrative of the exodus was transferred to the south, and was consolidated at the time of Jerobam's division of the kingdom. According to radical interpreters of Maimonides, he thought that the Bible was not given to Moses by God; but rather Moses, our teacher, composed it as a result of his examination of nature, using his exalted abilities as a philosopher- prophet. The interpreters of Maimonides, Efodi and Narboni, went so far as to claim that he held the narrative of the Sinaitic revelation to be an allegory. Personally, I am drawn to the approach of Martin Buber, Moshe David Cassuto and Abraham Joshua Heschel who hold that the Bible was written after the era of Moses, based on early traditions which were popular among the people, and that it contains a kernel of historical truth. The essential point concerning these traditions is that the ideological message of ethical monotheism is divine, revealed by means of man and transmitted orally until it was codified, whether at once or in stages. It seems undeniable to me that the possibility certainly exists that the Bible is a compilation of several documents, which are the product of several authors who had different perspectives. However, the subject of this work is not the clarification of the origin of the texts or their historical accuracy, but rather the meaning that the text in its current formholds for the reader. To this end, there is no reason to assign excessive significance to the identification of the source or sources, and the identity of the author or authors and that of the editor or editors. Granted, contradictions and difficulties in the text may be resolved

Introduction

by means of breaking the text up into different source documents and varying traditions, or inserted texts and the like; however, I generally follow the approach of the traditional exegesis, which attempts to harmonize the text and thereby understand the intent of the author or editor. I briefly note the critical approach for the benefit of the enlightened reader where I deem appropriate, or in the footnotes. However, for the purpose of this book, the key questions are: What did the author of the text before us intend in the context of his time and place, the surrounding internal influences- the culture in which he lived- as well as the external influences? What did he want to teach the reader who was his contemporary? What in the text before us is relevant to us? Of course, I am aware that it is impossible to be certain of the author's intent; it is only possible to attempt to approach it. This is true both because of the historical and intellectual gap and the difference in mindset between the author and the commentator; and because of the realization that all commentators, including this writer, inevitably inject their own understanding and that of their school into the commentary. Like any commentator, I seek out my own spiritual world in the text, consciously and certainly unconsciously; that is to say, that of a modern scholar who is an observant Jew.[2]

In my opinion, the resolution to the tension between 'modern' and 'observant', that is to say, between the results of academic research and belief in the sanctity of the Bible, is to be found in Luzzatto's 'dual truth'. This approach establishes an unresolvable dialectic

---

2. Concerning the tension between the conclusions of the literalists and academic scholarship on the one hand, and the Halakhic interpretation on the other, cf. Uriel Simon, 'Mashmautam Hadatit Shel HaPeshatot Hamithadshim' pages 133-152 in *Hamiqra Veanachnu* (Tel Aviv: Dvir, 1979); Yeshayahu Maori, keitzad Nityaches Lmidrashei Hazal Behoraat Hamiqra Beveyt Hasefer Hadati' pages 209-219, ibid; Sara Japhet, *Dor Dor Uparashanav* (Jerusalem: Bialik, 2008), 35-54.

Introduction

tension between two truths; a cosmic rift between **the scientific truth,** that the human intellect discerns with respect to the text's sources, which were humanly authored (although Luzzatto denies this point); and **the religious truth,** which was established by the Sages (as the transmitters of the Sinaitic tradition, or by means of their genius and inspiration ascribed to them by Luzzatto). This rift can only be fused in the divine realm, not the human. Man must live with this dual truth. According to Luzzatto, it is incumbent on him to investigate the text as far as his intellect allows, while following the Halakhah as established by the Sages, who established the awesome narrative of the nation, and its children's shared experience.[3]

Finally, I would stress that the commentary which I present is my suggested formulation of the Torah's view on many matters. Whereas my commentary is based on modern scholarship, it attempts to avoid expressing modern ideas and opinions, including my own. That said, the biblical ethic and thought is much more compatible with modern sensibilities than we tend to think.

The original kernel of this work is the brief lecture series on the portion of the week which I composed for myself and taught

---

3. Regarding the approach which I am advocating, cf. Luzzatto,, Intro to *Hamishtadel* (Vienna, 1847); Meir Weiss, Besod Siach Hamiqra Miqtzat Derakhav Shel Buber Beparashanut Hamiqra, pages 15-16 Intro to Buber, *Darkho Shel Miqra* (Jerusalem: Bialik, 1964); F. Rosenzweig, *Naharaim*, 32-33; Moshe Greenberg, 'Cheqer Hamiqra Vehametziut Hayisraelit,' pages 70-85 in *Hamiqra Veanachnu*. With respect to the relationship between the commentator and the text, cf. Moshe Halbertal, *Mahapechot Parashaniot Behithavutan* (Jerusalem: Magnes, 1999), 39-40, 181-197; Gili Zivan, *Dat Lelo Ashlaya* (Jerusalem: Shalom Hartman Institute, 2005), 42-45, 221-224. Concerning Maimonides' opinion with respect to the origin of the Torah, cf. Moshe Halbertal, *Maimonides: Life and Thought* (Princeton and Woodstock, 2007), 328-329 ;328-329 Micah Goodman, *Secrets of "The Guide for the Perplexed,"* Philadelphia, 2015), 107-113.

in the synagogue over the course of forty years, primarily in the communities of Judah Halevi and Renanim in Jerusalem. It also incorporates insights which I heard or read during that period of time. I particularly wish to note the integrative-immanent interpretations of my father and teacher, Dr. Haim Yitzchak Chamiel, of blessed memory; who, together with his beloved wife, my mother, Hava (Hertz), 'may her light shine', instilled in me a love for the Torah and its study. This book is dedicated to them. Ever since I was old enough, I absorbed my father's teaching regarding the portion of the week at the Sabbath table, in his lectures and lessons, articles and books (*Maaynei Miqra* and *Limudim BeFarashat HaShavua*).

Two modern commentaries have a central place in this work:

(A) The commentary of Rabbi S.R. Hirsch on the Torah. While this commentary is strongly connected to the interpretations of the Sages, particularly to the halakhic Midrash, and saturated with fundamentalist pathos; the modern ideas which are embedded in it - many of which express, in my opinion, the depths of the peshat - are extremely significant and have been adopted by Modern-Orthodoxy to this day.

(B) The commentary of Luzzatto on the Torah. This outstanding commentary, which follows the peshat, is a guide to the primary reading of the text.

In addition, I heard and internalized many Torah lessons from many sources, including: My teachers in Midrashiat Noam and Yeshivat Kerem B'Yavne, my colleagues in the synagogues of Judah Halevi and Renanim in Jerusalem, Rabbis Maurice Lamm and Abner Weiss in Congregation Beth Jacob in Los Angeles, R. Leor Broh in Congregation Mizrachi in Melbourne, Rabbi Benny Lau in Congregation Ramban in Jerusalem, whose lectures later were consolidated in his book, *Etnachta*, as well as various teachers of the class on the portion of the week in the synagogue Ohel Nechama.

Introduction

Steve Bailey of Los Angeles introduced me to the depths of Rabbi S.R. Hirsch's commentary and initiated my interest in it by means of the weekly lessons held in his home during the 1980s. Additional sources include the articles in *Hatzofeh* and *Mekor Rishon* as well as radio and television programs on the various stations on the weekly portion (by Benny Lau, Dov Elbaum, Micah Goodman and others). I also gained knowledge from various weekly portion sheets which are distributed in synagogues, especially *Shabbat B'Shabbato, Shabbat Shalom* and Bar Ilan's weekly sheet.

Nechama Leibowitz's work, *Studies in the Books of the Pentateuch*, was extremely helpful to me. My father, of blessed memory, was the driving force behind the dissemination of her teachings. Yeshayahu Leibowitz's books, *Hearot Leparashiyot Hashavua* and *Sheva Shanim Shel Sihot Al Parashat Hashavua*, provided me with my first encounter with commentary which was liberated from the ideology which holds that there is a divine plan for the world embedded in the holy writings, although I do not accept this interpretation as the biblical perspective. I also benefited from Yehuda Nachshoni's *Studies in the Weekly Parashah*, which is a treasure chest of commentaries of varying perspectives. These four works collect much varied exegetical material, and contain excellent discussions relating to the topics found in each portion. The modern reader who wishes to understand the historical-philological position of the biblical scholarship will find references to *Olam Hatanakh*, edited by Menahem Haran, Alexander Rofe's *Mavo Lesifrut Hamiqra* and Yisrael Knohl's *Meayin Banu* in the footnotes of the book. These books also clarify the relationship between the Bible and traditions and narratives of the ancient nations of the region. "In order to bring redemption to the world," I attempted to attribute the interpretations which I chose to present in this book. It was simple to reference the central commentaries, both

Introduction

medieval and modern. However, other sources, which I mentioned here, among others, are jumbled in my consciousness and it was difficult to reference them. I offer my apologies to the authors of these sources.

I arrived at the decision to write this book during the course of my doctoral work, which dealt with the religious responses to modernity in the philosophy of Z. H. Chajes, S. R. Hirsch and S. D. Luzzatto. That work was published in 2011 by Carmel as *"Haderekh Hamemutzaat" Reshit Tzmikhat Hadatiyut Hamodernit,* and in English by Academic Studies Press in 2014 as *"The Middle Way" The Emergence of Modern-Religious Trends in Nineteenth-Century Judaism.* That research compelled me to delve into modern biblical interpretation, and instilled in me the drive to make the teachings of Luzzatto and Hirsch, who are among the central pillars of this interpretation, available to the general public. In order to ensure that the reader understand the text which the commentary relates to, namely the biblical text itself, and in light of the fact that biblical Hebrew had become further and further removed from spoken Hebrew, I saw fit to attempt to briefly convey the sense of the text and to direct him/her to learn the text and attempt to delve into the commentaries which I refer to in the notes throughout the book. These references are mainly to those interpretations which I selected, but the notes also reference worthy alternatives. Sometimes they also refer to, for the sake of comparison, interpretations which I rejected. The reader who examines the works referred to in depth will acquire a broad view regarding the perspective of the Bible and its commentaries with respect to whatever topic interests him or poses a difficulty for him in the portion; and will assist him in preparing a lesson or 'Devar Torah' suitable for his particular audience. I pray that this work will contribute to the growth of the study of Torah, the greatest asset of the Jewish nation, and to its glorification.

Preface

Even those who favor a later date for the composition of the Torah agree that the Pentateuch, in its present form, is over 2,500 years old; and that the process of its composition began in the tenth century BCE. For thousands of years people of monotheistic faiths lived with the awareness that these texts originated from a real historical event of divine revelation which occurred following the exodus of the Jewish people from Egypt (dated between the 15th and 13th centuries BCE). The sole question which they dealt with in this regard was whether Moses heard the generalizations along with the details from God and wrote them down during the forty days which he spent on the mountain, such that he descended the mountain holding one scroll which contained the entire Torah; or whether he only heard the generalizations at Sinai and wrote the Torah (on the mountain and throughout the journey) as separate scrolls, which he gave the nation in accordance with the events that occurred in the desert and the details which were given to him by God, or only at the completion of the journey.

Either way, the basic belief that the Torah was given by the Almighty was the basis for the claim that it, the Torah, concealed within it mystical-kabbalistic or philosophical secrets, which only the initiated could uncover. Therefore, alongside the mainstream of commentary, there existed two other streams: The first, the philosophical, based on the thought of Maimonides, interpreted the Bible as an allegory for philosophical ideas concerning the nature of the divine and as a guide to the path of study which a person ought to be devoted to. The miracles were for the most part portrayed as dreams. The second stream, the kabbalistic, interpreted the Bible, including the miracles described therein, as symbols for mystical concepts regarding the various strata of the divine realm, and as a guide to its perfection by means of the human theurgy, i.e. through the fulfillment of the commandments.

This acceptance of God's having given Moses the Torah at Sinai lasted in Judaism almost without anyone contesting it (with the possible exception of Maimonides, and excluding some of his disciples) until the beginning of the nineteenth century, the very heart of the modern era. Approximately 150 years earlier, in the mid-seventeenth century, modern Bible criticism, which viewed the Torah as a human creation, commenced.[4] The most profound and systematic of the early Bible critics was actually the excommunicated Jew, Baruch Spinoza, in his book *Tractatus Theologico-Politicus*. Biblical criticism, which is based on scientific-philological research, was begun by Christian scholars in the eighteenth century. In the course of the criticism, the scientific position coalesced which held that the Torah is the product of editing which took place long after the time of Moses, and integrated ancient fragments in its possession. These fragments were composed by

---

4. The term 'criticism' is not used here in the negative sense, but rather in the sense of 'inquiry, analysis and clarification.' The term is used this way, for example, by the philosopher Immanuel Kant in the titles of his books, *Critique of Pure Reason, Critique of Practical Reason, Critique of the Power of Judgment*. The conclusions of the critique may negate opinions or actions which the critique deals with. Some attribute the beginnings of Bible criticism to medieval Moslem scholars. This position is prominent in the writings of Hava Lazarus-Yafeh. It says in the Koran itself that the Bible, in its current form, is distorted, or was edited to conceal the prophecies ascribed to Mohamed. There are many who note the blossoming of Bible criticism in Thomas Hobbes' *Leviathan* (ch. 33) in 1651. Nonetheless, these critiques are of an entirely different sort than that of the modern criticism beginning with Spinoza, this criticism being philological-historical on a scientific basis.

various authors, and reflected different theological and social outlooks. These were intelligently and expertly joined together, without substantial differences in their content, out of recognition of their antiquity and sanctity.

At the end of the eighteenth century, Moses Mendelsohn and the *maskilim* forged a path for the Jews to break out of their spiritual ghetto. Already before this, secularization, acculturation and emancipation had spread in many areas of Europe; and had begun to seep beneath the religious and social foundations of the community's ancient form. All of this caused Bible criticism to spread among the Jews as well, and to find its way into their hearts. The Reform movement, which set out to correct Judaism, its beliefs and commandments, in order to fit in with the changing European culture, adopted Bible criticism. They believed that if the source of the Torah is human rather than divine, then it is possible to correct many of its norms, which are antiquated and contrary to reason, and to present to the world the eternal values which Judaism has imparted to mankind, i.e. ethical monotheism, whose light the Jews are uniquely qualified to use to lead the world to its redemption.

The Torah is primarily a book of laws, supported by a powerful ethical code. Modern commentators greatly emphasize the ethical dimension of the Torah, which, in their opinion, is the focus of the stories of the patriarchs. These narratives, which predate the giving of the commandments, point to the natural ethics which the family of Abraham adopted for themselves, as a result of which they merited a direct connection with God. However, this sort of commentary does not portray Abraham and his descendants as perfect individuals, nor as mythological characters, but rather as flesh and blood. The ethics of Abraham is built on monotheism and universalism, and this was the foundation of the commandments - and of the revelation which contained the given commandments -

which were given to the nation that grew out of this family.

The biblical narrative takes place along the axis of creation – revelation – redemption, and reflects desirable relationships, as opposed to undesirable ones, between man and God and between man and his fellow man and nature. Perhaps surprisingly, and perhaps not, the Torah does not contain lengthy discussions regarding the three constitutive events on the axis. The main discussion in the Torah concerns the path which man took from the creation to revelation, and the path which he needs to take from revelation to redemption; how must he conduct himself in order to merit redemption. Some of the commentators throughout the generations attempted to fill this lacuna, and to pour more content into the creation narrative, the revelation at Sinai and the end of days. However, other classical commentators concentrated on interpreting the narratives of the Torah, and on giving rational explanations for the commandments and their significance. Modern exegesis follows this latter approach. It deals with the Torah as a guide to the here and now for the Jewish people and through them for all of mankind, in an attempt to give an aspect of divine holiness to man's daily conduct in the world, and to establish a society which fulfills the ideals of justice, equality, human rights and mutual assistance; to bring paradise to our world and to minimize the importance of involvement with supernatural utopian Messianism, relating to the end of history, the world to come, or the divine structure and influence on it (see Hirsch Genesis 2: 7-9; *Iggrot Zafun* no. 2).

Judaism of the nineteenth century was characterized by stormy ideological clashes. Those faithful to tradition denounced the leaders and thinkers of the Reform movement as traitors, fawning toward the educated and the Christian establishment, rebellious and honor seeking, who were endangering the continuity of the nation; for according to the traditionalists, the Jewish nation can only exist based on belief in a complete Torah given at Sinai, and the fulfillment of its commandments. The historical consciousness developed in the camp of the innovators, which placed Bible criticism as a foundation, and this led to criticism of the Halakhah. Those who wished to modify the religion, both the Reform and the Conservative, opposed Orthodoxy, which viewed the Torah and the Halakhah as an eternal, super-historical phenomenon. The Reform viewed both the written Torah and the oral Torah as evolving phenomena; and in some instances they presented the Sages as power-hungry and manipulative characters; whereas, the early Conservative (who belonged to the Positive-Historical School) tended to accept the written Torah as divine, but held that the oral Torah reflected human innovation, and was the product of Sages who were spiritual giants and understood the needs of their generation very well.

Simultaneous with these clashes, the documentary hypothesis, which views the Torah as a collation of fragments ('documents') from various sources, was enhanced by means of the advances of modern science using laboratory experimentation and philological-historical research tools. This development intensified the objections to the Bible as a historical narrative, regarding the historical truth of the events described in it, and it presented the traditional commentators with severe challenges. The main stream of biblical commentary, the Orthodox, struggled to retain its naive faith that it is possible to limit the validity of the scientific statements or emphasize its evanescence where it contradicted that which was stated in the Bible, or to interpret the text such that it conforms to reason. It is true that scholars and commentators have established, based on newer discoveries of ancient documents and archeological finds that the narratives of the Bible are generally consistent with

Preface

the periods that they describe, and contain a kernel of historical truth. Nonetheless, the dispute regarding this, and the documentary hypothesis, remains in place.[5] In any case, it is difficult to accept

---

5. Cf. Julius Wellhausen, *Akdamot L'divrei Y'mei Yisrael* (photoprint, Jerusalem 1978); Y. *Kaufman, Toldot Haemunah Hayisraelit Vol.1 Book 1* (Tel Aviv, 1937), 26-27, 31. According to them, the documents which comprise the Torah were written between the ninth and fifth BCE. Martin Buber, *Darko Shel Miqra*, 65-67, 310-311, 318-320; idem *Moses*, 6; F. Rosenzweig, *Naharaim*, 26-27, 31. In their opinion, throughout ancient generations until the days of Solomon, various editors worked on its ongoing composition; initially based on oral traditions which were later written down and then expanded on, while preserving its uniformity. According to M. D. Cassuto, *MeAdam ad Noah* (Jerusalem: 1953), 1-5, idem, *MeNoah ad avraham* (Jerusalem, 1959), 203-205, idem, *Torat Hateudot Vesiduram Shel Sifrei Hatorah* (Jerusalem: 1959), 83-86; idem, *Sefer Bereshit Umivnehu* (Jerusalem: 1990), 329-333, the Torah was authored as one unit, not before the end of the monarchy of David, by a single genius, based on ancient literary and poetical traditions which were known orally within the Jewish nation and its sages, rather than based on documents. See the critique of Cassuto's approach in 'MeAdam ad Noah' by Y. Kaufman in his book, *Mikivshona Shel Hayetzira Hamiqrait* (Tel Aviv: 1966). Also, cf. A. Rofe, *Mavo Lesifrut Hamiqra* (Jerusalem, 2006), 21-117, in which he summarizes the various opinions including that of Cassuto and his critique of it. He details the latest developments in the biblical research, including innovative opinions concerning the approach to the history of traditions, and suggests (113-117) a revised position, according to which the composition of the Torah spanned the period from the twelfth century through the fourth century BCE. Also, cf. *Olam Hatanach Bereshit* (Tel Aviv, 1993), 89-91; Y. Knohl, *Meayin Banu* (Ohr Yehuda, 2008), 11-18; L. Ravid, *Hatanach Hayah Beemet* (Tel Aviv, 2009); Y. Meitelis, *Lahpor Et Hatanach*, 115-131. For an overview of biblical criticism from Spinoza until the modern age, cf. Ephraim Chamiel, *"The Middle Way" The Emergence of Modern-Religious Trends in Nineteenth-Century Judaism* (Academic Studies Press, 2014), ch.1. According to scholars, the Torah is composed of the following primary sources: the book of Hashem (the kingdom of Judah) and the book of Elohim (the kingdom of Israel) - which were added gradually between the 12th and the 8th centuries BCE, the book of Deuteronomy - 7th century

that the narrative in Genesis is actually the personal story of the first human, that the cosmology described in the creation narrative is scientific fact and that the biblical dating of events reflects historical precision. On the other hand, Maimonides' unique view on the creation narrative sounds speculative, and apparently reflects his world and not that of the Bible; and the kabbalistic-mystical exegesis is not acceptable to the rational mind. Therefore, the mainstream modern exegesis maintains that the Bible, whatever its origin, is intended to educate man and to guide him/her to reach ethical and theological perfection, resulting from free will, rather than to provide scientific and historical truth. Modern commentary sought a masterplan in the Bible, built in stages, for educating man toward ethical freedom, i.e. toward an ethics that is rooted in free will and is integrated with attachment to God, with the objective of redeeming all of humanity, and not just the Jewish people. Modern exegesis's universalism is one of the distinctions between it and the educational perspective of the philosophical commentary as formulated by Maimonides.

In the twentieth century, the storm of dispute between the traditionalists and the innovators, which shook the nation and even tore it apart into different trends hostile to each other and divided by both belief and communal frameworks, died down. The dispute continued and was carried on exclusively in scholarly circles. The Jewish people faced total obliteration, and they united in the mission of physical existence and survival. Before and after World War Two, the ideological trends developed, primarily in the United

---

BCE, the Priestly and Holiness code (priestly sect of the temples) - written between the 6th and 5th centuries BCE. The priestly code re-edited the books of Hashem and Elohim. The Pentateuch was completed between the 5th and the 4th centuries BCE. In recent times it has been demonstrated, by means of a sophisticated computer program, that there is a clear distinction between the Priestly source and the others.

States and Israel, in open, liberal and capitalistic societies. Among the traditional scholars, who wrestled with the documentary hypothesis of the Bible critics and who maintained the unity of the Torah, two camps stood out. The first camp included two approaches. Martin Buber, father of the method of objectives, held that the Torah was composed by a number of authors over the course of generations: Originally this was oral, and then it continued in a written kernel, which was expanded by authors who maintained its unity. The second approach is Moses David Cassutto's theory of traditions. He held that one genius composed the Torah, based on oral traditions. By contrast, in the other camp there was Rabbi Joseph B. Soloveitchik, of the dialectic theory, which we will clarify below; and Rabbi Mordecai Breuer, of the theory of aspects (or, in contemporary parlance, viewpoints), who continued his path, and held that God instilled in His Torah from the start different and even contradictory ideologies, in order to teach us about the diversity which exists in His world and within ourselves. Breuer raised the possibility that the divine author deliberately created a text, which appears as if it were put together by authors having divergent views, who present different divine behaviors, a world and mankind which are diverse. By means of proper synthesis, these texts reach perfection and harmony.[6]

In the mid-twentieth century, the post-modern era began. As usual in the case of transitions between eras, the majority of the innovators in the range of fields of research and thought and their audiences, as well as the general public, were unaware of the first influences of the new era. The generation's Modern-Orthodox thinkers were indeed influenced by the academic world,

---

6. M. Breuer, "Emunah Umada Beparashanut Hamiqra," *Deot* 11(1960), 18-25 and 12 (1960), 12-27; *Pirkei Moadot* (Jerusalem, 1986), 11-22; *Pirkei Bereshit* (Alon Shvut, 1999), 82-122.

and post-modernism came into existence there, before it spread to the general public. However, they were not always aware of the thought of post-modernism's meaning and implications. The post-modern philosophers asserted that there was no room for searching for one comprehensive truth regarding the meaning of human existence – a search which runs like a scarlet thread through the history of civilizations, each in its own way. Post-modern thought asserts that each nation, each society, each group which maintains any ideology of any sort, has a narrative which it adopted for itself – a faith narrative of revelation, or a secular equivalent (such as that of Marxism) – which defines its norms of behavior and their aspirations for the future. According to this view, historical events have no religious significance, there is no ultimate narrative which humanity strives for based on some sort of divine guidance, and there is no one narrative which is truer than another. In post-modernist circles there exists a liberal-skeptical pluralism in which each group develops its own discourse; and recognizes that it does not have a monopoly on the truth. The most sacred texts are the product of a particular narrative, and reflect the world of those who produced them. The interpretation of these texts takes place within the dialogue between the world of the author and that of the reader-commentator. These opinions took hold among the general public in the end of the twentieth century and continue to spread more and more in the Jewish world. As such, new dilemmas face the biblical commentator who has internalized these new views, at least partially, and is uncertain how to incorporate the new skeptical consciousness into the belief that the text of the Torah before him reflects the true revelation, and the norms contained in this text embody the correct and pure ethic – belief that the divine masterplan for human history is built upon the Torah, its ethic and its bearers, the Jewish nation. He must continue to act with a consciousness replete with modesty and humility, that there are other beliefs and opinions, perhaps parallel to each other, and their truth is not inferior to his truth for those who maintain it, and that he should, therefore, aspire to a fruitful dialogue with them, despite the differences in the discourse.[7]

The post-modern commentary, unlike that of the modern, does not attempt to harmonize the scientific approach with that of traditional faith. The sources of the text and its unity, and the nature of the historical and scientific knowledge contained in it, are less important to this commentary than is the ideological message of the text, and the experience it creates for the individual and the community who adopted it as their narrative. This commentary examines the human-psychological aspects in the biblical narrative, aspects which find expression in the character of the people in those stories. The Jewish post-modern commentators seek out the redemption of the individual and his community from within their narrative, rather than seeking a universal solution for all of mankind.

---

7. For a philosopher's perspective on religiosity in the post-modern age, cf. Gili Zivan, *Dat Lelo Ashlaya* (Jerusalem, 2006), especially part.1, ch.5 and part.2, ch. 1, 3-7. For a historian's perspective on post-modernism and the mutual critique between it and modernism, cf. Yoav Gelber *Historia, Zikaron Vetaamula* (Tel Aviv, 2007), 104-157.

The Book of Genesis

Part one - the Beginning of the World and of Mankind

Parshat Bereshit
The Narratives of the Torah – Historical Truth, Myth or Message?

The act of creation and the formation of man is related exceedingly briefly in our parasha, in two descriptions which contradict each other in terms of significant details. The first – from chapter 1 verse 1 through chapter 2 verse 3, and the second – from chapter 2 verse 4 through chapter 3 verse 24. This is one of the primary difficulties for the traditional exegesis.[1] A further fundamental difficulty is the fact that the biblical cosmology is in conflict with the accepted scientific cosmology.

Biblical criticism approaches the contradictions between the two creation narratives from the stance that every text is of human origin and reflects the world of its author. The undertaking of

---

1. Concerning the repetition and contradictions in the Pentateuch, cf. Rofe, *Mavo Lesifrut Hamiqra*, 26-32. For Cassuto's position cf. Cassuto, *Torat Hateudot*, 61, *MeAdam ad Noah*, 45. For examples of harmonization of the two sources cf. Netziv's, *Haamek Davar*, Gen.2:4; Buber, *Darkho Shel Miqra*, (Jerusalem: Bialik, 1964), 54, 68; F. Rosenzweig, *Naharaim*, 27; Joseph B. Soloveitchik, *Lonely Man of Faith* (Jerusalem, 5738); the criticism and exegesis of D. Hartman, *Mesinai Lezion*, and the position of M. Fisch, "Mishnayim L'Echad Ubechazara: Sipurei Habriah Veanthropologiat Habrit," 659- 694 in D. Hartman, *Mechuyavut Yehudit Mitchadeshet* (Tel Aviv, 5761), from which I made use of several principles both here and in *Vayakhel-Pekudei*. Apropos to this context I will reiterate what I wrote above concerning Rav Mordecai Breuer, whose theory of aspects utilizes Rav Soloveitchik's approach to the Torah throughout the Pentateuch.

criticism was conducted based on this stance, proposing that the Bible is a blend combination of assembled documents written by ancient authors, each according to his tradition and worldview.[2] According to Bible critics, the two narratives before us come from two different and irreconcilable sources, each of which reflects its own ideological, theological and cosmological world. Others, who are more traditional, attempt to deal with this conclusion of the research. Cassuto asserts that when the Torah was written (by one person), two basic traditions existed in the nation concerning the creation of the world and of man: one had its origins in wisdom literature, and the other, in popular circles, and the Torah cited both after reworking them, for the edification of the generations.

Others, including Rav Soloveitchik, suggest another explanation which suits the traditional exegesis. They hold that the Torah is divine and unified; however, by means of its presentation using two separate narratives, it deliberately speaks of two prototypes of man:

In the first, Adam is presented as a romantic creature, a being of nature who is subservient, passive and obedient; who was created last in the creation in order to rule over it and conduct it in the name of his dispatcher, the Creator.

By contrast, Adam is presented in the second narrative as a rationalist functionary who is active, assertive, rebellious and conquering. In this narrative, Adam is created first, and after the creation of vegetation and animals, he is ensconced in the Garden of Eden to work and guard it (2:15). While Adam's body was formed from the earth, God blew his *ruah* (his soul according to the Ramban, his breath according to Sforno) into him. Therefore, he alone among the creatures is a composite of both physical matter and divine spirit. Adam names the animals, as one who is their

---
2. Cf. nt. 5 in the foreword to this book.

parashat Bereshit

master, and as an independent individual who acts based on his intellect, and was not satisfied until Eve (as he chose to refer to her) was offered to him as a mate.

The male and female are an additional pair of prototypes. In the first source, the female is presented as being created alongside the male in the divine image with absolute equality, the two of them being called Adam (1:27; 5:2);[3] whereas in the second source she is presented as inferior, since she was created from the *tzela* (the side) of the male, who alone is referred to as Adam. From then on, when a man marries a woman, it is as if his *tzela* is returned to him, and the two of them are transformed into psychological and emotion completeness ("one flesh" – 2:21-25); to the degree that a man prefers his attachment to his wife over his relationship with his parents and other relatives. This is in contrast to other animals, most of whom are not faithful to each other.[4] The woman is presented in this narrative as easily tempted, a temptress and as one who was sentenced to be subjugated to the male.

Rav Soloveitchik explains that these two prototypes of man represent human characteristics and traits which find expression throughout the Bible. These characteristics and traits are not only expressed in the biblical narratives, but also in each and every one of us. The Torah wishes to teach us that God instilled them in every

---

3. Compare S. R. Hirsch, 1:27. Cf. also Rashi 1:27; Nachmanides 2:18 based on Midrash *Bereshit Rabbah* 8:1; BT Berakhot 61a and Zohar Bamidbar 117a, according to which Adam was created as a male and female connected to each other at the back, and subsequently divided; a Midrash which amplifies the message of equality between them.

4. Regarding translating *tzela* as 'side' cf. Rashi 2:21, based on Bereshit Rabbah ad loc. 17:6 and *Vayikra Rabbah* 14:1. Regarding man's commitment to his mate in contrast to animal behavior, cf. Nachmanides and Luzzatto 2:24. Note that in this narrative the Torah ignores the fact that the woman also remains faithful to her husband. Cf. the discussion on the status of women in the Bible ahead in Parashat Naso.

person, and that a dialectic occurs between them within every person. Above and beyond this psychological lesson, we need to learn theological and ethical principles contained in the Torah, beginning with the radical monotheistic principle, according to which the world was created by one God, who is responsible for all of the contrasts in the world – good and evil, darkness and light, heaven and earth – as He was the one who brought them about and distinguished between them. We need to recognize God's transcendence (God is not nature), His free will by means of which He created the world, and His absolute control of the laws of nature which He created, and of human history. We need to be aware of our obligation to recognize the gift of life which we have received, and to attempt to understand the purpose for which we have been granted it, and how we are obligated to show gratitude to our creator. We need to learn about the nothingness of man, and at the same time of his greatness; and at the same time, about God's transcendence, and simultaneously, His closeness to us. We must learn about the divine unity, and by means of it – about the unity of mankind in all of its diversity, about love and respect toward one's fellow man, who – like us – is created in the divine image, and thereby about the value of pluralism. Indeed, already in parashat Bereshit the Torah presents to us the personal and social aspects of the principles of ethical monotheism contained in the biblical religion. These principles will be developed and clarified later on, both as lessons derived from the narrative sections of the Torah, as well as explanations for commandments and laws which it demands that we observe.

In terms of the problem of the relationship between the cosmology of the creation narrative and that of science: The exegesis associated with the mainstream, which maintains the divine origin of the Torah, holds that the Torah's cosmology is not meant to be consistent with modern scientific knowledge. According to this approach, the Torah aims at teaching us theology and ethics, rather than history and natural sciences. Indeed, the scientific truth is known to God, but the author (or authors) of the first creation narrative saw fit to formulate this knowledge in "the language of man" of ancient times. Therefore, the contemporary scientific truth is not relevant to the biblical cosmology and historiography: That truth is incapable of judging the presentation of the earth as the epicenter of creation, rather than as an insignificant planet somewhere in the Milky Way; the description of the firmament (raqia) as a partition dividing between the water above it, containing the stores from which God brings down rain for us, and the water of the oceans; the description of the *kochavim* – whether we view them as fixed stars or as planets in the solar system – as being smaller than the sun and moon; all of these are descriptive statements rather than judgmental ones, as they relate to topics which are not within the Torah's purview. These and similar descriptions ("Stand still, O sun, at Gibeon" in the book of Joshua) suit the cosmology which the civilizations at the time when the Torah was given believed in, and the direct experience of even contemporary people: Indeed, we speak about the sun rising and setting despite the fact that every child today knows that it is the earth which rotates around the sun. According to this exegetical approach, the Torah did not intend to reveal scientific matters which people were not capable of understanding. Rather, it was written anticipating from the outset the development of man's knowledge, which would eventually reveal the truth regarding the universe and its creation, this also being its objective.[5] The dating in the Torah was also not given for

---

5. Cf. Luzzatto on Parashiyot Bereshit and Noah (1:4, 6, 26; 8:21), A. Y. H. Kook, *Eder Hayakar*, 37-38. Compare with Cassuto, *MeAdam ad Noah*, 17-18, 208-209. Cf. U. Simon, *Bakesh Shalom Verodfehu* (Tel Aviv, 2002), 282-285.

the purpose of historical precision, but rather to lend perspective to the history of the world and mankind, and it does not contradict the scientific dating of the theory of evolution, for example. The Torah wishes to present the essential act of divine creation *ex nihilo* at a specific moment and its stages, including Adam and his progeny. It conveys this in a fashion which is clear and simple for the listener, even if that listener is unfamiliar with modern science.[6]

The Creation Narrative

The Torah opens with a caption-verse which asserts that God created the world. In the beginning of time, the heaven and earth – the two components of the world – were created as a fresh start, *ex nihilo*, as opposed to as an actualization of that which already existed in potential. One who can create ex *nihilo* is by definition supernatural, unique and primordial. The Torah asserts its view that the world and nature, and all of their forces are not gods, but rather God's creations; thereby rejecting the approach of idolatry, mythology, Christianity and pantheism.[7] Starting with the second verse, the Torah describes the stages of this creation. In the lower portion of the world there was initially an unformed and void state (desolation in the land and emptiness in the water that overflowed it); and in the upper portion – darkness (clouds and black mist) and a strong wind hovering above the deep water which filled the lower portion ('the depths'). Then light was created by God's decree, and God called it day. The darkness, which is the absence of light, was

---

6. Cf. Hirsch (1:6-7, 14-19) and *The Collected Writings*, VII (1997): 263-264; Luzzatto, 1: 1, 16, Cassuto, 27; compare with Y. Leibowitz, *Sheva Shanim shel Sihot al Parashat Hashavua*, 1-2, 369, in addition to many other parallels in his writings.

7. Hirsch 1:1, 4; M. D. Cassuto, *MeAdam ad Noah*, 1-2, 4, 10, 18, 21-23, 25, 30-31; Y. Leibowitz, *Hearot Leparashiyot Hashavua*, 13, *Sheva Shanim shel Sihot al Parashat Hashavua*, 13-15.

parashat Bereshit

separated from the light and called night. Afterwards, the firmament was created, this being a clear, hard partition which was erected in the midst of the water, above which was the water which became the upper water. The firmament divided between the upper blue water and the blue water which was beneath it; and God called it *shamayim* (*sham-mayim* [there-water]). At God's command, the lower waters pooled to their proper places, the dry land was revealed and was called earth, vegetation sprouted from the earth, the heavenly bodies and their courses were set in the sky – the sun, the moon and the stars – to shine on the earth and to distinguish between the day and the night, living creatures appeared in the water and on land (the crocodile is specifically mentioned as part of nature which was created, since it is considered to be a supernatural power in the mythology of Mesopotamia and of Canaan) and, in the end, man was created in God's image and likeness. This final creation was created with two forms – male and female – as a single copy, and named Adam (man).

The Torah thereby asserts that all human beings are equal in every sense: There is no room for racist claims, and no man can proclaim concerning himself (or another) that he is divine, to claim intellectual or physical superiority, or to demand a status of dominance over another person for himself – without being chosen for it by others.[8] God blessed Adam and his mate, and assigned them and their progeny dominance over the entire earth and defined the vegetation as food for them, and blessed them to multiply, fill the earth, dominate nature and succeed.

The creation – according to the first narrative – was concluded with its final stage of creation, the Sabbath. God ceased his labors on the Sabbath and sanctified it and raised it above the other six days, these being six eras or stages. The Torah does not require the six days

---

8. Mishna Sanhedrin 4: 5.

parashat Bereshit

for chronological purposes, but rather to explain the meaning of the Sabbath, which is an integral part of the creation, and is one of the most important gifts which Judaism bestowed on humanity.[9]

The second creation narrative – or more precisely the combination of the two narratives – come, as was mentioned, to depict both aspects of man: On the one hand – as the God's handiwork, formed of matter ("And the Lord God formed man from the dust of the earth" – 2:7), insignificant relative to the unfathomable powerful God, who created the universe and controls its laws; and on the other hand – created in God's image and possessing the breath of life which God blew into him; that is, unlike animals, he is sovereign, possesses reason and will, the power of speech and choice.[10] Each time a new component of the creation (not merely a distinction between components which were already created), "it is good" was declared. The one exception is the creation of man, who possesses free will to also choose evil. At the conclusion of the creation, "and behold it is very good" (1:31) was stated concerning it as a whole.[11]

9. Regarding the biblical Sabbath in contrast to what was accepted amongst the ancient peoples cf. Cassuto 40-43. The claim that the text here doesn't refer to actual days, and evening and morning as we know them, but rather to stages, is based on the fact that there was no sun until the fourth day; and the earth's rotation around the sun determines evening and morning.

10. Luzzatto 1:26 disagrees with all of the biblical commentators who ascribe to God's statement *'betzalmenu'* only an abstract interpretation; cf. Maimonides, *Guide to the Perplexed*, 1:1; Meshekh Hokhma, 1:26. Luzzatto ascribes to the Torah's words here, as well, to the beliefs of the ancients that all of the heavenly hosts, including God, are made of invisible spiritual substance, and man was created in God's image. The Torah however was not intended solely for philosophers, and speaks in the language of the masses at time it was received. The word *'kidmuto'* and the term *'tzelem Elohim,'* Luzzatto explains to mean "omnipotent." Compare with Cassuto, 34-35.

11. Hirsch, 1:31; H. Y. Chamiel, *Limudim BeFarashat HaShavua* Genesis 3, 20. Note that the word *'vehine'* in the Bible indicates a turning point, a surprise or a new situation. Cf. Rashbam, 25:24; Malbim, 24:15, *Haketav*

parashat Bereshit

In the two creation narratives, several names of the Creator appear; and Cassuto delved into the matter in an attempt to understand the connotation of these names. The distinctions between the names of the Creator were the starting points for the documentary hypothesis, which Cassuto opposed. According to his approach, the different names represent different perspectives regarding God, as they appeared in different traditions and ancient ballads, which were utilized by the author of the book: In the traditions of wisdom literature it speaks about a transcendent God [*Elohim*] who is distant from material nature and from man – this name is used in the first description of creation (which, as was mentioned, concludes in chapter 2 verse 3); whereas Lord [*Hashem*], using the letters Yud-He-Vav-He is used by the traditions of the popular literature, in which God is near and involved in an intimate dialogue with man, and later – with the Jewish people with whom God established a covenant, and to whom man offers sacrifices. "Hashem" first appears in chapter four. The second description of the creation, despite belonging to the popular literature, adopts the appellation "Lord God" [*Hashem Elohim*] on a one-time basis in chapters 3-4; for the sole purpose of teaching us that both names relate to the same being.[12]

There are those who are inclined to see the theory of "the Big Bang" held by contemporary science, in the creation narrative. They claim that the statement, "God said, 'let there be light,' and

---

Vehaqabbala, 1:31; H. Y. Chamiel, *Limudim BeFarashat HaShavua,* Vayetze, p, 50; *Daat Miqra* throughout the book of Genesis.

12. M. D. Cassuto, *Torat Hateudot Vesiduram shel Sifrei Hatorah* (Jerusalem: 5719), 14-16, 19-38, *MeAdam ad Noah,* 54-61. Sacrificial offerings are always for *Hashem* according to Sifrei *Pinchas* 38 and TB Menahot 110a; cf. Cassuto, *MeAdam ad Noah,* 138; A. Rofe claims that this explanation does not stand up to criticism. Cf. nt. 48 in the book of Exodus.

there was light," accurately expresses the event of "the Bang."[13] However, in my opinion, this interpretation falls into the same trap as Maimonides fell into when he identified the Aristotelian science with the biblical creation narrative, and argued that Aristotelian philosophy was the secret of the creation narrative and of the entire Torah. The same is true of Gersonides (Rabbi Levi ben Gershom), who identified the worldview of the Torah with the scientific theories of Aristotle and Ptolemy. Tomorrow a new theory in physics may come along and replace that of "the Big Bang." This sort of modern commentary follows in the footsteps of the classical exegesis, according to which the Torah furnishes, among other things, scientific knowledge. This theory brings the scientists closer to the concept of biblical creation, however it does not stand up to scrutiny; as according to modern science, the sun and the fixed stars were formed before the earth, and the earth is not in the center of the Universe.

The Garden of Eden Narrative – Historical Truth or Lesson?
The Garden of Eden narrative is part of the second narrative of the creation of the world, according to which Adam was created before the vegetation and animals (2:4, 19). At this stage, God did not yet cause rain to fall for the benefit of man, but rather the vegetation was irrigated by means of vapors which arose from the earth. Previously ("*miqedem*"2:8[14]), God planted the magnificent Garden

---

13. N. Aviezer, *Bereshit Bara* (Tel Aviv, 5754), 24-25. Cf. regarding such approaches, M. Buber, *Darko shel Miqra*, 49.

14. Nahmanides 2:8. The term '*kedem*' in the bible may be understood in three different ways: east, before, or as the name of a particular place. The reader must decide which definition seems most reasonable to him. Here it is possible to interpret that the Garden of Eden was located east of the Land of Israel, which is at the center of the biblical geographic orientation. This places the Garden of Eden in the basin of the Tigress and Euphrates rivers.

of Eden, and after He created Adam, He placed him there, in order to work this divine portion and guard it from harm. In addition, God prohibited him from eating from the "tree of knowledge of good and evil" which was in the garden, under pain of death. The serpent enticed Eve to eat from the fruit of the tree. She ate, and gave of it to Adam. When they ate the fruit, knowledge developed within them – the knowledge of good and evil. God punished them for this sin with expulsion from the Garden of Eden and sentenced them to a life of hardship and toil.

Maimonides was the first to break the consensus that the creation narrative is a simple historical description of the history of the first human couple. Maimonides saw the biblical text as being intended for the simple masses, while the wise may glean philosophical knowledge which is concealed in the text. As a key for understanding the narrative, in the Guide for the Perplexed, Maimonides raises his famous questions: How could it be that man merited attaining knowledge of good and evil and free will as a reward for his sin? If he did not know how to distinguish between good and evil and did not possess free will before the sin, how was it possible to command him and to punish him? What sort of human being was he prior to the sin? Was he not a perfect man from the time of his creation, and more so before the sin than after?

In order to answer these questions, Maimonides distinguishes between truth and falsehood on the one hand, and good and evil on the other. He asserts that Adam's intellect before the sin could differentiate between truth and falsehood, and that "knowledge of good and evil" – which is a limited type of 'knowledge,' as he goes on to clarify – is attained by him when he eats the forbidden fruit. That being the case, Adam originally recognized the divine truth and

---

As a rule, the entire region east of the Jordan River, which encompassed Assyria, Babylonia and Aram, is referred to as the Land of Kedem, (cf. 29:1).

the falsehood which distances it, and he was supposed to conduct himself accordingly, but the serpent clouded this distinction: He caused Eve to think that God's admonition regarding the fruit of the tree of knowledge ("You shall not eat of it or touch it, lest you die," as she herself quoted) was not true: "You are not going to die!" (3:3-4). The belief in the words of the serpent won out over the words of God because of her inability to resist temptation, a shortcoming which is specifically tied to a lack of knowledge of good and evil. The serpent based his enticement on this lack of awareness.

After the sin, Adam's intellect was corrupted. According to Maimonides, he chose to conduct himself in accordance with his "imagination" – the human distinction between good and evil which is subject to environmental and social influences, according to the era, rather than in accordance with the "intellect," the divine distinction between truth and falsehood. In the serpent's statement, "… and your eyes will be opened and you will be like *Elohim* who know good and bad," the word "*Elohim*" means a judge, representing the human judgment based on imagination and logical consensus accepted by the society and not based on the intellect which conforms to the divine truth. This is how man acts when he uses his judgment.

This explanation of Maimonides is surprising. How did Adam's imagination, which is based on environmental and social consensus, come into being, in the absence of a human society at that time? And if before the sin he possessed pure intellect – and particularly, if he knew how to distinguish between truth and falsehood – before the sin, how did he fail to see the falsehood in the serpent's words? Essentially, the distinction between truth and falsehood and good and evil sounds artificial. Man is unworthy of his status without the distinction between good and its antithesis; he is not complete if he is only capable of abstract reason (which deals with truth and falsehood) but not practical reason (which deals with good and evil).

Therefore, some of Maimonides' interpreters claim that from what he says, and from his hints in other chapters in the Guide for the Perplexed, one may reach a bold conclusion, which Maimonides wished to conceal from the average reader. They maintain that Maimonides held that the creation narrative is not a historical account, but rather an allegory about the man's status before God. Each man or woman contains two components: on the one hand, the "Adam" – the spiritual intellectual faculty, the form (in the Aristotelian sense), and on the other, the "Eve" – the physical imaginative faculty, the matter. There is a struggle between these two faculties for control of the man or woman. The man or woman's task is to overcome the imaginative faculty and to subjugate it to the intellectual faculty by means of the study of philosophy in light of – or from within – the Torah, belief in its truth and the observance of its commandments. When a person sins, he subjugates his intellect to the imaginative faculties, to society's consensus and popular conventions, and to hedonism. Maimonides himself writes that one must read the creation narrative with great care: to investigate each mention of the words "*Adam*" and "*Hava*" and to determine whether it refers to the Adam aspect in a man or a woman, the Eve aspect in a man or a woman, to the entire species, to part of the species, i.e. the common masses, or an individual thereof.[15]

This bold interpretation of Maimonides' words was not accepted by the mainstream commentators, if they were even aware of it. Some of them found it difficult to accept that this is not a realistic

---

15. Maimonides, *Guide for the Perplexed*, I:2; II:30; Sarah Klein Breslavi, *Peirush HaRambam Lasipurim al Adam BeFaarshat Bereshit* (Jerusalem, 1987), 254-261.

historical depiction. The more modern among them did, in fact, agree with Maimonides that it does not make sense that man was unable to distinguish between good and evil before the sin, however they found it difficult to accept the philosophical interpretation of the text which is contained even in the more conservative interpretations of Maimonides' words. They preferred an alternative to his interpretation. They hold that the message of the Torah is an ethical one, and according to it, although God is transcendent, exalted and holy, the creator of the world, he connects with man, turns to him with ethical demands, examines his secrets and imparts to him of His goodness if he, i.e. man, is worthy of it. According to these commentators, we learn from the Garden of Eden narrative that the source of evil and human suffering is man's free will and divine punishment, rather than nature which God created, and is exceedingly good. Man is also composed of matter and is therefore weak; he is unable to resist the temptations of the inclination and requires ongoing ethical education. The essence of the sin of Adam was not the eating of the forbidden fruit, nor favoring good over truth, but rather failing to obey the divine command. The failure to obey derived from man's preference for using the ability which enabled him to distinguish between **truth and good** and **falsehood and evil** even before the sin, in accordance with his inferior and flawed personal judgment, rather than in accordance with the divine command which reflects absolute truth and good.[16] What is more, Adam and Eve did not take responsibility for their actions, and attempted – each in turn-- to cast the blame on the other.

The clever and cunning serpent is the evil inclination which nestles in man and unceasingly tempts him.[17] The dialogue between

---

16. Cf. the statement of Rabbi Pinhas ben Yair in *Midrash Tadshe* ch.7. Cf. also S. R. Hirsch 3:1; Cassuto 44; compare Luzzatto 3:24.

17. Sforno, 3:1; compare Ibn Ezra and Kimhi ad loc.

Eve and the serpent is actually an internal dialogue which she engages in with herself. The "serpent" tempts her by telling her a half-truth: that the fruit of the tree will not cause their death, but will rather benefit them. He craftily conceals the complete truth, that the knowledge of good and evil based on purely human standards is dangerous, and in fact is liable to cause death, albeit spiritual death, which not everyone is sensitive to. The evil inclination turns to Eve and tempts her verbally, by exaggerating the scope of the prohibition – "You shall not eat of any tree of the garden" (3:1) – and by refuting the promised punishment. Eve invites the continuation of the incitement when she also exaggerates "and do not touch it" (3:3). The inclination takes advantage of this opportunity, and suggests that God established the prohibition for his benefit rather than for theirs, to prevent them from being like him. Eve chose to eat from the fruit, based on judgment by human standards – that it was good for eating and a delight to the eyes and desirable as a source of wisdom – and ignored God's command which reflects a holy, spiritual standard which is above man.[18] God calls to man, through the Torah, to accept the divine commandments out of the free will of human reason, based on the understanding that the commandments are beyond imagination, sensuality and materialism.[19] In other words, man must understand that the commandments are beyond his understanding and that they express a greater intelligence than his own. The moment that Adam and his wife chose to follow their imagination and passions, "and the eyes of both of them were opened and they perceived that they were naked" (3:7). The discovery of sensuality necessitated the covering of their bodies with clothing, symbolizing the loss of

---

18. Compare Abarbanel 3:1.

19. S. R. Hirsch 2:25. Concerning the dialogue between Eve and the snake cf. Cassuto 94; N. Leibowitz, *Studies in Bereshit (Genesis)*, 28-35

parashat Bereshit

natural freedom which existed previously, when the body served as the protection for the soul.

The post-modern commentators, by contrast to their predecessors, return to the Maimonidean allegorical reading. They too seek instructions regarding the way to conduct themselves vis-a-vis God and his world and vis-à-vis their internal world (this is in light of their psychological and anthropological readings, which seek out human archetypes in the biblical narrative). Their conclusion is that every person must always seek out a dialectical harmony between one's reason, which was given to him by God in order to deal with life's dilemmas, and between the divine commands which guide him based on a super-intelligence, which man reveres but is incapable of fully comprehending. God constantly calls out to man and asks him "where are you?" (3:9): Where are you situated in these dialectical processes? If your path is not carried out honestly (that is to say, prepared to stand at any moment before God's gaze and to reveal yourself with the response of "I am here!") and out of a multi-dimensional deliberation which takes into account the divine command, then you will be banished from God's closeness, from the Garden of Eden.[20]

The first attempt at educating man failed. The Garden of Eden is not a suitable place for such education. Adam and his mate were indeed banished both because of their faulty judgment and because they did not have the courage and inner strength to take responsibility for their actions, each trying to blame the other for the sin. True, they both were enticed (their responsibility therefore was partial), and therefore the death sentence was not carried out, however the punishment was severe. From that moment, their

---

20. Compare with M. Fisch, nt.1 above. Luzzatto writes in one of his letters, *Igrot Shadal*, 247, that the stories of Bereshit are none other than ethical parables.

parashat Bereshit

lives would be short and difficult; they will enter into an incessant reproductive cycle, bearing offspring to preserve mankind and have to see to their own survival, to support themselves and to support others. The serpent – the symbol of the evil inclination – was sentenced to crawl on its belly (to be considered degraded), to eat dirt (not praying to God for its food- isolation from God) and to wage a constant battle with man for survival. Man was created as a mortal – "For dust you are, and to dust you shall return" (3:19) – however, he was meant to live a comfortable life in fellowship with God, as he worked the garden and guarded it. Now it was decreed that he could not live a perfect life without affliction. The land, from which he was created, and from which he was supposed to derive sustenance for himself comfortably, will now be cursed because of him, his livelihood will be attained through hardship and great effort. The woman was sentenced to be dependent on the man in terms of her sexual life, livelihood and family, and to suffer pain during pregnancy and childbirth.[21] Adam and his mate understood that they were both responsible for their new situation, for better or worse, and they did not look backward, but rather forward. Adam

21. Rashi, S. R. Hirsch 3:16. An important trend in modern exegesis explains the Garden of Eden as a kind of a playground for Adam and Eve. Adam's rebellion against God's instruction was for him a kind of a growing up process which resulted in his achieving independence and the awareness of his sexuality, existence and mortality; developments which harbor a fair share of danger. The events which revolve around the original sin are not exclusively punitive; rather they are challenges intended to advance man, (compare 3:5 with Deutoronomy 1:39). Cf. Cassuto, *MeAdam ad Noah* (Jerusalem, 1953), 73-74. Compare with Luzzatto 3:24. U. Simon, a student of Cassuto, adopted this approach and other aspects of his teacher's interpretation of *Parashat Bereshit*. The classical interpretation, by contrast, understood the verse '*vehu yimshol bakh*' as reinforcement of the accepted notion at the time of the inferiority of women, whose role was to serve and to please man. Cf. Kimhi, Ibn Ezra, Nahmanides, Bahya ben Asher, 3:16; Gersonides, 3:20.

gave his mate a forename, Eve [*Havah*] – the mother of all living creatures [*Hai*], in the sense of mankind. Their partner in their new path – God – made garments of skins for them, in preparation for their removal from the Garden of Eden. Their expulsion from the garden ensured that Adam would lose the possibility to live forever, as he would not be able to eat from the tree of life and thereby be attain eternal life, or, at least, a lengthy and healthy life.[22] To be on the safe side, cherubs armed with swords (perhaps winds, lightning and storm clouds[23]) were placed as guards before (*"miqedem"* 3:24) the Garden of Eden. They replaced man in the task of guarding. This exile begins a process of repair and building in this world which we are familiar with, in which Adam and Eve and their descendants were forced to deal with domestic problems – murder in the family as a result of jealousy and rivalry; difficulties of livelihood – exhausting agricultural work and shepherding; the burden of toiling in order to meet the increasing physical and spiritual needs of humanity was placed on them – and this was carried out by means of building cities, crafts, art and theology (calling out in God's name). Outside of the Garden of Eden, Adam hastened to engage in sexual relations with Eve and reproduce, as

---

22. Cassuto, 108-109. Most of the commentators agree that Adam was supposed to have lived eternally, however his sin shortened his lifespan. I prefer Cassuto's realistic interpretation, despite it being problematic in terms of the *peshat*. Nonetheless, it is possible that this is another difference between the two stories of *Bereshit*. According to the first, Adam, about whom the story is told, was an ordinary man, a mortal who didn't reside in the Garden of Eden. According to the second story, Adam was supposed to have lived in eternal tranquility in the Garden of Eden. His sin resulted in his death sentence, which is why he then hastened to establish progeny. Regarding woman's economic dependence upon man, cf. Saadia Gaon 3:16. Regarding the tree of life, cf. Saadia Gaon 2:9; 3:22; Nahmanides and Kimhi ad loc.

23. Cassuto, 117.

a replacement for the perfect and lengthy life which was lost to him. The proud Eve named her first son Cain, to mark the creation of the first child in partnership with God: The name Cain [*qayin*] derives from the same root as *q'niyah*, which also means 'making'; and Eve says: "I have made [*qaniti*] a man together with the Lord" (4:1). The second son was called Abel [*Hevel*], possibly because of his premature end.[24] In His unique way, God continues His plan for mankind.

The Cain and Abel Narrative – the First Murder and its Significance

The problems begin as soon as the first two sons of Adam grow up. The two of them have very different natures, and it appears that there was ongoing tension between them. Cain, whose name alludes to his being a person of material possessions, chose to work the land, while his brother Abel, whose name alludes to his being a spiritual person, chose shepherding and a life of detached wandering. Both brothers spontaneously carried out a religious rite for the first time, expressing their desire to maintain a connection with God even outside of the Garden of Eden. It turns out that the background for the dispute and the first murder was religious. Cain was the one who initiated the rite, however, Abel who followed his lead chose his offering well, and sacrificed it properly. Abel brought a burnt offering from the firstborns of his sheep and the choice meat and roasted them on the fire, as they are eaten; whereas Cain was not careful to bring the best of the first fruits of his land, and may also have roasted the fruit which he brought, which is not how they are normally eaten (Leviticus 2:11-12). It is also possible that Cain was an unethical person, violent or sensual, and therefore God did not pay heed to Cain's offering, as all of the prophets of Israel preached

---

24. Cassuto, 133-136.

thatrite without an ethical foundation is abhorrent. God paid heed to Abel's offering (perhaps a fire came down from heaven and consumed Abel's sacrifice[25]). Cain's jealousy was aroused and God turned to him and clarified for him that only man's actions and his control over his sensuality and evil inclination, which lie in wait for him to tempt him in order to cause his downfall, are what determine his relationship with God. "Surely, if you do right, there is uplift. But if you do not do right, sin couches at the door; its urge is toward you, yet you can be its master." (4:7[26]). However, Cain did not internalize this warning, he did not introspect and did not examine where he erred; but rather, he decided to "correct" the injustice which he believed was done to him with his own hands. Abel, due to his naiveté, did not discern the tempest of emotions overcoming his brother, and complied with his request that they go out to the field – an isolated location – where he was mortally struck by his brother.

Cain apparently knew the nature of death, from his father's conversations with God ("As soon as you eat of it, you shall die" – 2:17. "For dust you are, and to dust you shall return" – 3:19), conversations whose content was surely transmitted to him. However, when a person is incapable of self-control, his spontaneous and awful response is to dispense with his rival by force and violence. In addition to his catastrophic behavior, Cain behaved like his parents: He did not take responsibility for his actions and even denied them. After the difficult dialogue with God, he digested the significance of his irreversible actions and the severe punishment of exile to which he was sentenced: isolation from human company and from the land which was so dear to

---

25. Rashi and Ibn Ezra 4:4; Kimhi 4:5.

26. Regarding the explanation of the word '*se'et*' cf. Ibn Ezra 4:7; compare Kimhi and Nahmanides ad loc. Cf. also S. R. Hirsch, 4:3-6.

him, to become a wanderer in the land, without rest or livelihood from it, vulnerable to attack by those seeking revenge in the future. Only then did he feel remorse. Here, for the first time, we learn of the power of repentance. He confessed his sins and accepted the sentence "My sin is too great to bear!" (4:13), but asked that the severe punishment be diminished.[27] God accepted his request, and guaranteed his survival by placing a sign on Cain indicating that he was not to be harmed.

The Torah's message which emerges from the verse cited above ("Surely, if you do right," etc.) is as clear as day: The choice is placed in man's hand. No original sin hangs over him and prevents him from overcoming his inclination by means of his free will, and thereby sanctifying his body – which is accomplished, first and foremost, by means of refraining from harming others – and reaching the pinnacle of ethics and spirituality in this world. The Christian exegesis of the original sin does not dovetail with the biblical viewpoint.[28] Man's free will means that God does not usually interfere to prevent human acts of evil, or to promote acts of righteousness: Responsibility for the existence of good and evil in the world rests with man, as an individual and as a society. So too, the Torah teaches us that man cannot escape divine punishment and that a person is not selected as being worthy based on superficial criteria (being the firstborn – as in the case of Cain – or strength, wealth or pedigree), but rather based on his actions. Abel, who was worthy in God's eyes, died because of man's wickedness.

---

27. Nahmanides 4:13. According to other interpretations Cain had difficulty accepting the verdict: A) Rashi and Nahmanides' first interpretation ad loc. based on Bereshit Rabbah 22:1, according to which Cain's remarks are interrogative. B) Ibn Ezra and Kimhi ad loc. who understand *'avon'* to mean punishment here - my punishment is too great to bear. Cain only now comprehended the ramifications of his actions - cf. *Tanhuma Bereshit* 9.

28. S. R. Hirsch 3:19.

parashat Bereshit

Cain is not worthy, and therefore Seth, the third son, was tasked with continuing the human race. Cain and his offspring, who were forced to abandon working the land as they were banished from it, developed civilization and human culture by building cities (Cain), raising sheep (Jabal), developing metal implements (Tubal-Cain), musical instruments and music (Jubal), and the accumulation of possessions. However, it seems that all of these are insufficient for preservation of a society. A human society cannot exist without ethics and a spiritual life, and these were not developed, as the majority of the people were distanced from God.[29] The legacy of Cain's civilization was indeed preserved for future generations by Noah and his sons, who were the descendants of Seth; however the offspring of Cain perished in the deluge.

The conclusion of chapter four, in which the text adopts the name "Hashem," as mentioned above, describes the genealogy of Cain through Lamech and his four children from his wives, Adah and Zillah. Lamech was the first to marry two wives, and they were, apparently, rivals to each other. It would appear that he suffered from them even more than they did from each other. He asked them, in his anger over their mistreatment of him: "Have I slain a man for wounding me, or a lad for bruising me?" (4:23) Did I kill anyone as Cain did? One who harms Cain can expect a sevenfold punishment ("If anyone kills Cain, sevenfold vengeance shall be taken on him." 4:15); However, the vengeance for your actions toward me – who did not sin, as Cain did – will be seventy-sevenfold.[30]

---

29. Malbim 4:23 and Cassuto, *MeAdam ad Noah*, 130, 164-165, 181, 184; compare with S. R. Hirsch 6: 1-2.

30. Rivash (Joseph ben Isaac Bekhor Shor) 4:23; Luzzatto 4:19, 23. Another possible explanation is that Lamech is boasting before his wives about his ability to kill and the vengeance on his behalf, which was infinitely greater than that on Cain's behalf; as a result of which no one was able to cause him

parashat Bereshit

The fifth chapter once again uses the name "Elohim" as did chapter one, and it enumerates the generations from Adam, by way of his son Seth and by way of Enosh, the son of Seth. The similarity in names between the two genealogies demands explanation.[31] In the era of the birth of Enosh, Seth and his offspring began to once again call out in the name of God, and to attempt to renew the connection between mankind and its God. The meaning of 'calling out to God' is not clear. It is possible that it refers to praying to God, or to receiving prophecy – direction from God – and its transmission from the prophet to the community. The tradition of calling out to God was continued by Abraham (12:8; 13:4; 21:33), Isaac (26:25), Moses (Exodus 34:5) and Samuel (based on Psalms 99:6). The chain of Seth continues forward to Lamech (not to be confused with the Lamech of the chain of Cain), his son, Noah and his sons Shem, Ham, and Japheth. Noah was the first baby born after Adam's death – on whose account the land was cursed (3:17) – and Lamech hoped that the curse was removed, and that his son would be the first to derive abundant produce from the land ("And he named him Noah, saying, 'this one will provide us relief from our work and from the toil of our hands, out of the very soil which the Lord placed under a curse'" 5:29).[32] However,

---

harm, for he was even more protected than Cain. His behavior represents unmitigated violence which points to the moral degeneration of mankind leading up to the flood. Cf. Cassuto, 162-165.

31. One explanation for this is the one proposed by Bible criticism; according to which, different documents recounting a similar story were assembled together by a single editor of the Torah. Cassuto thinks that the Torah presents two ancient oral traditions here which existed side by side, whose purpose was to present an unworthy physical tradition which was washed away by the deluge, alongside a tradition devoted to knowledge of God from which Noah sprung. Cf. Cassuto, 180 - 182. Concerning the chronology of the generations, see below in the discussion of the generations from Noah until Abraham.

32. Rashbam (from a manuscript in *Torat Haim*), Kimhi according to the *peshat*, and Hizkuni 5:29.

parashat Bereshit

Seth's offspring did not follow the ways of ethics and justice. The exception among them, other than Noah, was Enoch who found the connection to God and acted ethically, and God gathered his soul to Him prematurely, in order to free him from the society of his time, and their fate.[33]

The Second Failure

In the wake of the jealousy, rivalry and act of murder which are manifested in the narrative of Cain and Abel, corruption spread throughout the earth, primarily in the form of sexual sins ("And took wives from among those that pleased them" – 6:2) and acts of murder, robbery and theft ("The earth was filled with lawlessness" – 6:11). The stronger dominated the weaker.[34] God observed all of the evil which man was performing, was saddened and regretted the creation of humans and animals.[35] The divine plan to educate man toward ethical freedom within the context of attachment to God failed in the second attempt as well, namely that which

---

33. Concerning the meaning of the word '*huchal*' cf. Rashbam, Ibn Ezra and Sforno 4:26. Regarding Enosh and Enoch cf. Bekhor Shor 5:24 and Cassuto 166-167, 193-196.

34. Inter alia, they took wives for themselves by force, as they saw fit, as it says "the divine beings [*benei haelohim*] saw how beautiful the daughters of men were and took wives from among those that pleased them." (6:2) – '*benei haelohim*', according to the commonly accepted explanation are powerful violent people. Cassuto, (following *Midrash Pirkei D'Rabbi Eliezer* 22), 201-206 accepts the opinion that these were the fallen angels, the demons and angels of destruction, whose relationships with the daughters of man produced giants and corrupted warriors who were mortal like the rest of mankind. According to him, the term '*benei haelohim*', (as opposed to using mythological names) gives expression to the Torah's opposition to mythologies including traditions regarding giants and mythological heroes.

35. For the classical exegetical rationale for the destruction of the animals cf. R. Yehoshua ben Korha in BT Sanhedrin 108a and Kimhi 6:7.

parashat Bereshit

took place outside the Garden of Eden. Man did not learn from his sins, did not deal with the challenges of rational natural law,[36] forsook ethics and the divine spirit and sunk in the existence of physicality and lust. The world which had been "exceedingly good" was ruined by the elite of the creations utilizing his free will for evil. Science and technology, urbanization, industry, economy, music and art are incapable of making up for the lack of an ethical basis.[37] God reached the conclusion that his aspiration to establish a world in which the exalted man will live and rule harmoniously over the animals and vegetation is not likely to reach fruition. His indecision as to whether to punish mankind, or to take into account its weakness, stemming from their being flesh and blood, was resolved. He decided to wipe out all life from the world (with the exception of that which was in the water) and to recreate everything anew, from one family, the ethical behavior of its head – Noah, having found favor in his eyes – and from selected animals. In the new world, the life span of man will gradually be reduced to approximately a hundred and twenty years.[38] This would ensure

---

36. Nahmanides, 6:13, Hizkuni, 7:21. Cf. also *Derashat Torah Temimah, Kol Kitvei Haramban*, 1: 173. Nahmanides determines there that mankind's obligation to behave morally does not stem from the seven Noahide laws, (as these laws are a Midrash and are not the *peshat* of the verses), but from reason.

37. Cf. the explanation of Malbim and Cassuto on the beginning of ch.6, and Y. Leibowitz, *Sheva Shanim shel Sihot al Parashat Hashavua*, 16-17. Regarding the '*benei haelohim*' and their transgression cf. Saadia Gaon, Rashi, Bekhor Shor, Kimhi, Ibn Ezra, Nahmanides, Bahya ben Asher, Hizkuni 6:2, according to Rashbi in *Bereshit Rabbah* 26:5.

38. Saadia Gaon, Netziv, 6:3 and Cassuto 204; Ibn Ezra and Luzzatto bring this explanation and reject it. It is possible that the lifespan of hundreds years of the people who lived between Noah and Abraham's time are not to be taken literally. This is indicated by Abraham's and Sarah's doubt about the possibility of having children at the age of one hundred. According to what is

that even the biggest villains and tyrants would not live too long on the land, and there would be hope for the oppressed.[39]

Parashat Bereshit is the story of the failures of the human race, whether it is a historical account of the beginning of mankind, or whether it is lesson about the nature of man, who God wishes to teach how he should live his life, and serves as a preamble to explaining the mission of the Jewish nation.

Parashat Noah
Noah, a Righteous Man

The corruption of the human race reached an intolerable zenith and God decided to destroy it and begin anew. Noah, the lone perfectly righteous man of the generation, was chosen to be the one to start the human race anew. The parasha begins with Noah's genealogy (toldot=his offspring) – Shem, Ham, and Japheth – and recalls that which occurred to him and his family. The Torah twice describes Noah as being a righteous man in the generations in которых he lived: "A righteous man; he was blameless in his generation" (6:9), and "You alone have I found righteous before Me in this generation" (7:1). The emphasis on the "generation" led the

---

told at the end of *Parashat Noah*, Terah, the father of Abraham, lived for 205 years and had Abraham when he was 70 years old?! According to Cassuto the years recorded in the Bible are, indeed, the same as ours; however the lists of chronologies were not fully synchronized by the author who combined the different traditions. The chronology was less important to him than the moral lesson, and he preferred preserving every literary tradition to the degree possible. While he did attempt to unify, he forewent full harmonious synchronization. The tradition concerning Abraham and Sarah's wonder then is an independent tradition, like the rest of the traditions. In this way all of the biblical contradictions in chronology are resolved. Cf. *Sefer Bereshit Umivnehu*, 318-319.

39. S. R. Hirsch, 8:22.

parashat Noah

classical commentators[40] to debate whether righteousness in that generation, which deserved to be destroyed due to evil and ethical corruption, increases the prestige of the righteous man, or decreases it, as the viewpoints of the age certainly influence all of the people of that generation. On the one hand, Noah is to be praised for the fact that in such a terrible generation he managed to preserve the divine image within him and to be elevated. On the other hand, it is possible that Noah would not have stood out at all in a generation of righteous people. Those who mitigate his stature compare him to Abraham, about whom it is said: "and he put his trust in the Lord" (15:6); that is to say that his faith, given the circumstances of his age, is his great virtue and in it we see his superiority over Noah. What is more, concerning Noah it states: "Noah walked **with [*et*]** God" (6:9), whereas concerning Abraham it states: "Walk **before me [*l'fanai*]** and be blameless" (17:1). It would seem that the one who walks before God and lights the way for everyone by the force of his character and actions is greater than one who walks alongside God and is guided and reactive.[41] The difference between Noah and Abraham is: A) God carried out an ongoing dialogue with Abraham over the course of many years, in which Abraham played an active role, whereas Noah heard a divine monologue, to which he merely listened passively. B) Noah heard that God was planning the total destruction of mankind together with the animals, aside from two representatives of each creature, a male and a female, and did not react. Like his predecessors, Adam and Cain, he did not take responsibility. In this case, it does not refer to responsibility after the fact and for one's own actions, but rather responsibility ahead of time for the fate of others, in fact – for the fate of all of

---

40. "In his generations" - cf. Nahmanides 6:9. Regarding the dispute cf. Rashi 6:9 based on *Bereshit Rabbah* 30:9.

41. Rashi ad loc. based on *Bereshit Rabbah* 30:1.

nature – before the misfortune befalls them. Noah did not attempt to change the harshness of the decree, as Abraham tried to when he heard that God was planning to destroy Sodom and Gomorrah together with all of its inhabitants. Abraham did not hesitate to stand before the Divine Presence and raise the possibility that the divine justice could err in failing to distinguish between a wicked person and a righteous one, between one who deserves death and one who deserves to live, and he tried to change the decree. It was only when God tried him by means of an individual-personal test – at the binding of Isaac – that he did not object, and trusted in the divine justice. In this one can see the difference between Noah and Enoch (5:22) and the patriarchs, as Jacob attests to concerning them: "'The God **before [*lefanav*]** whom my fathers Abraham and Isaac walked" (48:15). On the other hand, those who praise Noah claim that he knew, based on God's testimony, that there were no other righteous people besides him, and he did not see fit to protest the destruction of the wicked.[42]

It is appropriate to note here that the connotation of the terms "righteousness [*zadikut*]" and "faith [*emuna*]" in the Bible is different than that which these words acquired in the language of the Sages. In the Bible, a righteous person is not someone who separates himself from this world in order to immerse himself in the service of God and in attempts to cleave to Him. Rather it is a person who is vindicated in the divine judgment, and whose path in this world is one of integrity. The biblical meaning of *emuna* is trust in the fulfillment of God's promises, or the quality of trustworthiness, integrity and acting justly; and not – as in later eras – awareness of God's existence without tangible verification

---

42. Cf. Zohar 106a, and on the other hand H. Y. Chamiel, *limudim BeFarashat HaShavua*, 28-29. Cf. also nt. 69 below. Compare with M. Buber, *Darko Shel Miqra*, 72-75.

or proof. The righteousness and blamelessness of Noah, and that of all who are called a righteous person in the Bible, therefore refers to his ethicality and integrity vis a vis others, as opposed to the degree of his religious attachment to God. This is the manner in which one should interpret that which is said in the Torah regarding Abraham (15:6): "And he put his trust [*v'heemin*] in the Lord" – Abraham, despite his and Sarah's advanced age, trusted in the fulfillment of the promise of offspring which God had promised him; "He reckoned it to his merit [*lizedakah*]" – God viewed him as vindicated. "Walk before me and be blameless" (17:1) – walk in the path of integrity. "Will You slay people even though innocent?" (20:4) – Does God not differentiate between one who ought to be found guilty in the judgment and one who ought to be vindicated? "Declaring the righteous in the right and the other in the wrong" (Deuteronomy 25:1) – vindicate the one who is in the right, and condemn the one who is in the wrong. "And they had faith in the Lord and His servant Moses" (Exodus 14:31) – the Jewish people trusted in God's promise delivered through His servant, Moses. This is not referring to belief in their existence, as Moses, after all, lived and acted in front of their own eyes! "And thus his hands remained steady [*emuna*] until the sun set" (Exodus 17:12) – Moses's hands were pointing straight up, strong and steadfast. "But the righteous man is rewarded with life for his fidelity" (Habakkuk 2:4) – not as per the Christian interpretation, that the righteous man will live in the merit of his faith (in the divinity of Jesus) and his attachment to this belief; but rather, that the righteous man will live in the merit of his trusting in God, his being faithful, honest and one acting justly.[43] Returning to our parasha: Noah's status relative to the people of his generation comes to teach us that the

---

43. Luzzatto, *ketavim* I 74-75. Compare with Y. Leibowitz, *Sheva Shanim shel Sihot al Parashat Hasahavua*, 78-79.

majority is not always correct, even when it is an overwhelming majority. One should not accept the societal convention in ethical and spiritual matters if it demands performing sins, over which a black flag waves.

The Ark and the Deluge – the Destruction of Mankind and Noah's Salvation

God revealed Himself to Noah and commanded him to build a large ark, which could hold him, his wife, his three sons together with their wives, and pairs of animals. The length of the ark – which was made of gopher wood (cypress) – was 300 cubits (approximately 150 meters), its width was fifty cubits (approximately 25 meters), and its height was thirty cubits (approximately 15 meters), and it consisted of three stories. The walls of the ark were slanted, and one of them contained a door; and on the strip of the ceiling there was a skylight the width of a cubit (approximately 50 cm.) – a window for lighting – or a lamp (or a roof covering). All of the walls were to be coated within and without with tar, to prevent infiltration of water. God explained to Noah that he intended to bring a flood (deluge) which will wipe out all of mankind and the animals on the land, and that the ark was meant to save its occupants from drowning, so that they will live.[44]

---

44. Moshe's ark also saved him from drowning. For parallel flood stories from the Ancient Near East cf. Cassuto, *MeNoah ad Avraham*, 4-19. Cassuto compares and contrasts between the Bible and other traditions, emphasizing the morality and monotheism of the Bible versus the arbitrary gods of the Eastern tradition. In addition, Cassuto brings there his assumptions about the coalescing of the biblical text. According to Bible critics the flood story was written down by ancient cultures, based on traditions of a large ecological disaster which transpired, wiping out men, children and animals. The Torah made use of these stories to teach a moral lesson. For more on the reason for the destruction of animal life in classical biblical exegesis, cf. R. Yehoshua ben Korha in BT Sanhedrin 108:71; Kimhi 6:7.

The Torah tells about God's instructions regarding the identity and number of those entering the ark four times. It speaks three times about a male and female (or perhaps two pairs[45]) of each species; and once (the second time) the pure domesticated animals and birds are singled out. These serve, from the offering of Abel, as sacrifices to God; and after meat is permitted to those leaving the ark, the Torah will sanction the Jewish people eating these animals. In the case of these, Noah is commanded to gather seven pairs of each species; that is to say, six pairs in addition to the original male and female. The modern commentaries note that the second section, which includes the instructions regarding the pure animals, is said in the name of *Hashem* [the Tetragrammaton] rather than *Elohim* [God][46] as sacrifices were offered from these animals, which serve as a connection with *Hashem* rather than with *Elohim* (which, as was mentioned, connotes God in a general sense – the deity of nature. Recall, "Cain brought an offering to the Lord [*Hashem*] and the Lord [*Hashem*] paid heed to Abel ..." (4:3-4). For this reason, in these matters this name is always mentioned, along the lines of "Whoever sacrifices to a god [Elohim] other than the Lord [*Hashem*] alone shall be proscribed" (Exodus 22:19). Bible critics believe that there are at least two sources here, and that the second source which relates to sacrifices is priestly; however, verse 16 in chapter seven poses difficulties for this approach, as both the name *Hashem* and the name *Elohim* appear in it.[47]

---

45. Luzzatto 6:19.

46. The name '*Elohim*' is used in this context in 6:17-22, 7:7-10, 7:10-16. The name '*Hashem*' is found in vs. 7:1-6.

47. Luzzatto, 6:9. Cf. the detailed discussion by Cassuto, 22-29, in an attempt to reconcile the documentary hypothesis regarding the names of God, redundancies (which he attributes to biblical style which is generally like that of the Ancient Near East), various expressions and contradictions between verses. In 31-32 he rejects the attempts to correlate the deluge with a natural

parashat Noah

God's initial address to Noah involves the preemptive command – presumably a year or more before the event – in order to allow Noah to build the ark and gather food. The second directive was given seven days prior to the deluge: to prepare for entry into the ark and to get organized in its vicinity. The third occasion, during which the order was given regarding bringing the animals into the ark, was at the inception of the implementation of the process of bringing the animals into the ark. The fourth was said at the time of Noah and his family's entry into the ark on the day on which the first rains began. The classical commentators explain that the impure animals came to the ark from their locations throughout the land, at the command of God, master of nature; and Noah was only required to usher them in and settle them in the ark. In the case of the seven pairs of pure animals, which were destined for domestication for the purpose of sacrificing, consumption and working the field, Noah was required to gather those animals which were domesticated by him. For this reason, he was commanded regarding this a mere week before the entry into the ark.

The water of the deluge flowed from the windows of the heavens, which were fully opened and gushed mightily from the springs, over

---

phenomenon which has any historical or archeological basis. On p. 50 he suggests that Noah needed to bring seven additional pairs of ritually pure animals, in addition to the original pair, or eight pairs of each ritually pure animal. On p. 51 he explains that the sacrifice of exclusively domesticated animals to the gods was accepted in the Ancient Near East even before the Torah. On the confliction of a believing modern bible critic cf. U. Simon, *Bakesh Shalom Verodfehu*, (Tel Aviv, 2002), 274-285. Bible critics assume that that there is an integration of two documents here: In one, the ritually pure animals were set aside as the name *Hashem* was known in the generation of Noah, and these animals were utilized as sacrificial offerings after the flood. The second document doesn't distinguish between the animals, and stipulates one set from each species, since Noah sacrificed to *Elohim* and not to *Hashem*, who was known only to those who underwent the Exodus from Egypt.

the course of forty days; until the water reached the height of 15 cubits (9 meters) above the summit of the highest mountain; as of the world reverted to the pre-creation state of being unformed and void. All living creatures on the surface of the land died by drowning. Toward the conclusion of the deluge, the rain and the gushing continued at a normal rate; the water began to decline slowly as a result of evaporation and absorption of the soil, and the rain and gushing also gradually lessened, until they ceased entirely. After 150 days (five months) from the start of the deluge, the bottom of the ark reached the height of the tops of the mountains, and came to rest on the mountains of Ararat. After about another month and a half, the summits of the mountains could be seen from the window of the ark. Another forty days passed, and then Noah sent the raven out through the window of the ark, to see where it would find dry ground to land on;, although he was not willing to be separated from the ark, consistent with his practice of only being concerned about himself, and he remained in the vicinity of the ark. Noah waited seven days and then sent the pleasant and friendly dove. It flew far away, from morning until evening, like an experienced carrier pigeon; but was forced to return empty-handed, and Noah retrieved it into the ark. After an additional week, it was sent out again, and this time it returned in the evening with an olive leaf or branch in its mouth. The olive tree is an evergreen which grows in the mountains, and Noah understood that these trees were already visible above the water. After another week, he sent the dove out again, and it did not return.[48] About two more months passed until there were no longer accumulations of water on the land, and fifty-seven more days until the ground was entirely dry. One (lunar) year and eleven days (adding up to a solar year) after the beginning of the rain,[49] he received

---

48. Cf. regarding the raven and the dove in the different traditions versus the biblical tradition, Cassuto, 73-77. Cf. Kimhi 8:7.

49. Cassuto, 78.

parashat Noah

the divine directive to leave the ark. A process similar to that of the creation of the world occurred once again (water, dry land, vegetation, animal life, man),[50] however, it appears that little changes.

After the Deluge – A New Beginning

Noah's first act upon leaving the ark was to sacrifice an offering as thanksgiving to God. In contrast to Adam, who never sacrificed to God – and on the contrary, took for himself produce belonging to God, namely the fruit of the tree of knowledge – and in contrast to Cain and Abel, who did not build an altar, Noah built an altar, took from the pure birds and animals in his possession and offered them entirely as a burnt offering to God. God carefully examined Noah's gesture in offering this sacrifice and found it pure and consistent with total dedication to God, and accepted it ("The Lord smelled the pleasing odor" – 8:21). Since Noah's gesture found favor in God's eyes and gave Him satisfaction,[51] He decided to no longer curse the land in terms of its refraining from producing crops easily and plentifully, as He did to Adam, to no longer destroy large portions of the creation concurrently and to not change the natural order, as He did in the deluge. All of this was in spite of the fact that "although [*ki*] the devisings of man's mind are evil from his youth" (8:21: "*ki*" is used here in the sense of although).[52] Hence, God recognizes that

---

50. Cassuto noted that the description of the recovery from the deluge is similar to the creation of the world. Cf. 67, 69, 78, 79, 85, 86.

51. According to Luzzatto, 8:21, ancient man believed that God experienced pleasure from the aroma of the sacrificial offerings which placated his anger; and the Torah speaks in accordance with the beliefs of those who were the recipients of the Torah. According to the rest of the commentators (aside from the Kabbalists), the phrase simply means a sense of satisfaction.

52. Saadia Gaon 8:21. The possibility of reading the word '*ki*' in this way is raised by Jonah Ibn Janah in his *Sefer Hashorashim*. This is brought down by Ibn Ezra in his commentary on *Shemot* 34:9, although he prefers a different

parashat Noah

the new man is like the old, and that the new world is no different than the one which preceded it. God blessed Noah and his sons with the same blessing as he blessed Adam and his mate – "Be fertile and increase, and fill the earth" (9:1),and placed control over the animals in their hands. Since there is no longer any expectation that man will be a spiritual elite, who rules the world in harmony, and also in order to mitigate man's punishment in terms of his livelihood, God permitted man to not only eat vegetation; but rather, all that he desired, including the flesh of animals – "Every creature that lives shall be yours to eat" (9:3).[53] This time, the prohibition against eating is not directed against the fruit of a specific tree, but rather against blood. In addition, God explicitly prohibited the murder of all who were created in the divine image. Murder will be avenged by God, however it is man who must judge the murderer without bias and kill him. The murder of Abel, and the acts of murder which typified the generation of the deluge, were the reason for the explicit admonition not to murder. Apparently, the natural laws of reason are insufficient; and, therefore, God must become involved and command that which is the primary and most fundamental natural law.

After the traumatic experience which Noah and his sons underwent and with their exiting the ark into a desolate world, it appears that they were hesitant to return to the routine of life, to production and construction, in a world which is so vulnerable to

---

explanation there. Another plausible explanation is that God said to himself that there was no longer any purpose in the total destruction of mankind, as man's nature and desires will always bring him to sin. Cf. Rashi and Nahmanides 8:21.

53. Abravanel ad loc. The root 'rms'[רמש] in the broad sense means 'moving', therefore that term relates to all of the living creatures like in this verse; or in a more narrow sense, 'crawling', and therefore relates to *sheratzim*. For the broad sense cf. also 1:28, 7:21, and for the narrower sense cf. 1:25, 7:23.

the wrath of God.[54] It is possible that Noah's offering was also a plea to God for reassurance. Therefore, God saw fit to promise that the event would not recur. He established a one-sided covenant with Noah and his sons and with the living creatures, for which the rainbow in the cloud – a natural phenomenon which existed from the time of the creation – will from now on serve as a sign: He committed Himself to turn His bow – which He had used to shoot His arrows at the world – backward, and to no longer use it, and to not cause another deluge. When rain falls, the sun will break through every now and then, and then the rainbow will appear and remind God of His promise.[55]

The Descendants of Noah – Archetypes of the New Mankind
Noah too disappointed God, as Adam had in the Garden of Eden. He did not retain his righteousness, despite the experience which he went through; or perhaps, specifically because of the trauma which he did not succeed in overcoming. Indeed, in order to fulfill his father's vision and hope ("And he named him Noah, saying, 'This one will provide us relief from our work and from the toil of our hands, out of the very soil which the Lord placed under a curse'." – 5:29), he returned to working the land, planted a vineyard and saw success in his efforts. However, he did not use its produce wisely and with self-control; but rather, he went overboard drinking, reveled and got drunk and rolled around naked in his

---

54. Rashi 8:16, 9:9, based on *Tanhuma* ed. Buber, Noah 17, and Kimhi 6:18, 8:16 and Hizkuni 8:16, based on TB Sanhedrin 108b, *Bereshit Rabbah* 31:12, 34:7, 35:1. The Midrash noticed that at the exit from the ark the men and women also left separately, and from this he deduces that they refused to engage in propagation despite God's command that each man leave the ark together with his mate. Compare Abravanel ad loc. regarding the concerns of those who exited the ark.

55. Midrash Lekah Tov, Nahmanides 9:12, Cassuto, 93-94.

tent. In contrast to the fruit of the tree of knowledge which opened Adam's eyes and led him to cover his nakedness, the fruit of the vine led Noah to nudity and loss of his senses. He lacked guidance to maintain his righteousness and overcome his sensuality. His youngest son, Ham – the father of the nations of Canaan – favored this situation; however, his two brothers, Shem, and Japheth, covered their father's nakedness by walking backward, and did not see it. They, thereby, atoned for his act, and allowed mankind to advance anew.

The conduct of the sons in this event reflects and symbolizes the three archetypes of people: Ham, the youngest of the brothers, is the sensual, instinctual and hot headed – from him descends Cush, Egypt and Canaan (Leviticus 18:3, 27). He fails to overcome the temptation of seeing his father's nakedness; and the descendants of his firstborn Canaan, who were defective and corrupt as symbolized by their ancient father, were cursed by Noah to be degraded slaves to the descendants of their father's brothers, Shem and Japheth. And so already here, the Torah promises the land of Canaan to the children of Israel, the descendants of Shem.[56] The firstborn, Japheth, represents the aesthete, artist, statesman, philosopher and commander:Greece comes from him. The middle son, Shem, is the wise man, the scholar, prophet and intellectual – the forefather of Abraham the Hebrew. Shem and Japheth (and their offspring) are blessed by Noah that they will build the human race collaboratively.

---

56. According to BT Sanhedrin 70a which is also quoted by Rashi 9:22, the gazing was accompanied either by castration or sodomy, cf. Rashi 9:24. Compare with Cassuto, 103-104. Cf. also Buber, *Darko shel Miqra* 274-278 as well as the discussion on the Canaanite women in *Parshot Hayei Sarah* and *Toldot*. Regarding the Torah's agenda of giving basis for the transfer of the land from the sons of Canaan to the sons of Abraham, for which it makes use of the curse to Canaan, cf. *Olam Hatanach, Bereshit*, 69-70.

parashat Noah

Shem holds the compass and directs humanity; and is blessed in the name of **Hashem**, the God of ethics. Japheth is invited to dwell in the tents of Shem, and there to make his great contribution and he is blessed in the name of **Elohim**, the God of nature. Both of them will utilize Ham's abilities for their purposes.[57]

The section concludes with a description of two genealogies. To begin with (10:1-32), seventy offspring of Shem, Ham and Japheth are enumerated, from whom the nations spread out throughout the world. Among the descendants of Ham are Egypt, Cush, Sheba, Philistines,[58] Canaan, Heth, Hivites and the other nations of the Land of Israel who lived in Sidon, Gerar, Gaza and the cities of Sodom. One of the sons of Cush was Nimrod, who excelled as a hunter and as one of the great rulers of his generation,[59] who established a mighty empire which included inter alia Babylonia, Acadia and Ninveh. Among the offspring of Shem were Elam, Assyria, Aram and Hazarmaveth.[60]

The first inhabitants on the face of the earth initially settled in one mountainous region, "the hill country to the east" (10:30), and

---

57. Cf. TB Megillah 9b, the commentary of S. R. Hirsch on 9:25-27 and Cassuto, 102-106. Cassuto explains that the author was influenced by the way in which he views the Jewish people as representing the Canaanite nation and other nations, and recalls the story accordingly. Regarding the seizure of the land from the Canaanite nations cf. Ibn Kaspi, *Tirat Keseph*, 70. Ham was the youngest son of Noah and Canaan was Ham's eldest son. Cf. Nahmanides 9:18.

58. The tradition of the seventy nations of the world originates here. Regarding the identity of the Philistines and their tribes cf. Cassuto, 141-143.

59. Kimhi, Nahmanides 10:8-9. On possible identifications of Nimrod in Mesopotamian culture cf. *Olam Hatanach, Bereshit*, 78-80.

60. Cassuto, 124, 126-127. Cassuto here lists the sources which in his opinion comprise the book of Genesis. On 130-152 the commentator attempts to identify the nations and their cities.

parashat Noah

then traveled "from the east" (11:2[61]), and descended into a valley in Shinar. They wanted to build a fortified city there, with a tower (Babel) in its midst, with its summit in the heavens, in order to make a name for themselves. They were punished for doing so, as I will show and explain in the section which follows.

In the end of the parasha, the lineage from which Abraham descended is described. This description serves as a transition from dealing with all of mankind to dealing with the father of the Hebrew nation. The description opens with one of the five sons of Shem, the one from whom Abraham (who was originally called *Avram*) descended. It is interesting that in contrast to the ten generations from Adam to Noah – who lived close to the time of their creation by the Creator and whose life span extended between 900 and 1000 years – in the first ten generations after the deluge, from Noah until Abraham, there is an almost totally consistent decline in longevity.[62] In the end, the Torah focuses on Abraham the son of Terah, and recalls that he married Sarah (who was originally called *Sarai*, and may possibly have been born to Terah from an additional, later marriage). Terah emigrated from Ur of the Chaldeans to the land of Canaan, together with his family. His sons, Abraham and Nahor, together with their families left with him (cf. 24:10), as well as his grandson Lot. Lot was the son of Haran, who was the brother of Abraham and Nahor, who had died. Terah remained in Haran, which was in Aram-naharaim (Paddan-aram 25:20), together with his family; and Abraham continued on his way to Canaan. Terah died in Haran sixty years after Abraham departed from there.

---

61. Rashi 11:2 according to *Midrash Bereshit Rabbah* 38:6.
62. Cassuto, *MeAdam ad Noah*, 179, 204, *MeNoah ad Avraham*, 172-174. Cassuto shows that chronologies such as these also existed in Mesopotamian tradition, although in them the kings lived longer and were more like demigods, a position which is in opposition to the stance of the Torah.

parashat Noah

The narratives of the lineages are not meant to teach us anthropology and history. Rather, they aim at teaching us that God is the one who establishes nations in their lands and distinguishes between the Israelite and the other nations; and He is the one who fashioned the diversity of languages and cultures within the human race, which originates from one father and therefore its children are equal to each other.[63]

The Generation of the Divide – the Danger of Uniformity and the Third Failure

Modern exegesis views the first sections of the book of Genesis as a narrative of God's attempts, as it were, to teach mankind an ethical lesson. The first attempt at an idyllic life in the Garden of Eden failed. The second attempt at allowing man (outside of the Garden of Eden) to independently attain recognition of the lone God and the necessity of an ethical life for the preservation of society also failed. Man preferred his baser physical, sensual foundation, and brought the deluge upon himself. After the deluge, with the restoration of the human race and the establishment of new world orders, including instructions which were given to Noah's descendants, the third attempt to enable the existence of society for mankind took place, based on ethical and spiritual values. This attempt also did not work out well. The people of the divide [*hapalaga*] (they lived close to the birth of Peleg, who was fourth generation to Noah[64]) wished to develop and advance mankind without divine guidance. In order to achieve this, they negated the value of the individual and harnessed all forces for the

---

63. Maimonides, *Guide for the Perplexed*, 3:50 and Cassuto, *MeNoah ad Avraham*, 97, 119, 123. Regarding possible identifications of *Ur Kasdim* cf. *Olam Hatanach, Bereshit*, 89.

64. Kimhi, 10:28.

tyranny of the society: They congregated in one place and erected a monumental structure there for the purpose of consolidating their rule through preservation of ideological and linguistic homogeneity ("Everyone on earth had the same language and the same words" – 11:1). They thereby violated the commandment to "Be fertile and increase, **and fill the earth**" (9:1). Indeed, this time man chose to develop and strengthen his power as a result of hubris, extreme pretentiousness and tyranny.[65] They viewed the state, the nation, steeped in the accumulation of possessions and the development of civilization and technology, as an end in of itself, rather than as a means for the betterment of its citizens, enabling spiritual advancement. The government harnessed the citizens in an absolute fashion for the building of the tower, with its summit appearing as if it were in the heavens – a symbol of power, of acquisition, of success and of centralization. God, who is higher than high, descended to observe their actions, and was not pleased by the situation, the outcome of which would be rebellion against God and ethical corruption resulting from the negation of the value of the individual as a reflection of the divine image. Therefore He dispersed the people of the generation of the divide, and they were scattered in all directions, and He mixed (or confounded) their languages. The construction of the tower was halted and the city surrounding it was named for the mixing [*b'lilah*] (or confusion [*bilbul*]: Babel [*Bavel*]. The original divine objective was thereby achieved: the spread of the human race over the entire face of the earth. God shattered the pursuit of communal honor, prevented uniformity, the totalitarian centralization, and enabled subjectivity and diversity from which derive a diversity of languages, opinions, efforts, and struggles. This diversity gives meaning to the human experience, and the

---

65. Rashbam, Ibn Kaspi, *Mitzraph Lakeseph*, 11:4, and Cassuto, 166.

parashat Noah

truth of the Torah would ultimately be clarified through it by means of ongoing dialectical processes.[66]

The colors of the rainbow symbolize this diversity, which ensures the development of humanity, and it is a sign for the fact that diversity saves the life on the earth from a further deluge.

The descriptions of these first three attempts come to teach the biblical view according to which the source of evil is within man, who is given free will to do good or evil. He is liable to err, to be negligent or to sin knowingly as a result of laziness, foolishness or wickedness, as he is ensnared in the net of desire for honor, greed or lust. Evil exists in the world in order to thereby distinguish good from it. This is the best of all possible worlds. A world without evil and without suffering is a world without challenge, without a lesson and without reward, an empty world. It is clear from the course of human history up to this point that man requires divine direction toward the good: without it he finds it difficult to identify it, to strive to maintain it and to succeed in it. According to the modern exegesis, God adopted a new means for this purpose: the appointment of an emissary from among the human race, who will guide them in the ways of God. This emissary is not one person, but rather a nation, which God chose for this purpose. The history of the patriarchs of this nation, the Jewish people, begins here.

---

66. Cf. the commentary *Aqedat Yitzchak*, S. R. Hirsch and *Haamek Davar* on the sin of the generation of the divide. Compare with Gersonides and Abravanel ad loc. and Y. Leibowitz, *Hearot Leparashiyot Hashavua*, 15-16, *Sheva Shanim shel Sihot al Parashat Hashavua*, 29-36. Cassuto, 154-155 and 157-158 sees the story as biblical satire directed against the materialism of ancient peoples, especially the Babylonians, who glorified themselves with great wealth;, and as substantiation of the position that nothing can stand in the way of the actualization of God's plan for the dispersal of man upon the entire Earth. On p.156 he explains where the remnants of the tower are found and on p. 157 he explains the source of the Acadian name '*Babel*', which means the gates of the *El[God]*, (*B'ab Ilu*).

According to the modern exegesis, from this point on, the Bible describes and explains the place of the Jewish people in human society and its mission to bring it back, by means of a long journey, to the Garden of Eden, to closeness to God.[67]

The Jewish post-modern exegesis is more modest. According to its approach, the Bible presents us now with the narrative of the Jewish people – one of several parallel and, to a large degree, similar ones – which existed in the region of the Fertile Crescent in ancient times. This commentary views them from a pluralistic perspective; and accepts that each of them reflects the truth for its bearer. The Jewish people, in whose consciousness the biblical text developed, did not at all question the sanctity of the work; and their commitment to the norms contained in it remained strong, as well.

Part two - Abraham

Parashat Lekh Lekha
The Divine Plan – Why was Abraham Chosen and What was his Mission?

In *Parashat Lekh Lekha*, we encounter the image of Abraham for the first time.[68] The Torah conceals from us the description of the first seventy-five of his 175 years. We know nothing of those years, other than his birth, marriage to *Sarai* and his emigration, together with his father Terah, from Ur of the Chaldeans to Haran. The

---

67. This is the theory of S. R. Hirsch and M. Buber. Cf. for example Hirsch 3:19, 6:22-24, 11:10, and many more; Buber, *Darko shel Miqra*, 68-71, 93-94.

68. For the sake of convenience, I use the later names of *Avram* and *Sarai*'s, which God changed to the more familiar names, Abraham and Sarah.

parashat Lekh Lekha

Torah does not view them as being relevant. The Midrash, seeking an explanation for God's sudden selection of Abraham to be the person through whom all the families of the earth will be blessed, adds information concerning his childhood and youth; however, this information is not our concern. For the modern exegesis, Abraham represents a new phase, a fourth attempt in human history for the divine masterplan. Man failed in the Garden of Eden with respect to his relationship with his creator, he failed in the generation of the deluge in his relationships with his fellow man and he failed in the generation of the divide with respect to his relationship with society. Now, providence abandons global solutions for human education toward ethical monotheism. One man will be chosen, and from him, in the course of numerous stages, a family will grow, and from it – a nation, which will be a light for the nations, and will lead to their redemption.

The medieval commentators disagree as to the reason for the selection of Abraham. Rabbi Judah Halevi, the Neo-Platonist, held (in his work, the Kuzari), that Abraham embodied the quintessence (in contemporary terminology we might view this as a sort of "gene") of Adam, the uniqueness of prophecy; transmitted to him by way of the elite. This capability is realized in the Land of Israel (or on its behalf), as it has the exclusive capability to enable prophecy. Abraham transmitted this capability to Isaac; and it was transmitted via Isaac to Jacob and the children of Israel. The author of the Zohar and the Kabbalists viewed the uniqueness of Abraham in that he was the *sefirah* of *Hesed*. His connection to the Land of Israel, which is the *sefirah* of *Malkhut*, allowed for the beginning of the correction – a renewing unification of the *sefirot* - which were separated through the sin of Adam – a correction which the descendants of Abraham were going to continue by means of the fulfillment of the commandments. The *Hasidei*

Ashkenaz viewed the uniqueness of Abraham in his absolute self-sacrifice to the point of martyrdom, which was actualized in the binding of Isaac. Maimonides, the Aristotelian rationalist, rejected these particularistic, exclusive positions. As a universalist, he held (Mishneh Torah, *Hilkhot Avodat Kokhavim* chapter 1) that every person created in the divine image has the capability of prophecy, and that the Land of Israel does not possess any special sanctity. In his opinion, which is based on a Midrash, Abraham was chosen because he succeeded in maximizing his intellectual potential, and in attaining an intellectual recognition of God; and the Land of Israel was chosen for historical reasons.

Modern exegesis did not accept these medieval positions. It found the reason for the selection of Abraham in the text in *Parashat Vayera*, which follows the one we are dealing with. There, God Himself explains the selection of Abraham prior to His informing him of his decision to destroy Sodom and Gomorrah, whose sexual and societal corruption cried out to the heavens. God said to Himself that He could not fail to share his plan with Abraham, since Abraham was his candidate to father a great nation, through which all of humanity would be blessed. What distinguishes Abraham? "For I have singled him out, that he may instruct his children and his posterity to keep the way of the Lord by doing what is just and right" (18:19). One may conclude from this that Abraham was not chosen by virtue of his intellect, nor because of some special mental quintessence, which is not contingent on him, but rather because he formed himself into a spiritual-ethical person, and developed his potential to be a knight of ethics, a teacher-educator for his immediate family and a source of ethical influence on the generations after him.[69]

---

69. Cf. H. Y. Chamiel, *Maaynei Miqra Miqraei Kodesh,* 220-231, *Limudim BeFarashat HaShavua, Lekh Lekha,* 1:29-32. As opposed to Noah, about

parashat Lekh Lekha

Indeed, Abraham demonstrated in that very context that his selection was justified. He was not afraid to confront the providence which was about to harm the "other", and he rushed to defend Sodom despite the fact that its inhabitants were notorious. He argued that it is possible that there are innocents (*tzadiqim*) in the city, who the attribute of justice was not taking note of among the general public. A society which allows for the existence of such innocents in its midst testifies about itself that it has not reached its nadir, and that, therefore, there is a chance for its recovery. The lighthouse of ethics only relinquished the struggle after daring to repeatedly confront God – six times – and understood that there were not even ten innocents in Sodom. That being said, God respected the ethics of human reason, with noteworthy patience, and did not rebuke Abraham for his insolence.

This parasha, then, is fundamental to the modern interpretation of the selection of Abraham. The modern commentators internalized the principles of the French Revolution and the Enlightenment, and rallied around the egalitarian approach that all humans possessing reason were entitled to freedom and happiness without distinction based on race, gender or status. They recognized the significance of this stance for the Jews struggle for emancipation in particular, and for their existence in the world in general. Therefore, they were not able to accept the approach of Rabbi Judah Halevi, who asserted that the Jewish people, the chosen people, innately have qualities which are fundamentally-immanently superior to those of members of other nations. The parallel stance was also rejected by the modern exegesis, namely, the stance of the Kabbala and Nahmanides (whose stature as a kabbalist is no less than of his stature as a biblical commentator;

---

whom the text speaks in the past tense "*was a righteous man*", the text speaks of Abraham in the future tense, "*and be blameless*", and in the verse cited above it says "that he may instruct".

parashat Lekh Lekha

however, his public stances reflected a medieval rabbinic position), that only the Jewish soul, and not the souls of members of other nations, are of divine origin. In this regard, the modern exegesis preferred the position of Maimonides, that a Jew has no fundamental superiority over a non-Jew, and the Land of Israel has no innate superiority over other lands. According to modern exegesis, Abraham was selected, then, not because of his natural superiority, which he received from Adam by way of Shem and his descendants; but, rather, because of the historical fact that in the generations of pagans immersed in lowly bestiality, he alone – a person of justice – had the ability to grasp the oneness of God, from which the true ethical stances flow. He thereby became the senior representative of mankind, and from him comes "My firstborn son, Israel" (Exodus 4:22) – the first among equals. Abraham and the nation which came from him were chosen due to their suitability for the task of ethical-monotheistic guide for mankind. Luzzatto had a unique approach to this topic, that it was not God who chose Abraham; but, rather, it was Abraham who chose God, and God responded by selecting him. From this point on, the essence of human history is the Jewish nation's being educated by God, and the education of mankind by the Jewish nation. The first attempt at this mission was carried out when the nation dwelt in the Land of Israel (including the interruption of the Babylonian exile), and it failed. The second attempt occurred when the nation was in exile, after the destruction of the second Temple. Its success – the redemption – will occur when all of humanity reaches the highest level of divine service, in accordance with the norms established by God, and the Jewish nation will, once again, find its place in its land, and dwell in it in tranquility and security.[70] The post-modern

---

70. It is possible to find positions such as these in the biblical commentaries and selected writings of S. R. Hirsch and Luzzatto; although the older Luzzatto retracted the idea of the mission. Cf. Ephraim Chamiel, "The

exegesis forgoes the pretentiousness of ascribing the education of mankind to the Jewish nation, and makes do with the individual's ongoing search for self-fulfillment within his community, based on the lesson of Abraham and his descendants.

Abraham in the Land of Israel

God appeared to Abraham in Haran, and commanded him to disassociate himself from his past, from the culture in which he and his family lived; and go to the Land of Israel, where he will establish his mission to mankind. Abraham was destined to be an important person there, from whom a large and blessed nation was to grow; and through him, and in his merit, all of the people and nations would be blessed. Abraham left his father Terah, who was 145 years old at the time; and took his wife Sarah, Lot, the son of his brother Haran, and all of his possessions – slaves and maidservants, livestock and chattel, with him. In the end of the previous parasha, the Torah recalls that Haran dies prematurely, and that Sarah was barren. It is possible that it was for this reason that Terah, Abraham and Sarah wished to emigrate from Ur of the Chaldeans to a new location; along the lines of "changing one's place changes one's fortune". Sarah's barrenness was, apparently, the reason for Abraham's responding to God's call to emigrate from Haran to Canaan; a call which was accompanied by the promise that he would become a great nation there. We will see in

Middle Way," (Jerusalem, 2014), especially in the sections on their approach to ethics in the second chapter and in the sections on their position regarding the emancipation and universalism in the fourth chapter. Concerning Luzzatto's unique position cf. *Al Hahemla Vehahasgakha- Yesodei Hatorah*, 39, 62. Cf. also M. Buber, *Darko Shel Miqra,* 95-97, N. Leibowitz, *Studies in Bereshit (Genesis)* 164-170 where she adds and identifies the ethical "*derech Hashem"* (18:19) with "*daaa et Hashem"*, in Jer. 9:22-23, 22:15-16. It should be noted here that Micha Goodman recently suggested a different and revolutionary reading of the position of Rabbi Judah Halevi, in his book *Halomo shel HaKuzari.*

the continuation that Sarah's barrenness serves the Torah as a means for emphasizing how miraculous the formation of the Jewish nation was from its very outset.[71]

Abraham came to the land of the Canaanites and there, in Alon Moreh which is next to Nablus, he merited a second revelation; in which God told him that this is the land which is promised to his progeny, and that the rule of the Canaanites over it was transient.[72] Abraham built an altar as a sign of gratitude for the revelation and for the promise, and also to mark his spiritual territory. He continued southward along the mountain ridge on his spiritual conquest of the land and settled "east of Beit-El" (12:8), that is eastern Beit-El, between Beit-El in the west and Ha'Ai on its east. Abraham built an altar there and called out in the name of God, i.e. he made a monotheistic announcement about the oneness of God; as is appropriate for any place of permanent dwelling, conquered for God's honor and needing His blessing.[73] Afterwards he continued southward, and

---

71. Note that the story at the end of Noah 11:26-32 is dissimilar to the story told at the beginning of 'Lekh Lekha'. In that story it is God who commands Abraham to leave Haran. It wasn't Terah's initiative to leave for Canaan; an initiative which came to an end in Haran. The commentators see two stages in the journey from Ur of the Chaldeans to Canaan; God is involved only in the second stage (cf. Luzzatto 11:31). Bible critics claim that there are two traditions preserved here, and that the second is more reliable, for the Chaldeans ascended the stage of history later than the time of the patriarchs. Cf. Knohl, *Meayin Banu*, 2008, 38-40. For the reason for Sarah's infertility cf. ben Asher, Abravanel, Luzzatto and *Daat Miqra* 11:30, S. R. Hirsch 12:2, 17:17.

72. Luzzatto 12:6- "*vehakenaani az baarez*", *Torah Nidreshet*, ch.24. According to Ibn Ezra 12:6, *Devarim* 1:2, this is one of the verses which was implanted into the ancient text, from comments in the margins, at a later editing. Bible scholars view this verse as proof that the Torah was written, or edited after the inhabiting of the land. Cf. A. Rofe, *Mavo Lesifrut Hamiqra*, 23.

73. Luzzatto 12:8, cf. also Nahmanides, Kimhi 12:8, Cassuto, 227. According to the Midrash, commentators and Bible critics, many of the stories of the patriarchs allude to events which occurred in the early days of Israel's settling

concluded his journey in the Negev. Abraham, thereby, transformed the one-time transient acts of Noah (who built an altar one time) and Enosh (in whose days "it was caused to begin that they called out in the name of God" – 4:26) into a permanent practice; whereby, after an extended period of detachment, God once again played a role in the human consciousness. Abraham's calling out in the name of God also contrasts with the behavior of the people of the generation of the divide, who wished to create a name for themselves (11:4), and to accumulate power through detaching themselves from God. Abraham knew that only attachment to God and his ways and calling out in His name would enable man's elevation.

Abraham – the Man

Despite all of his uniqueness, Abraham is presented in the Torah as a human being possessing weaknesses, including mistakes and errors: He did not rely on God's promise, and in the face of hardships of drought – he abandoned the land which was promised to him and he went down to Egypt. Knowing the ways of the Egyptians – murder and lust – he, thereby, endangered himself and his wife, Sarah. It is possible that he did so out of recognition that God only helps those who attempt to act in all human ways to help themselves, and do not rely on miracles.[74] Prior to their arrival in Egypt, out of

---

of the land. David's (and Solomon's) Empire based itself on these Biblical stories of the Patriarchs and on the Divine promises to give them the land (whether understood as prophecy or as post facto reality), and on stories such as the corruption of the Canaanites and their subsequent curse. Cf. *Bereshit Rabbah* 40:8, Tanhuma Buber *Lekh Lekha* 12. Nahmanides 12:6, 10, and nt. 137 below, as opposed to nt. 56 earlier and Cassuto, 207-209, 220-221, 224.

74. Kimhi 12: 12, S. R. Hirsch, 12: 10, along the lines of "The discerning man will learn to be adroit" (Prov. 1:5), "With the pure You act in purity, and with the perverse You are wily." (2 Sam. 22:27) and "we do not rely on miracles" (TB Pesachim 64b).

parashat Lekh Lekha

fear that they would kill him in order to obtain his beautiful wife,[75] he instructed her to say that she is his sister rather than his wife. He said to her that it will thereby be good for him in her merit, that is to say, that he will survive and they will both remain alive, and be spared the indignity of starvation.[76] It is possible that he expected the local dignitaries would engage him in protracted negotiations in order to acquire her legally, rather than forcefully; and, thereby, he would gain time until he and Sarah could return to the Land of Israel. He did not expect that the king himself would desire her; and the king is, obviously, above the law.[77] Abraham's plans never came to fruition; on the contrary, Sarah was taken to the palace of Pharaoh. Abraham was, thereby, punished for his mistakes; and became entirely dependent on divine salvation.[78] Nonetheless, he received a significant dowry of cattle[79] and slaves.

---

75. Regarding the claim that Abraham erred here cf. Nahmanides, S. R. Hirsch and D. Z. Hoffmann, 12: 10-13. For an explanation of this issue connected to the nature of the trait of faith, cf. the discussion on *Parashat Vayishlakh*. Regarding the beauty of the aged Sarah cf. Cassuto, *Sefer Bereshit Umivnehu*, 318-319, *Menoah ad Avraham*, 236-237.

76. Kimhi and Nahmanides 12:13. In this way the claim of Israel's detractors is contraindicated. They claim that Abraham, the patriarch of the nation, lied and abandoned Sarah in order to acquire property and wealth. Cf. also M. D. Cassuto, *Sefer Bereshit Umivnehu*, 181-183, *Menoah ad Avraham*, 237-239.

77. Abravanel, Sforno, S. R. Hirsch and Luzzatto ad loc., based on Rabbenu Nissim, who disagrees with Nahmanides and believes that Abraham did not sin.

78. Cassuto, *Sefer Bereshit Umivnehu*, 183-186, *Menoah ad Avraham*, 240-241.

79. The cattle which Abraham received included camels. The question of whether or not there were domesticated camels in Abraham's time has been the subject of debate since W. Albright determined in 1949 that camels were first domesticated after the patriarchal period. Other Bible critics concurred, although there were those who disagreed. Cf. Y. Knohl, *Meayin Banu*, 31, 52, who takes the later opinion and Cassuto, *Menoah ad Avraham*, 242-243,

God accepted both Abraham's human frailties and his human efforts to escape famine and the Egyptian sword; and ultimately saved the couple from the claws of Pharaoh. He afflicted the king and his family with disease (perhaps leprosy) and Pharaoh immediately understood the cause (perhaps Sarah revealed the truth in her distress). Pharaoh, lecherous snatcher of women, summoned Abraham, and – in the height of hypocrisy – admonished him for misleading him, and then instructed his people to send Abraham and Sarah back to Canaan.[80]

We will note, in the context of Abraham's mistakes that he erred once again in his debate with Sarah regarding the banishing of Hagar and Ishmael, in the following parasha. God advised him that in this case Sarah was more correct than he; as Ishmael, lacking ethical inhibitions, was not worthy to be in his father Abraham's household. Sarah also erred on this occasion, by oppressing her maidservant, and Abraham did not object.[81]

Y. Klein, *Olam Hatanakh*, *Bereshit* 12:16, Meitlis, *Lahpor et HaTanakh*, 125-126, who take the earlier perspective. It seems that Meitlis decided this debate in favor of those who view domestication as having taken place earlier.

80. This story repeats again in a different version in the story of Abraham, Sarah and Abimelech, the king of the Philistines (20:1-18), and in the story of Yitzchak and Rivka and the king of the Philistines who bore the same name (26:7-11). Those subscribing to the Documentary Hypothesis attributed the story to three different sources. Cassuto, *Sefer Bereshit Umivnehu*, 256-264, *Torat Heteudot*, 69, *MeNoah ad Avraham*, 228-235, explains that there were three different traditions in Israel which aimed to teach that God helps those who are faithful to him, before the story was written in the Torah. According to him these three traditions contribute to this educational-religious principle. This kind of repetitious writing was practiced in the Roman and Babylonian traditions. The stories of the patriarchs also contain many repetitions of the same motifs, and the events of their lives were similar.

81. Nahmanides 16:6. S. R. Hirsh, 12: 10-13, expresses his opinion that the Torah presents historical fact, and doesn't hide the weaknesses of its

parashat Lekh Lekha

After he was respectfully sent off with all of the possessions which he had accumulated in the form of money, cattle and slaves, Abraham returned to the south of the Land of Israel, and from there he gradually went up northward to the point which he constructed for himself – Beit-El east. Abraham apparently shared his possessions with his nephew, Lot, and, as a result of this, a quarrel broke out after a while between Abraham's shepherds and Lot's shepherds. The local grazing fields and wells were insufficient for both of their flocks, flocks which grew and increased, as the Canaanites and the Perizzites had already settled in the Land of Israel at that time.[82] The quarrel which broke out might have been symptomatic of differing world views, which surface at times of material abundance. Lot, being a man of physicality, viewed wealth as an end unto itself, and apparently did not recoil from unworthy acts in order to increase his assets; whereas Abraham, being a man of spirituality, viewed it as a means to increase righteousness and justice, and rejected Lot's

---

role models. It is impossible to see superhumans as a model from which to learn lessons; only human characters who have struggled and overcame their sensuality in order to elevate themselves may serve as role models. Cf. also S. R. Hirsch 25:27, 28, 27:1, 34:25-31. Cf. the discussion on *Parashat Vaera* regarding the characters of Moshe and Aaron and the commentary of S. R. Hirsch on Exodus 6:14-30.

82. Bekhor Shor, and Hizkuni 13:7. Ibn Ezra maintains that several verses spread out in the *Humash* were implanted in the text a long time after they were written by Moses, apparently for the purpose of clarification. Our verse here (13:7 like 12:6) is, in his opinion, one of them. According to him this is secret, and is similar in nature to the final twelve verses of the *Humash*, which were written by Joshua, (cf. his commentary on Deuteronomy 1:2, 34:1- the secret of the twelve). Regarding similar scattered verses cf. Ibn Ezra Genesis 22:14, Deuteronomy 3:11, 31:22. Additional verses which pose difficulty: Genesis 26:33, 36:31, Numbers 12:3, 14:45-21:3, 32:41, Deuteronomy, 2:12, 11:30, 19:14. Compare with Luzzatto, *Torah Nidreshet*, ch.24, *Mehkrei HaYahadut*, 1:98-105; A. Rofe, *Mavo Lesifrut Hamiqra*, 23-25. Cf. Deuteronomy, notes 228, 230.

parashat Lekh Lekha

actions. Here, too, Abraham showed a certain weakness. He was unable to peacefully resolve the problems which led to conflict in the family. After the quarrel, he told Lot that it would be better for them to separate; and he gave Lot the option of choosing between the north of the land or the south. Lot left the residence which was common to him and Abraham – "east of Beit-El" – and traveled from that "east of" to Sodom, which was in the Jordan Valley.[83] Abraham did not protest Lot's decision to dwell alongside the wicked sinners of Sodom, merely because the Jordan Valley was fertile and wealthy. The Torah tells us in a parenthetical remark, that this area, where the Jordan spills into the Dead Sea, was irrigated by the Jordan at that time, and was particularly fertile without dependence on rainfall. It was like the Garden of Eden, which is at the delta of the Tigris and Euphrates in Mesopotamia, and like the delta of the Nile in Egypt. However, Lot would ultimately pay a high price in life and property for his pursuit of wealth, and for his preferring to live among the wicked of Sodom, rather than in the vicinity of Abraham, a person of righteousness and justice. After the separation from Lot, God again revealed Himself to Abraham, in order to strengthen him and to promise him that despite his weaknesses he is still the chosen one – all of the Land of Israel would belong to him and his numerous progeny – and He urged him to continue to travel throughout the land. Abraham went back toward the south and settled in Hebron, where his ally, Mamre the Amorite, allocated Elone Mamre to him. Here too, as appropriate for a permanent dwelling for him and his family, and in gratitude for the confirmation of the divine promise, he built an altar.

---

83. On '*miqedem*' cf. M. Z. Segel ad loc. On Lot's choice cf. Bekhor Shor, 13:10.

Abraham and His Neighbors – Respect Him and Suspect Him

Simultaneously with the difficulties in the family, Abraham demonstrated in his conduct with others, that his being chosen as the representative of ethical monotheism and its emissary was correct. He went to war without hesitation against the four kings led by Chedorlaomer, who ruled over the eastern bank of the Jordan and who subjugated the five kings led by the king of Sodom, who ruled over the valley of the Dead Sea west of the Jordan, for twelve years. In the thirteenth year, the subjugated kings rebelled. A year later, the four went to war to subjugate the rebels anew, and on their way south-west they defeated important, powerful kingdoms on both sides of the Jordan. The five kings who fought against them were defeated as well and the subjugators took a large amount of booty and captives, including Lot. Abraham heard of these events from one of the fugitives of the defeated; he did not cringe from the proven might of the four, left Hebron with his men and his allies, the brothers Mamre, Eshkol and Aner, in order to rescue his nephew and the rest of the captives and the rest of the enslaved. He ran after the vanquished northward until Dan, split his men, surprised Chedorlaomer and his partners with a nighttime attack from several directions and defeated them. He pursued the fleeing army to the north (left) of Damascus, recouped all of the captives and their property, and took the booty of the vanquished. The king of Sodom and the priest, Melchizedek, who was king of Salem, went out to greet the victor with bread and wine, and blessed him in the name of God, the Most High. As per the custom regarding priests, Abraham conferred a tithe of the captives and the spoils of the war on Melchizedek.[84] The king of Sodom thought that Abraham saw himself as the owner of the balance of the spoils;

---

84. Rashi, Ibn Ezra and Nahmanides, 14:20. *Smol*= *zafon*- cf. Luzzatto 14:15.

parashat Lekh Lekha

however, he himself was the master of the land and a significant portion of the spoils were rightfully his according to the customary law. He suggested to Abraham that they divide the spoils such that Abraham receives all of the property and the king of Sodom all of the captives. Abraham rejected the offer: He refused to take of the spoils "so much as a thread or a sandal strap" (14:23). He asked only for compensation, as per the law, for his soldiers and allies in the battles – the brothers, Eshkol and Aner and Mamre. It is God who enriches, and let the wicked and corrupt king of Sodom not say that he enriched Abraham.

It is worth paying attention to the veiled theological polemic between Abraham, the king of Sodom and Melchizedek, king of Salem (Jerusalem?) "a priest of God Most High," (14:18) who, as mentioned, went out to greet Abraham with bread and wine to bless him on his victory. Melchizedek blessed Abraham with the words: "Blessed be Abram of God Most High [*Elyon*] Creator of heaven and earth" (14:19). The blessing is in the name of the Canaanite deity *Elyon*, who Melchizedek believed was supreme over the other deities.[85] In his response to the king of Sodom's suggestion regarding the spoils of the war, Abraham presented his theological stance, together with his refusal to take anything: "I swear to the Lord [*Hashem*], God Most High, Creator of heaven and earth" (14:22): Indeed, there is a God who is supreme over all of the deities, a God who created the world, and the world is His possession; however, it is not the deity named *Elyon* but, rather, the one and only God, the Lord [*Hashem*].

---

85. Ohr Hahaim and Luzzatto 14:18. Cf. also M. D. Cassuto, Sefer *Bereshit Umivnehu*, 61-62, 66-67, *Yerushalayim BeSifrei Hatorah, Sifrut Miqrait VeSifrut Cnaanit*, 1: 92, and Y. Knohl, *Meayin Banu*, 2008, 95. Regarding Abraham's refusal to take property from the king of Sodom cf. *Haamek Davar*, 14:23.

The Covenant between the Pieces – the Fear and the Hope

After the victory against the kings, God appeared to Abraham and reassured him, that he should not be afraid that the kings will return to avenge their defeat. God promised Abraham much reward for forgoing the spoils of the war; however, Abraham forewent also this, because he did not see the purpose of his possessions as he was childless, without a familial heir. After the separation from Lot, Eliezer, the manager of his household, was destined to inherit Abraham's estate.[86] God responded to these issues with two promises. The first – the blessing of progeny, which was said outside of the tent in a nocturnal vision: "That one (Eliezer) shall not be your heir; none but your very own issue shall be your heir," (15:4) and your progeny will be as numerous as the stars above you. Abraham believed in this promise without question, and God counted this to his credit.[87] The second promise is the blessing of the Land of Israel, which was said during the daytime: "Then He said to him, 'I am the Lord who brought you out from Ur of the Chaldeans to assign this land to you as a possession'." (15:7) Here Abraham suddenly asked: "How shall I know that I am to possess it?" (15:8). Did he doubt this promise and ask for a sign? From God's answer it would appear that Abraham did not cast doubt on the fulfillment of the promise itself; but, rather, he wished to know when it would be fulfilled, when would his descendants begin to inherit the land: How will it be known that the time has come, and how will it take place?[88] Regarding this, God established a

---

86. Cf. the opinion of R. Nehemia in Bereshit Rabba 41:8. Cf. also Luzzatto, 15:2.

87. Cf. Psalm 106:31, Targum Unkelos and Johnathan, Rashi, Kimhi, Sforno, *Habeur*, Reggio, 15:6, and Maimonides, *Moreh Nevukhim*, III:53 and *Haiqarim*, I:21. Compare with Luzzatto ad loc.

88. Behor Shor, S. R. Hirsch, Luzzatto and D. Z. Hoffmann, 15:8.

parashat Lekh Lekha

covenant with Abraham – the covenant between the pieces, which defined the time frame and the events leading up to the inheritance of the land by the offspring of Abraham.

This covenant was added to the covenant of the rainbow, which God established with all of mankind, and this is God's first covenant with Abraham and his descendants. Abraham took three fattened[89] animals – a heifer, a goat and a ram, as well as birds – a turtledove and a young bird; he divided the first three and remained to guard the carcasses from birds of prey until evening. After darkness descended, Abraham fell asleep. While dreaming, he experienced a dark dread – an awful dread – and heard the divine promise, which inspired both fear and hope simultaneously. As is the case with all of the dreams recalled in the book of Genesis, the numbers which appear in them represent time.[90] The four animals, which the birds of prey (the enemies) threaten to destroy, represent four hundred long, bleak years of slavery and oppression in Egypt, to the threshold of the mental, and even physical, destruction of the nation (in Pharaoh's order regarding the killing of the infants), or four generations of subjugation and exile, until the Egyptians receive their punishment and the fourth generation will go free, leave Egypt with great wealth and conquer the Land of Israel.

The Promised Land extends from the Nile to the Euphrates. At the time of the promise, ten nations dwelt there. The region of the land which was meant to be conquered first belonged to seven of them, and this latter group included the Amorites and Canaanites (cf. 15:20-21). At the time of their being freed from Egypt, the time would arrive to exact retribution from the Amorites for their

---

89. Behor Shor, Hizquni, Luzzatto, 15:9, based on *Tosafot* TB Gittin 56a, s.v. *'egla tilta'*. According to Targum Jonathan and others – three year old animals.

90. Cf. more on this discussion in *Parashat Vayeshev*.

parashat Lekh Lekha

sins; in other words, to conquer their land, which was promised to the Israelites.[91] As was typical for covenants in ancient times, a flaming torch emitting thick smoke appeared from the midst of the darkness,[92] representing God, and passed between the pieces which Abraham cut; and the covenant between God and Abraham was thereby completed and sealed. The Torah does not explain why Abraham's descendants were sentenced to exile and subjugation in Egypt. Modern exegesis holds that the land of Canaan posed a danger to the expanding family becoming assimilated among its neighbors; whereas in Egypt, whose culture was diametrically opposed to that of the Israelite culture – and the Egyptians were revolted by the Israelite culture – the Israelites would flourish in isolation from the Egyptian nation. In addition, the total subjugation of the Israelites ensured no one can claim that the Israelite nation was formed like any other nation, through natural human processes.[93]

Our Brother Ishmael

In this parasha, the Torah presents the character of Ishmael for the first time, the father of the Arab tribes. Ishmael is the son of Abraham, a descendant of Shem, the blood of noble and wise men flows through him; at the same time, the blood of the Egyptian maidservant Hagar, descendant of Ham and his son Egypt, also flow in him. From this mix is born a son destined for greatness; but he is also a nomad,

---

91. Regarding the interpretation of the vision cf. D. Z. Hoffmann and the commentary of Benno Jacob which is brought in N. Leibowitz, Studies in *Bereshit* Genesis, 149-150. Compare with Ibn Caspi, *Tirat Keseph*, 80-82. Regarding the stages of the actualization of the promise cf. Rashi, Hizquni, 15:19, based on Bereshit Rabbah, 44:23, PT Shvi'it, 6:1.

92. Rashi 15:10. This torch will reappear later, representing God at the splitting of the Reed Sea.

93. S. R. Hirsch, Genesis, 45:11, 46:33; Exodus, Sforno, Genesis, 46:3. Cf. the discussion regarding the subjugation in *Parashat Shemot*.

parashat Lekh Lekha

hot tempered and sensual, married to an Egyptian woman.[94] The barren Sarah hoped to have a son through her maidservant Hagar, transcended herself and gave Hagar to Abraham in marriage. Hagar indeed became pregnant, however Sarah's plan backfired. Instead of creating a new atmosphere in the tents of Abraham, during her pregnancy, Hagar demonstrated contempt toward the barren Sarah, and superiority toward her,[95] and evoked tension and jealousy. Sarah sensed Hagar's bad character traits, was angry at Abraham for not acting to correct the situation, and held him responsible for her denigration. Abraham informed her that Hagar still had the status of being her maidservant, and permitted Sarah to act as she saw fit. As the events developed, Sarah did not succeed in maintaining her ethical standard, she forced hard labor on Hagar and oppressed her; and Hagar ran away from her to the desert. A divine angel found her beside a spring in the desert, and engaged her in conversation so that she would not be startled: He asked her where she was coming from and where she was headed. When she replied that she was running away from Sarah, he instructed her to return to the home of her mistress, despite the suffering, and to fulfill her task as a maidservant. Hagar was too stunned to respond. The angel understood that she was concerned, among other things, about the status of her son, who was destined to be a slave in the household of Abraham. Again, in the absence of her reply, the angel promised her, that the son, who she was going to give birth to in the home of Abraham, would be considered Abraham's son, with full privileges, and that his offspring would be very numerous. He will be a free man, free of masters – "He shall be a wild ass of a man [a free nomad, dwelling in deserts]; his hand against everyone [eager to battle, his opponents

---

94. S. R. Hirsch, 16:14, and in *Parashat Vayera*, on the 'binding' of Ishmael, 21:21.

95. Kimhi, 16:4.

being unable to defeat him], and everyone's hand against him; he shall dwell alongside of all his kinsmen [attaining prolificness and greatness]." (16:12) – a description suited to the descendants of Ishmael throughout the generations, through our days.[96]

The Circumcision and the Tidings

Abraham merited an additional revelation in our parasha, this time, it was not by means of "I am the Lord;" but, rather, by means of "I am El Shaddai" (I will return to the revelations by means of "I am the Lord;" and by means of "I am El Shaddai" below[97]). This revelation takes place fourteen years after the previous one. During these years, Ishmael was born and was raised in the household of Abraham. This new revelation was meant to renew and update the covenant which was established between the pieces. Abraham thought that the divinely promised family and nation would grow from Ishmael; however, the divine plan was clarified for him when he was ninety-nine years old, in the current revelation: "I am El Shaddai, Walk in My ways and be blameless (faithful and committed). I will establish My covenant between Me and you, and I will make you exceedingly numerous" (17:1-2). God repeats the promises which were given to Abraham in the previous revelations and changes his name from Avram to Abraham – symbolizing the fact that he will be fruitful and multiply and be "the father of a multitude of nations" (17:5). Indeed, from Abraham came Ishmael, the Midianites, the Edomites – the descendants of Esau – and the Israelites. The covenant between God and Abraham is an eternal covenant, and the chosen descendants of

---

96. Ibn Ezra, 16:12 and S. R. Hirsch, 12:11-13. Regarding the oppression of Hagar cf. Nahmanides, Kimhi, 16:6 and compare with S. R. Hirsch ad loc. It seems that the promises to the family of Abraham are predicated upon preemptive subjugation, maybe for educational purposes.

97. Cf. the discussion later on *Parashat Vaera*.

parashat Lekh Lekha

Abraham will ultimately acquire the Land of Israel, which will be an eternal inheritance for them. In this covenant, God summed up all of the clauses of the covenant in detail and with clarity: The land of Canaan as the eternal inheritance of the Israelites, and a progeny which will greatly multiply and become a nation, which will be utilized by kings, and for whom the Lord [*Hashem*] will be its God.

Abraham and his descendants' part in this covenant is circumcision. This time, the covenant is established in Abraham's flesh, and not in the dividing of offerings. Abraham is commanded to circumcise all of the males in his household, including male slaves which he purchased, immediately; and, in the future, to circumcise all eight day old infants in his family and in the family of his slaves whom he purchases. Whoever does not undergo circumcision will be punished – will be cut off from the nation, in other words, will not be gathered to his nation in death, and will not be considered as a member of the nation, servants of God, who bear his seal in their flesh. The cutting off of the foreskin of the organ embodying lust and sensuality is to be the sign of the covenant between God and the descendants of Abraham, who control their sensuality through His ethical guidance.[98] God instructed Abraham to change his wife's name from *Sarai* to Sarah, and told him the amazing news that Sarah would become pregnant from him and would give birth to a son in exactly a year. This news created an indiscernible tension for Abraham. He falls down on his face, shocked and agitated; not knowing whether to laugh or cry at hearing this wonderful prophecy. Feelings of astonishment mixed with joy surge within him, and in an attempt to break the tension, he declared that he would settle for Ishmael. He had difficulty digesting the fact that he and his wife were

---

98. Kimhi, 17:11; Nahmanides, 17:9; S. R. Hirsch, 17:10-11. Compare with Maimonides, *Moreh Nevukhim*, 3:49; *Aqedat Yitzchak*, ad loc. On the covenant as God's seal cf. Behor Shor, 17:11, 14.

worthy of a miracle which meant the drastic change of the laws of nature, according to which elderly people such as themselves were unable to father and give birth to babies.[99] God informed him that the miracle was part of his plan: It was meant to demonstrate that this family and the special nation were created by Him in such a way that no one would question their uniqueness.[100] This son, who will be named Isaac [*Yitzchak*] (in commemoration of Abraham's laughter [*zhok*] as a reaction to the absurdity of this birth), will merit that the promises of the covenant with Abraham will be fulfilled through him; although – as requested by Abraham – Ishmael will not lose out and will also become a great nation. Abraham, at the age of ninety-nine, fulfilled God's command. He, Ishmael, who was thirteen, and all of his slaves, were circumcised on that very day.

Parashat Vayera
Ethical Monotheism

Modern commentary views the book of Genesis as representing the conditions for the receiving of the Torah. The basis for receiving the divine Teaching [*torat haelohim*] is the education for the science of man [*torat haadam*]. "*Derekh eretz* precedes the Torah," and *derekh eretz* in this commentary is not merely conduct necessary for existence, or etiquette and manners; but, rather, the laws of natural ethics and the finest of human culture, which are attained by means of reason.[101] The cornerstone for all of these is monotheism,

---

99. Ibn Caspi, *Tirat Keseph*, 89. Compare with Rashi, Behor Shor, Nahmanides, Kimhi and Luzzatto, 17:17.

100. S. R. Hirsch, 17:17.

101. Concerning the importance of *derekh eretz* in Judaism, cf. N. H. Weisel, *Divrei Shalom VeEmet* (Berlin, 1782). This is also the approach of '*Torah Im Derekh Eretz*' of S. R. Hirsch. Cf. E. Chamiel, *The Middle Way*, ch.3.

parashat Vayera

as according to the Torah's viewpoint, ethics can only be acquired based on recognition of one God, who created one man as the father of the human race. Thus, relations between man and his fellow are based on the perspective that we are all shoots or branches of the same person; and the commandment "Love your fellow as yourself" comes from here. Similarly, it flows from this, that every person stands and is judged as an individual – responsibility for his actions is on him alone – before the one, the Creator, before whom he stands.

In our parasha, Abraham, who is associated with the one and only God, stands in all of his ethical glory, in contrast to the surrounding pagan society, whose ethics are lowly and corrupt. The beginning of the parasha is apparently inextricably tied to the end of the previous one; as evidenced by the opening verse, which does not indicate that Abraham was the subject of the divine revelation, indicating that we have before us the continuation of the verses dealing with circumcision which precede it. According to this reading, God appeared to Abraham in the very midst of painful days following the circumcision. In this revelation, Abraham noticed three figures from afar. He immediately demonstrated his good character and welcomed three strange nomads under his roof, which was an expression of universal love for his fellow man and of benevolence. The promise of a piece of bread turned into a royal feast, and Abraham exerted himself using all of his energy to make the meal pleasant for his guests.[102] These nomads turned out to be

---

102. Compare Rashbam and Luzzatto 18:1, in contrast to Rashi, (following the Midrash) and Nahmanides ad loc., who see in this revelation which is unaccompanied by speech, a sign of esteem for Abraham upon his circumcision, or possibly a sick-visit. Concerning Abraham's guests cf. Saadia Gaon, 18:2, Kimhi, 18:3, 5, 7. Cassuto suggests in his book, *Sefer Bereshit Umivnehu*, (Jerusalem, 1990), 163-165, that the three guests were God and two of his angelic servants, who came to destroy Sodom. While this interpretation is daring, it does eliminate a number of difficulties from the text.

parashat Vayera

God's angels, sent to herald the birth of Isaac, to destroy Sodom and to save Lot from the destruction. The Torah, by means of its formulation, deliberately blurs the distinction between God and his angels. Ostensibly, this is an additional version of the narrative of the announcement of Isaac's birth, this time in the name *Hahsem* and through the medium of angels.[103]

Maimonides[104] held that angels do not exist in the real world, and that prophecy takes place within the mind of the prophet, either awake or in a dream. Therefore he held, that all that is recalled from verse 18:2 through 19:26 was a prophetic vision of Abraham's, as he was sitting and dozing in his chair at the entrance of his tent in the heat of the day. It was only when Abraham arose in the morning that he saw that the prophecy was fulfilled and the cities of the plain were destroyed. In this way, Maimonides resolves the difficulties of heavenly angels who eat a meal, and the repetition of the announcement. Nahmanides[105] disagrees with Maimonides and argues that narrative is realistic and that this announcement is intended for Sarah and it is for this reason that the angels ascertain that the modest Sarah is in close proximity and hears what they say. She too (perhaps not realizing that they were angels of God)

---

103. This is what the Bible critics would say. The story of the tidings in the previous *parasha* uses the name *'Elohim'*.

104. *Guide for the Perplexed*, 2:6, 42, according to the way in which Nahmanides explains it, 18:1, and according to Abravanel's understanding of Maimonides' position, in his commentary on the Guide and on our parasha. Aside from the Abravanel, the following commentators also follow the approach of Maimonides: Kimhi, 18:1, and throughout the chapter. He holds that the dream concludes at the end of the chapter. Ibn Kaspi, *Tirat Keseph*, 91-94. So too, Isaac Ara'ama in his commentary *Aqedat Yitzchak*. See below the psychological approach to the binding of Isaac, and that which is stated there in nt. 132.

105. Ad Loc. According to BT Bava Meziah 86b. Concerning the discussion between the angels, Abraham and Sarah, see Nahmanides 18:15.

mocked the speaker, laughed to herself when she heard these things and said to herself: "Now that I am withered, am I to have enjoyment [menstrual cycle]?[106] — with my husband [Abraham] so old!" (18:12). The laughter apparently expressed frustration, bitterness and disbelief of despair, unlike Abraham's laughter. Therefore, God (or an angel representing Him) rebuked her with the rhetorical question: "Is anything too wondrous for the Lord?" – Is there anything which the master of nature is unable to do?[107] This question was directed at Abraham, and so God concealed from him that which Sarah said about him, i.e. Abraham. God changed what she said, and caused them to refer only to herself, by saying to him: "Why did Sarah laugh, saying, 'Shall I in truth bear a child, old as I am?'" (18:13). Rashi (ad loc.) explains, based on the Midrash, that God too changes what others said, for the sake of peace (in this case, marital harmony); that is for ethical reasons. Even the very fact that God (or an angel representing Him) directed Himself to Abraham concerning Sarah, rather than addressing her directly comes to teach *derekh eretz* of gentleness and humility. Abraham rebuked Sarah for the lack of trust in her heart, and when she denied it, he repeated his accusation.

In the continuation of the revelation, after Abraham escorted the angels on their way, and they headed to Sodom to investigate whether it was "according to the outcry" (18:21), while Abraham "remained standing before the Lord" (18:22), God decided to reveal his intent to destroy the cities of the plain, due to their corruption, to Abraham. Abraham heard and responded both by evoking the attribute of divine mercy and by force of his universal

---

106. Cf. Rashi ad loc.

107. Nahmanides, 18:15, Targum Unkelos and Johnathan, 18:12. Saadia Gaon adds that the first promise to Abraham was predicated upon the circumcision, and after it was implemented the angel confirmed it again.

parashat Vayera

moral judgment: He entered into a debate with God regarding the fate of Sodom. Abraham's image here accentuates the inferiority of all those around him. Sodom is the symbol of human wickedness, which is expressed in our parasha through sexual immorality, as I will show below.[108] The evil of Sodom influenced Lot and his family, as I will present and explain in the continuation.[109] Hagar educated her son in the spirit of freedom, sensuality, self-centeredness and hot-temperedness of the desert nomads. Therefore, Abraham had to remove him from his home and sever his ties to his family. Abraham's neighbors, the people of Gerar (and leading them, their king, Abimelech) were far from ethical perfection. Abimelech took Sarah for himself. Albeit, he was unaware that she was a married woman, as Abraham presented her as his sister, as he had done when he went down to Egypt, and for the same reason. However, isn't this very practice – taking a woman against her will, and without the consent of her family, and to subjugate her to the lust of the ruler – fundamentally unacceptable and corrupt? It is, therefore, no wonder that Abraham concealed the fact that Sarah was his wife, as he said to Abimelech: "I thought, surely there is no fear of God in this place, and they will kill me because of my wife" (20:11). From this statement – "there is no fear of God" – it is clear what the difference between Abraham, who is God-fearing, and others is: Abraham is an ethical person, because fear of God, that is monotheism, is a precondition for ethics. "The devisings of man's mind are evil from his youth;"Man's nature does not allow for ethics without divine guidance. The guiding God is transcendent, free of the bonds of physicality, who created

---

108. Nahmanides, 19:8.
109. Cf. D. Z. Hoffmann ad loc., N. Leibowitz, *Studies in Bereshit (Genesis)*, 178-180. Cf. the commentary of Ezekiel 16:49 regarding the sins of Sodom.

ex nihilo. He formed man in his image, and God's spirit is within him. This allows him to rise above the bonds of his sensual body and to sanctify the body, the physical, with the assistance of divine guidance. This assistance is given later in the revelation at Sinai in an expanded version.[110]

Divine Conduct Toward Man

God recognized Abraham's worth, and knew him well as a man of righteousness (integrity and social justice toward the weak) and justice (equality before the law); and as one who educates the members of his household in this spirit. He updated him, and shared with him His plans to destroy Sodom and Gomorrah, about which the great cries of their oppression reached Him, and the sin of the oppressors was too great to bear. Earlier, God descended to the area, through the medium of his angels, in order to examine up close whether the corruption – social and sexual – was indeed total and comprehensive. According to Rabbi David Kimhi this comes to teach that this is how any proper judge, or person who hears a report which is not accompanied by clear evidence, ought to act. At that point, God decided to destroy these cities together with their inhabitants. Abraham did not accept this decision, but rather stubbornly argued with God about the harsh decree; despite the fact that he was aware, in his great humility, that he was but "dust and ashes" (18:27), and apologized for speaking at length. Note the fact that Abraham addresses God at the time of the negotiations, using the name of "mastery" [*adon*], and not the name *Hashem*. This is a show of respect when directly addressing God, angels representing Him, or a person deserving respect. They are not addressed by their

---

110. This is S. R. Hirsch and Luzzatto's interpretation of the meaning of Judaism and the purpose of the Torah commandments. Cf. E. Chamiel, *The Middle Way,* ch.2.

personal name, but rather by use of a descriptive term: My master, or masters.

Abraham asked repeatedly whether it was possible that there were no righteous (innocent) in the city, who are not liable for the death penalty (wicked), and in whose merit the city would be spared. God did not reply with answers such as: "Do not interfere in areas where you are not able to understand," or "my bookkeeping is confidential, not everyone who appears to be righteous is actually a fully righteous person," or "that's the way of the world," or "thus I decreed". He agreed to suspend execution of the sentence until Abraham himself will reach the conclusion that there is no choice but to carry it out. As long as a direct connection and an ongoing dialogue exists between God and the just person, and so long as the fate of an entire community is hanging in the balance, there is a reckoning, and God's justice must be clear to man and compatible with his reason. Abraham addressed God six times, and each time lowered the number of righteous people required to save the city; beginning at fifty and concluding with ten. God responded each time patiently, and his final reply was "I will not destroy for the sake of the ten" (18:32). However, even ten righteous people were not found in the city in order to save it, nor to rescue them from the inferno. God only had compassion on Lot and his family, in the merit of his familial relationship with Abraham, and perhaps in the merit of his hospitality toward the angels. From the Torah's perspective, one who listens to God's voice, and fulfills His instructions merits life, health, livelihood and security. Anyone who leaves God's path is punished. The fate of a nation who goes too far in terms of their corruption is sealed, to be ejected from the land and be destroyed. This is what happened to Sodom and Gomorrah, and it is what will ultimately happen to the nations of Canaan, who went too far in the days of Joshua. Moses warned the nation repeatedly that this will also be their fate if they go too far.

parashat Vayera

Lot saw the two angels at the gate of the city, entreated them to stay and spend the night at his house, and prepared a feast for them, exhibiting –the trait of hospitality he learned from Abraham. At night, all of the people of Sodom surrounded the house, and crudely demanded of Lot that he bring the guests out to them in order to carry out homosexual relations with them. The hideous proposal by Lot, who had gone out to the crowd and closed the door behind him – to bring his two virgin daughters who were in his house out to them and to abandon them to the lust of the mob –, was met with outright rejection. This proposal shows Lot's loss of the human and ethical standards as a father and as a human being.[111] The furious bullies promised to harm Lot even more than his guests, and approached in order to break the door of the house. The angels quickly brought Lot inside, locked the door and afflicted the inhabitants of the city with temporary blindness and forcibly carried Lot (who tarried because he found it difficult to part with his property) outside with their own hands, together with his wife and his two single daughters. His married daughters, and his sons-in-law, who heard from him the warning of the destruction; thought that he was joking and made fun of him, and remained in the city. The angels brought the refugees to the outskirts of the city and instructed them to flee to the mountain and not look back. His wife did not obey the order: She was unable to forgo her life in Sodom and her daughters and their families; she was drawn back as if spellbound, lost her right to exist and turned into a pillar made of salt.

What the angels saw and heard was enough for them to conclusively endorse the sentencing of Sodom to receive the rod. Lot, who was concerned that they would not have enough time to reach the mountain, asked that he be allowed to flee to the small nearby city of Zoar. He further requested that they spare it for their,

---
111. Nahmanides, 19:8.

parashat Vayera

the refugees, sake. He answered in the affirmative, in Abraham's merit. In the morning, at the moment when Lot arrived at Zoar, God rained upon the cities of the plain sulfurous fire, annihilating them and their inhabitants, and transformed the entire plain from fertile earth to salty and desolate land (Deuteronomy 29:21-22). In the morning, Abraham looked from the mountain, where he dwelt, toward the Jordan Valley; and saw the smoke of the land rising from the area like the smoke of a kiln.

Lot and his daughters were afraid of remaining in Zoar and fled from there to a cave in the mountain, and they were certain that Zoar would be wiped out after they left it. Perhaps they believed that the whole world had been annihilated, or was about to be annihilated; and maybe they assumed that whoever fled from the place of evil is liable for excommunication.[112] In any case, the eldest daughter said to her sister: "...there is not a man on earth to consort with us in the way of all the world" (19:31) – there is no man from whom we can become pregnant and give birth. She influenced the younger sister to give their father wine to drink at night, and to become pregnant from him in order to give life to progeny; they did so during the course of two nights, without their father knowing about it. Lot's body was abandoned to the disposal of his daughters, which was poetic justice for his intending to abandon them to the unbridled lust of the people of Sodom. The two daughters became pregnant and gave birth to sons. The son of the eldest is called Moab, and that of the younger Ben-Ami. These are the sole offspring of Abraham's nephew who are known to us, and the nations Moab and Ammon.

The topic of reward and punishment, which Abraham raised as he stood before God, is repeated with greater intensity in the covenant

---

112. Rashbam, 19:30, and the commentary of Yoseph Kara, cited in Kimhi, 19:31. Concerning the number of Lot's daughters cf. Bereshit Rabbah, 50:9, Ibn Ezra 19:14.

parashat Vayera

which was established between God and the Israelites, and which is expressed in the blessing and curse (*Parashat Behukotai* and *Ki Tavo*). It applied to the community, and in exceptional circumstances to the individual, as well:[113] "Perchance there is among you some man or woman, or some clan or tribe, whose heart is even now turning away from the Lord our God to go and worship the gods of those nations … rather will the Lord's anger and passion rage against that man, till every sanction recorded in this book comes down upon him, and the Lord blots out his name from under heaven" (Deuteronomy 29:17-19). The documents of the covenant state that its abrogation by means of the nation will alter God's way of treating them, in terms of reward and punishment. The direct connection and dialogue will cease: "Then My anger will flare up against them, and I will abandon them and hide My countenance from them. They shall be ready prey; and many evils and troubles shall befall them. And they shall say on that day, "Surely it is because our God is not in our midst that these evils have befallen us." Yet I will keep My countenance hidden on that day, because of all the evil they have done in turning to other gods" (Deuteronomy 31:17-18). Indeed, after the destruction of the Temple and the beginning of the exile, the divine conduct changed. God hid His countenance, desisted from open intervention in history; and the world runs its course based on the laws of nature, physics and genetics. Man is neither directly rewarded nor punished by God for the choices which he makes, his mistakes, and the acts of wickedness which he inflicts on others in the course of his life in this world. The reward of a *mitzva* is – a *mitzva*, the consequence of a sin – a sin. A person's spiritual elevation is his reward and his spiritual descent is his punishment. God does not intervene to protect those who suffer from the foolishness or

---

113. Cf. the discussion on biblical reward and punishment in *Parashat Behukotai, Ekev* and *Nizavim*.

wickedness of human beings, in whose control He placed the world. Divine conduct is one of decree, not of compassion. The Torah leaves open an opening of hope for repentance, for the return of the Israelites to their land, and for the renewal of its direct connection and dialogue with God. This will bring back the previous conduct of reward and punishment for the individual and the community in this world and will return God to history, in order to enable redemption. This is in accordance with the promise: "And the Lord your God will grant you abounding prosperity in all your undertakings, in the issue of your womb, the offspring of your cattle, and the produce of your soil. For the Lord will again delight in your wellbeing, as He did in that of your fathers" (Deuteronomy 30:9). In the era of God's hidden countenance, the Sages gave hope by means of the promise of reward in the world to come, and thereby – a reason to continue observing the commandments and to cleave to God.

Abraham and Abimelech – an Encounter Between Cultures

After the destruction, Abraham went from Elone Mamre to Gerar, which is in the land of the Philistines (of the nations of Ham), in which Abimelech reigned. Based on what he had heard about the Philistines, Abraham thought that they were less corrupt than the Egyptians; however, like the Egyptians,[114] the Philistines also began to take an interest in Sarah. Abraham, who was surprised to a certain degree, was forced to adopt the old subterfuge and informed them that Sarah was his sister; hoping to thereby escape harm. However, Abimelech surprised Abraham again, and took the beautiful Sarah (who reverted to looking like a young woman when she became pregnant)[115] to his palace, in order to take her as a wife.

---

114. Cf. The discussion on this in *Parashat Lekh Lekha*.

115. Concerning Sarah's beauty cf. Nahmanides, Kimhi, 20:2, based on the assumption that the chronology of events was preserved. Bible critics

Abimelech did not consummate the marriage, because God blocked his reproductive organs, and those of his wives and all of the members of his household. God appeared to Abimelech in a dream and informed him that he was liable for death for the sin of the abduction of a married woman. Abimelech claimed that Abraham and Sarah had told him that they were brother and sister, he did not know that they were married; and he took her in good faith and his hands are clean. According to the laws of Gerar, the king has the right to force himself on any single woman, and therefore he is innocent (righteous) and blameless, and he therefore asks: "Will You slay people even though innocent?" – will you kill an entire nation together with their king, even if they are innocent? God answered that indeed it was known to Him that Abimelech did not know that Sarah was Abraham's wife, and that he acted in good faith. For this reason, He prevented him from touching Sarah, and thereby sinning to God. However, Abimelech's hands are not clean; rather, he abducts women without their consent and without the permission of the family. God commanded Abimelech to return the wife to her husband immediately, and to beg his forgiveness and ask him to pray on his behalf in order to remove the punishment of death which was anticipated for him and all who

---

say that this story is essentially another version of the story of Pharaoh and Sarah. According to Cassuto there were several traditions which existed before the writing of the Torah which needed to be integrated with the biblical chronology. Cf. nt. 80 above and Cassuto, 236-237. Note that as opposed to Rashi and the Midrash who do not flatter Abimelech, Nahmanides views him as a righteous man. Even so, Rashi and other commentators distinguish between Pharaoh and the Egyptians who were licentious, and Abimelech and the Philistines, who were not. Nonetheless, it would appear from the text that Abimelech did not pass any test and that Abraham didn't have any proof that there was any true fear of God in *Pleshet*, and that people did not kill there without a compelling reason. There was dread of God, but not true fear of Hashem.

parashat Vayera

were his – members of his household, slaves, perhaps even his nation – because Abraham is a prophet and has a strong connection to God. Abraham's divine ethics, which is identical to natural ethics, prohibits the king – just like anyone else - from forcing himself on women, even single ones.

Abimelech awoke early in the morning, worried and anxious, and told his dream to his servants. They were all very scared. He summoned Abraham and rebuked him for his unworthy deed; in other words, concealing the fact that Sarah was a married woman – a deed which nearly caused an ethical disaster. Abimelech played dumb, and ignored his own actions entirely, as if taking a woman by means of coercion is appropriate behavior. The perplexed Abraham did not reply. Abimelech did not let go of the issue, and demanded to know why Abraham acted as he did. Abraham justified himself and explained: Since I am unfamiliar with Gerar, I was concerned that perhaps its inhabitants are corrupt, and in my heart I thought, "Surely there is no fear of God in this place, and they will kill me because of my wife" (20:11).[116] Aside from that, Abraham added as justification: In fact, she is my paternal sister (the daughter of Terah from another wife). Ever since God instructed me to uproot myself and distance myself from my father's household, and directed me toward Canaan, which was unfamiliar to me,[117] I instructed her that each time that we arrived at a foreign place, whose practices are not known to us, she should say that she is my sister. Abimelech,

---

116. Rashi 20:11, based on BT Bava Kama 92b. Concerning Abimelech's ethical transgression towards Abraham cf. S. R. Hirsch, 20:2-10. Cf. also the discussion on the fear of God in *Parashat Shemot*. Cf. also Kimhi on v.6 which focuses attention on the fact that even in the absence of divine revelation, all men have a responsibility towards God and should be punished for every action which reason- God's representative- rejects. Concerning the need for asking for forgiveness, cf. Mishna Bava Kama 8:7.

117. Saadia Gaon, 20:12, 13, Rashi 20:13, Ibn Ezra, 20:12.

upon whom the fear of God had fallen, understood that Abraham is an asset, because God is with him. He recompensed Abraham and Sarah with money, cattle and slaves, and permitted them to dwell wherever they wished in his kingdom. He said to Sarah that this compensation would demonstrate that he did not touch her abusively, and that she remained spotless. Abraham accepted Abimelech's request for forgiveness and prayed for him to God, Who canceled the death penalty for Abimelech's household, and cured him and the wives in his household, such that they were once again able to beget and give birth.

Two 'Bindings'

A significant portion of our parasha was selected by our Sages for the Torah reading of the two days of Rosh Hashanah. The portion that is read includes the narrative of the birth of Isaac, the banishing of Hagar and Ishmael, the covenant between Abraham and Abimelech, the binding of Isaac and the information concerning the birth of Rebecca. It would appear that this collection was not chosen for naught. A hidden strand connects these events to each other and merges them into one narrative of great significance. Modern exegesis identifies two 'bindings' in our parasha, the 'binding' of Ishmael and the 'binding' of Isaac.[118] The Torah hints at the fact that there are two 'bindings' before us, by presenting similar events and

---

118. Cf. Rabbi Abraham ben HaRambam 21:14, M. Buber, *Darko Shel Miqra*, 313-314, U. Simon, "*Gerush Ishmael- HaAqeda Sheqadma LeAqedat Yitzchak,*" pages 56-59 in *Baqesh Shalom Verodfehu* (Tel Aviv, 2002). Compare H. Y. Chamiel, *Meiynei Miqra* (Jerusalem, 1983), 53-87. Concerning the monikers in the two *Aqida* narratives, by which the text refers to Ishmael and Yitzchak- *ben, yeled, na'ar*- cf. *Daat Miqra* throughout the narratives. '*Ben*' and '*yeled*' convey a closeness, love and dependence; '*naar*' conveys independence and distance. Reuben and Judah refer to Joseph as '*yeled*'- cf. *Daat Miqra* 37:30 nt. 43 ad loc.

parashat Vayera

similar terminology in the narrative of the banishing of Ishmael, his life being saved by the angel and the discovery of the well; and the narrative of the binding of Isaac, his life being saved by the angel and the discovery of the ram. However, it must be emphasized here that the trail of the binding of Isaac is far greater than the trail of the banishment, in which God informed Abraham from the outset that no harm would befall the youth. On the contrary – "As for the son of the slave-woman, I will make a nation of him, too, for he is your seed" (21:13). However, in addition to the similarity between the 'bindings,' there is also a cause and effect relationship between the events; and the Torah hints to this in the expressions: "**At that time**" (21:22) and "**Some time afterward**" (22:1, 20).

Sarah gave birth to her son precisely at the promised time; Abraham called him Isaac as per God's instructions and circumcised him when he was eight days old. When Isaac was born, his father was 100 years old, his mother was 90 years old, his grandfather was 170 years old and his brother was 14 years old. This time Sarah celebrated and laughed wholeheartedly, joyously, about the wonder that occurred; and said to herself: 'Who would have believed that all of this would happen to me and my husband in our old age?' Abraham organized a large feast when Isaac grew and was weaned, as was customary in those days. It would appear that during that feast, Sarah noticed that Ishmael, who was growing up, was being rowdy and was involved ("playing")[119] with the local girls in public; and was acting like the son of Hagar, the Egyptian – like the offspring of Ham – more than as the offspring of Abraham. Sarah understood, by means of her practical wisdom, that Ishmael's behavior endangers the continuity of the family of Abraham at their standard of righteousness and justice which is fundamental

---

119. Cf. 26:8, 39:14, 17, Exodus, 32:6, Bereshit Rabbah, 53:15 according to R. Akiba; Tosefta Sota 6, according to R. Eliezer; Ibn Caspi, 21:9.

parashat Vayera

to the divine blessing; and that he had no share alongside Isaac in the spiritual legacy of Abraham. She asked Abraham to banish the maidservant Hagar and her son Ishmael from the household. This request was bad in the eyes of Abraham, as it concerned his own flesh and blood son. He thought that it would be preferable to keep Ishmael in the household, in order to try and influence him positively, and not allow Hagar to raise him by herself.[120] However, God endorsed Sarah's arguments, and command him to listen to her.

The 'binding' of Ishmael was inevitable, despite the fact that it went against Abraham's ethical-logical code. Abraham learned once again, as he had in the Sodom affair that human ethics, whose reason is limited by the sensuality of the flesh, is finite compared to divine judgment, which expresses the ultimate ethics and good, which is identical to pure reason. The binding of Isaac will prove that he has internalized this lesson. Abraham unwillingly freed Hagar from her service; and sent her and their son from his home the next morning, after supplying them with food and a flask of water, which he placed on Hagar's shoulder. He apparently relied on God's promise that Ishmael will also become a nation. In this promise God referred to Hagar as "the maidservant" and to Ishmael as "the son of the maidservant" (21:12-13). In contrast to Sarah, who was concerned about her son and his proper education, Hagar exposed her selfishness when she wandered in the desert with her son and the water ran out: Instead of wrapping her son in her arms and consoling him until his inevitable death, she cast him under one of the bushes, distanced herself so that she not hear his cries and see his death, and she herself burst into tears of despair. God, in contrast to Hagar, specifically heard the voice of the youth and responded to him, and not to her unworthy voice. A divine angel

---

120. S. R. Hirsch, *Haketav Vehaqabbala*, 21:11.

parashat Vayera

commanded her to carry the youth, to take his hand in hers and not leave him alone, as he will ultimately be a nation. These words awakened and encouraged Hagar, who surveyed her surroundings and noticed a hidden well of water.[121] The mother and son settled in the desert and sustained themselves by means of the game hunted by Ishmael, who became "a *roveh* (youth) who was an archer" (21:20). He grew up and his mother married him to woman from her country, Egypt (of the offspring of Ham).

Abimelech, who knew of Abraham's military, spiritual and financial prowess, heard "**At that time**" (21:22) that Abraham was estranged from his firstborn son, the son of the maidservant Hagar, while giving preference to his younger son, the son of the mistress Sarah. Such conduct is inappropriate, especially for someone claiming to be God-fearing. Abimelech feared that Abraham, God's prince, demonstrated a pattern of alienation from loved ones out of selfishness, fickleness or vindictiveness. He invited Abraham to establish a covenant with him, to insure that Abraham would not "deal falsely with me or with my kith and kin," (21:23) and not do to them as he did to his own son.[122] Abimelech expected Abraham and his descendants to treat him kindly; as he had treated them, in providing them with refuge in his land. The perplexed Abraham acquiesced to all of the conditions. Abraham does not hide the difference of opinion prior to establishing the covenant. He demonstrates integrity by rebuking Abimelech regarding the fact that his servants stole a well from his people; Abimelech excused himself, saying that he had not heard about it until that moment.

---

121. Concerning the revelation of the well, cf. Kimhi, Abravanel, Sforno, 21:19, based on *Guide for the Perplexed* 1:2. Concerning Hagar's behavior cf. S. R. Hirsch, 21:15-18. Concerning Hagar's emancipation from slavery, cf. Saadia Gaon 21:14.

122. *Meshekh Hokhma* ad loc. And H. Y. Chamiel in nt.126 below.

parashat Vayera

The two of them established a covenant and swore to each other; and Abraham bestowed seven sheep (the number seven [*sheva*] also relates to the term oath [*shevua*]) on Abimelech, in exchange for and as testimony to the wellbeing recognized as his. From then on that place was called Beer-sheba. Abraham planted a tamarisk there, called out in the name of God, and resided in the land of the Philistines for a long time.

God examined this event and concluded that it must be proven to all, in the present and in the future, that Abraham's actions were free of any selfish, fickle or vindictive motivation; rather, they flowed from divine guidance. Without such proof, Abraham and his descendants could not serve as a paradigm of ethics for the nations of the earth. God's means of demonstrating this was the binding of Isaac. Through this it would become clear that even his beloved son from his beloved wife, his heir and successor, does not come between him and his God. "**Some time afterward**" (22:1) God decided to test Abraham. He called to him, "Abraham;" and when Abraham answered "I am here," He shocked him with the command to take his only son remaining in his household, his beloved son Isaac, and sacrifice him as a burnt offering on one of the mountains in the land of Moriah (derived from God shows [*mareh*] or God instructs [*moreh*]), as He will instruct him. Abraham arose early in the morning, without hesitation or protest, in order not to involve and worry Sarah, saddled his donkey, took his two servants and the young Isaac, chopped wood for the burnt offering; and left on the journey, in accordance with the precise instructions which he received from God that morning. On the third day, Abraham saw the place which God had described from afar, and he understood that they had arrived at the destination.[123]

---

123. Bekhor Shor, 22:2. Isaac was a boy of approximately thirteen years; cf. Ibn Ezra, 22:4. Concerning the feelings of the father and son, as well as the mother, the text remains silent. Cf. N. Leibowitz, 137-140, *Daat Miqra*, 122.

parashat Vayera

He instructed his servants to wait with the donkey until he and Isaac returned from serving God. The father and son continued on their way. Isaac carried the wood, and Abraham carried the fire (coals) and the knife. Along the way, Isaac asked his father where the sheep for the burnt offering was, and Abraham replied, as if prophetically, and in order to remove any apprehension from his son's heart, that God would take care of it, and He would select and find the sheep. When they arrived at the place, Abraham built an altar, arranged the wood, and bound up his son on top of the altar, on top of the wood. At the moment when he took the knife, a divine angel called out to him – this time, using terminology of affection and closeness: "Abraham, Abraham!" Abraham once again replied: "I am here!" The angel ordered him to halt and to do nothing to the youth; and informed him that he now knows that Abraham is so God-fearing that he did not even withhold his son from God! That is to say, now it will be known to the whole world, that Abraham is God-fearing to the highest degree.[124] Now the blissful Abraham raised his eyes and saw a ram – which until now had been hidden from his sight behind [*ahar*] trees or an incline - caught in the thicket by its horns ("When Abraham looked up, his eye fell upon a ram [*ahar*] caught in the thicket by its horns" (22:13): It is also possible that the word *ahar* is here as the result of the switching of a *reish* for a *daled*, [אחד-אחר] which was meant to be in the word one [*ehad*]). He took it and sacrificed it as a burnt offering in place of Isaac. Abraham named the place "Adonai-yireh," (22:14) and this is its name to this day (ibid.): "On the mount of the Lord there is vision" – God reveals Himself on this mountain.[125]

---

124. Tanhuma Buber *Vayera*, 46, Bereshit Rabbah, 56:7, Saadia Gaon, Rashi, Rashbam, 22:12, Kimhi, 22:1.

125. Saadia Gaon, Rashi, 22:14. Compare with Luzzatto ad loc, *Torah Nidreshet*, ch.24. According to Ibn Ezra, 22:14, Deuteronomy 1:2, this verse

109

parashat Vayera

The divine angel called to Abraham a second time, swore to him in the name of God [*Hashem*] and blessed him with abundance of progeny and with his offspring's victory over their enemies; and promised him that all of the nations will be blessed through his progeny, which will be a model nation. All of this was compensation for the absolute faithfulness which he demonstrated at this time. Abraham returned together with Isaac to his servants, and they all returned home together, to Beer-sheba.

The Torah reading of Rosh Hashanah concludes with hope for the future. Isaac is saved, and the wife who was destined for him, Rebecca, comes into the world. There is a future for the family of Abraham. Ishmael is finally cut off from this family, when Hagar marries him to an Egyptian woman, and thereby brought him into the fold of corrupt pagans from the lineage of Ham. From the viewpoint of the Torah, the offspring of Ham, Egypt and Canaan, were infamous for their sexual promiscuity and unbridled sensuality; their idolatry was exceedingly primitive and was blended with sexual immorality. The Bible explicitly testifies to this in the portion dealing with forbidden sexual relations and with the worship of the *Molekh* in the book of Leviticus: "I the Lord am your God. You shall not copy the practices of the land of Egypt where you dwelt, or of the land of Canaan to which I am taking you; nor shall you follow their laws. My rules alone shall you observe, and faithfully follow My laws: I the Lord am your God" (18:2-4). It is incumbent on the family of Abraham to completely distance themselves from them in order to accomplish its mission. I will also deal with this in *Parashat Toldot*, in connection with the

---

is among those verses which were later implanted into the ancient text. According to Bible critics, the entire text was written late, and this verse is brought as proof of that claim. Cf. A. Rofe, *Mavo Lesifrut HaMiqra*, 24. Concerning *ayil ahar= ehad*, cf. Arnold Ehrlich, *Miqra Kipeshuto*, (Berlin, 5659), 22:13.

parashat Vayera

family's separation from Esau. The future of the chosen family, which is taking shape, depends on the binding of Isaac. At the conclusion of the event of the binding, "**Some time afterward**" (22:20), Abraham is informed about the birth of Rebecca in his brother's family in Paddan-aram.[126]

The Binding – Attempts to Understand It
However, the tremendous question in our parasha remains. The classical commentators throughout the generations were not at all troubled by the great ethical question of how God gave Abraham a patently unethical command which contradicts natural ethics, the divine command "do not murder" and the prohibition against sacrificing children to *Molekh*. Granted that we, the readers, know that this is a trial, but Abraham does not know. A black flag waves above this command, all the more striking in light of the earlier promises concerning Isaac's future, which this command contradicts. Abraham's untenable passive reaction invites criticism, especially in light of his famous fearlessness in facing the divine judgment in the case of Sodom. He certainly had solid, reasoned arguments against the command to sacrifice his son.

This narrative was both simple and wonderful in the eyes of the pre-modern commentators. It was clear to them, that a direct command of God's was superior to the reason of his creations; as it is God who defines ethics and norms for man (not to mention the fact that this was only a test). Abraham was commanded "go forth" on two occasions: On the first occasion, he was called upon to forgo his past, and in the latter – to forgo his future and

---

126. Concerning the test of the *Aqeda* cf. H. Y. Chamiel, *Maaynei Miqra*, (Jerusalem, 1983), 28-87; *Maaynei Miqra Miqraei Kodesh* (Jerusalem, 1992), 231-235, *Limudim BeFarashat HaShavua, Vayera* 3, 36-37. Cf. also *Guide for the Perplexed*, 3:33, and *Shaarei Simha*, ad loc.

parashat Vayera

he rose to the occasion.[127] Abraham's greatness lied in his being completely prepared to slaughter his son without protest. It is also possible to offer an additional interpretation of verse 12: Abraham demonstrated at this time that **despite fear of God** – that is to say, his being deeply ethical – he did not question the divine command, which appeared to be completely unethical: "For now I know [says God] that [*ki*] you fear God, since you have not withheld your son, your favored one, from Me." (22:12) "*ki*" also has the sense of "despite the fact": Despite the fact that you fear God, and do not kill, nonetheless you have not withheld your son from Me. That is to say: Now I know that you fear God, **truly and without it being limited by your ethics and reason.**[128] This supreme willingness, which is not contingent on anything – a promise or reward of any sort – becomes a symbol in the Jewish tradition of self-sacrifice in the performance of *mitzvot*, to the point of martyrdom; and for the great hope of all generations, that in the end there will be a salvation by means of a divine angel.

The ethical questions were only raised in the modern period, in which the recognition took root that God upholds the ethics of universal-reason, which is reflected in the divine image of man, just as He upholds the laws of algebra and geometry. That is to say, from a modern perspective, human reason and the ethics which it entails became a yardstick for divine reason and ethics. From this perspective, God's judgment cannot be different than the best

---

127. M. Buber, *Darko shel Miqra*, 79-80, *Haamek Davar*, 22:12.

128. Cf. H. Y. Chamiel, nt. 126 above, as well as *Limudim BeFarashat HaShavua, Ki Teze* 5, 319. This reading removes the difficulty – how it is that only now it became known to God that Abraham was God fearing? Of course, it is possible to explain it the way which I explained above: Now I know, or have made known to the world, just how great your fear of God is; as you didn't withhold even your son, and you were prepared to sacrifice him to me.

parashat Vayera

of ethics based on human reason; otherwise the divine command may not be accepted and carried out. The modern and post-modern commentary, therefore, offered several suggestions for resolving the apparent contradiction between the command of the binding of Isaac on the one hand, and ethics on the other:

A) <u>The neutralizing approach:</u> According to this approach, there is no relationship between the section of the binding of Isaac and ethics. Ethical issues only exist between man and his fellow, whereas here Abraham struggles with himself and with his God. The Biblical view (the ancient paternalistic view) is that a man's son (and certainly his young son) is not an independent person, but rather is inextricably connected to the father. Therefore, the issue is a personal trial of Abraham's, which relates to him alone; meant to demonstrate to him and to the world how far self-sacrifice for one's God goes: Sacrifice of that which is most precious to the person – his future, hopes and aspirations, embodied in his son – despite the promises that God made concerning him.[129]

B) <u>The separation approach:</u> This approach uses modern tools to provide basis for the traditional approach. According to this approach, there is no correspondence between universal human ethics and the revealed ethics of the Torah; and human ethics is null and void when it conflicts with God's command, which defines the correct ethical and norms. By means of a leap of faith, Abraham was elevated above the stratum of ethical reason to the stratum of the religious and cleaved to divinity.[130] God blessed Abraham for his willingness not to withhold his son's life and sacrifice it to God. The more extreme of those who subscribe to this approach hold

---

129. Cf. M. Fisch, nt. 1 above, 691-692, and nt. 101 ad loc., based on Maimonides and Kimhi. Also, cf. *Haamek Davar*, 22:12.

130. This is the position of S. Kierkegaard, *Fear and Trembling*, (Princeton, 1968).

parashat Vayera

that there is a total and absolute detachment between the Torah and ethics. The commandments of the Torah are the path to service of God, which is the ultimate value; and any attempt to ascribe human-ethical meaning to them, essentially aims at meeting human needs. Such an attempt is close to idolatry, as attributing supremacy to human values is essentially idolatry.[131]

C) <u>The psychological approach</u>: The narrative reflects an internal conflict and struggle within Abraham's soul. The event was only a dream. One inner voice called on him to imitate the rite of sacrificing one's son – which, in his era, embodied the height of attachment to the supreme forces which ruled over the world and man – and to perform this rite for God in order to demonstrate his attachment to Him. The other inner voice called on him to abolish this type of rite, to erase it from the face of the earth as an ethical evil, repugnant in God's eyes, and to sublimate it through symbolic animal sacrifice. The latter voice won out. At the last moment, Abraham was prevented from sacrificing his son, sparing him from death and thereby did not withhold him from God, and for this God blessed him.[132]

---

[131]. This outlook finds its fullest expression in the thought of Y. Leibowitz. Cf. for example his book *Yahadut, Am Yehudi UMedinat Yisrael*, (Tel Aviv, 1975), 23, 393, passim; cf. also *Sheva Shanim shel Sihot al Parashat HaShavua*, 80-86.

[132]. This position was first presented by Ibn Caspi, (*Gevia Keseph*, 30-34, 39, *Mitzraph Keseph*, 22:18) and it was adopted by the *Judische Wissenschaft* in Germany, headed by Abraham Geiger. They claimed that Abraham's greatness lay in his obedience to the angel who instructed him to abort the sacrifice of Isaac, and not in his readiness to slaughter his son. This position was attacked by S. R. Hirsch (22:11-12) and D. Z. Hoffmann, and was more recently formulated again by Mordecai Breuer, *Pirkei Bereshit*, 409-413, and by Abraham Nuriel, *Galuy Vesamuy BaPhilosophia Hayehudit Bimei Habeinayim*, 151-157. I heard a lecture in this vein from M. Z. Nehorai. Nehorai is of the opinion that this is the true opinion of Maimonides,

D) The identicality approach: The divine command is identical to the ethical command. Abraham's trial is the exception which proves the rule. Abraham attained the highest level of intimate acquaintance with divine ethics, after over twenty-five years of deep and ongoing dialogue with God. Events such as the emigration to the land of Canaan, the battles against rulers of nations, the war of the kings, the destruction of Sodom and Gomorrah, the promises and the beginning of their fulfillment, the banishment of Hagar and Ishmael, and all of the trials and debates with God; established for him the identicality between the absolute good and God. He became worthy of demonstrating this to all of mankind by means of passing this final test. It was already clear to Abraham at this point that the divine command, while not comprehended initially, will ultimately be clarified and shown to be identical with the good and the universal rational ethics.[133]

E) The dual truth approach: According to this approach, which appears clearly post-modern, there is no possibility of reconciling the contradiction between the rational-ethical Abraham of the

according to *The Guide for the Perplexed*, 2:41-42, in contradistinction to what it says in 3:24. It seems that Ibn Caspi, who follows Maimonides, also thought that this was his master's opinion. M. Halbertal, in the eighth and final chapter of his book, *Maimonides* (Princeton and Woodstock, 2007), 321-329, explains his opinion, that according to Maimonides, all of the biblical prophets, including, it would seem, Moses, prophesied in dreams, or through an inner voice which they heard, and did not have a direct line of communication with God. M. Goodman, *Maimonides*, 32-37, also is of this opinion.

133. This position was formulated in the books of D. Statman and A. Sagi, *Dat Umusar*, (Jerusalem, 1993). Cf. especially 204-207. The commentary of S. R. Hirsch suits this position, (22:2, 8, 13-14), which identifies the location of the *Akeda* as Mount Moriah- the place at which God instructs concerning that which is desirable. He explains the name of the place, which Abraham called '*Hashem Yireh*', to mean: Even in the place where I am unable to see, Hashem chooses for me.

section dealing with Sodom and the believing-religious Abraham of the binding of Isaac. Parallel to the two prototypes of man, who vie dialectally within each individual (based on the Rav Soloveitchik's interpretation of the creation of man); the Torah presents here two facets of Abraham, which represent two facets of each of us. The "Abraham of Sodom" demands of God that He listen to human conscience and morality, which He Himself established, and act accordingly. And so he inspects the command of the divine Halakha, each time anew. On the other hand, the "Abraham of the binding of Isaac" subjugates his conscience and his rational ethics, with humility and subservience, to the divine command, which represents the absolute intelligence and good; and this is the way in which he relates to the command of the Halakha.[134]

Parashat Hayyei Sarah

Acquiring land in the Land of Israel – with humility or by force?
The parasha opens with the narrative of Abraham's acquisition of the Cave of Machpelah as a burial place for his family. The acquisition came about as a result of Sarah's death at the age of 127, thirty-seven years after the birth of Isaac. The Torah recalls at length – ostensibly needlessly – the dialogue and negotiations between Abraham, the Hittites and Ephron the Hittite, the owner of the field of Machpelah and the cave which it contained (which was in Hebron), which Abraham wished to purchase. In response to the request of Abraham – who referred to himself as a resident

---

134. This position was presented by D. Hartman, *Aseh Libkha Hadrei Hadarim*, 2005. Cf. also M. Fisch (nt. 1 above), 669 and nt. 55 ad loc. Also, U. Simon, *Baqesh Shalom VeRodfehu*, (Tel Aviv, 2002), 49-55, presents a similar position. Concerning the approach of the 'double truth' In Judaism from the middle ages until Luzzatto, cf. E. Chamiel, *Haderech Hamemuzaat*, 330-339.

parashat Hayyei Sarah

alien – to receive a burial site among them, they replied – referring to him as "my lord: the elect of God" (23:6) – by suggesting that he choose whichever site among their burial sites that he wished. They said that he would receive it from them without reimbursement, for the sole purpose of burying Sarah. No one, they say, will prevent you from burying your deceased, out of either stinginess or arrogance; on the contrary, we would consider it an honor.[135] Abraham asked them to address Ephron and pass on Abraham's offer to buy the cave of the field of Machpelah for its full price, in order to transform it into a familial burial site. The Hittites were not thrilled to sell an ancestral site to a foreigner. Ephron offered that Abraham bury Sarah in the cave which he requested – and was prepared to give Abraham the cave, together with the surrounding field as a gift. However, Abraham preferred an official sale, so that it would be clear to all that it was irrevocable. He was prepared to pay a high price, so long as the cave would serve as a burial site for the entire family in their possession. Ephron replied that there was no need to make a big deal of a field whose entire value was four hundred silver shekels. The mourning Abraham should bury Sarah immediately, and the sale could be pushed off for a more convenient time. Abraham took the hint, and immediately paid the high price which was sought, but insisted on an immediate sale. The sale acquired public validity, and was recorded in the records of sale. Abraham buried Sarah in the cave, which officially became the burial site of Abraham's family.[136]

There is tremendous significance to the narrative of the acquisition of the first land in the Land of Israel, which was promised to Abraham and his progeny. This is the beginning of the settlement in the Land

---

135. Saadia Gaon, Ibn Ezra, 23:6.
136. Kimhi, 23:18-20. Compare Rashbam, Bekhor Shor, Hizkuni and Sforno, ad loc.

parashat Hayyei Sarah

of Israel, and the beginning of the process of the fulfillment of the divine promise. The narrative informs us of the importance of the Land of Israel for the living and the dead. It testifies to the fact that when we settle the land we do not steal, or conquer that which is not ours; rather we acquire the land which was promised to us in order to bequeath it to our offspring. We, thereby, do our part in the fulfillment of the divine promise to give us this land. According to this, the acquisition of the first inheritance points to God's kindness toward the Israelites: He fulfilled His promise to Abraham while he was still alive. The classical commentators approached this narrative based on the famous exegetical principle: "The narratives about the patriarchs are a sign for the offspring" and asked: "How does this help us for the Torah and the message?"[137] Their answers indicate two opposite directions of commentary.

The First Direction:

In the course of the dialogue, Abraham said to the local residents, to the Hittites: "I am a resident alien among you" (23:4). According to this interpretation, the terms 'alien' and 'resident' are not precisely compatible. Rashi explains, based on the Midrash, that this combination of words implies a threat being made by Abraham – the warlord who triumphed over four kings and is "the elect of God" (23:6), who sees himself as the master of the land, promised him by God. Abraham gave the Hittites the choice: Sell me the cave as an alien (a tenant) or I will take it lawfully as a resident (resident, an owner with the rights of a citizen), as God told me "To your offspring I assign this land" (15:18). The approach is also adopted by Ibn Ezra (23:19), Nahmanides (23:4-6, 18 – who cites both directions) and Abravanel.

---

137. Malbim, *Hatorah Vehamitzvah*, the questions on 23:17-20. Concerning the principle of *Maaseh Avot Siman Labanim*, cf. Bereshit Rabbah, 40:8, Tanhuma, Buber, *Lekh Lekha* 12, and Nahmanides, 12:6, 10, and nt. 73 above.

The Second Direction:

Abraham was in an inferior position, relative to the Hittites, the owners of the land. He saw himself as an alien (foreigner) who settled among them (i.e. alien and resident are synonyms according to this approach). The Hittites respected him – perhaps this was only superficial, by way of etiquette – and they showed him goodwill, and he bowed to them twice. This gesture is far from showing the self-confidence of someone who was promised the land by God. Abraham could not rely on this promise in his attempt to acquire the piece of land which he sought, in other words: The promise does not play a role in this event. This shows that this event was not the beginning of its fulfillment. On the contrary, this is an additional trial for Abraham, a miniature version of the binding of Isaac. The parallelism to the binding of Isaac is as follows: After Abraham was promised that a great nation would emerge from his progeny; he was commanded to slaughter his only son, from whom the promised nation was supposed to be born. Here, despite the promise that this land would belong to him and his descendants, he had to negotiate for its acquisition, pander to the current lords of the land, talk sweetly to them and pay hard cash for land which he had been promised would be his (in chapter 15 verse 20 the Hittites are explicitly noted as one of the nations whose land will be given to the Israelites).

In both trials, Abraham was required to walk in God's way, despite doubts which arose for him, in light of the possibility that God did not intend to fulfill the promises which He Himself had promised. That is to say, Abraham was required to have faith in God, despite the mistrust – if not feeling of betrayal – which these circumstances naturally aroused! Therefore, after the binding of Isaac, Abraham had no difficulty passing this current test. He acted precisely according to providence's expectations. The

Midrash praises Abraham's humility, both before God and before the Hittites, for his willingness to pay a large sum of money for land which had been promised to him; and all of this without questioning God's ways, without criticism. The Midrash contrasts the exemplary behavior of the patriarchs with Moses's problematic conduct toward providence. Abraham was forced to buy land which had been promised to him, and did not question, Isaac was forced to give back wells which he dug in his land (again, based on God's promise), and did not question; whereas Moses did not refrain from criticizing, despite the promises of redemption: "And they ask me, 'What is His name?' what shall I say to them?" (Exodus 3:13), ""O Lord, why did You bring harm upon this people? Why did You send me?" (Exodus 5:22). Therefore, Abraham was promised that God would appoint him a lord and prince over his interlocutors, the owners of the land; as befits one who exhibits character traits worthy of a leader: modesty, humility and good judgment.

Abraham did not make use of the promise which he was given in order to forcibly take control of the Land of Israel which he had a right to although he had the power to do so, as he had defeated four kings without divine guidance and without a promise of divine help, but rather because of the obligation to free captives and save lives, which he took upon himself to fulfill, purely through his own power. He viewed going to war on that occasion as an ethical obligation; however, here, he did not see himself as being entitled – let alone obligated – to take the initiative for the fulfillment of God's promise, but rather left it to God alone. This direction is also found in the commentaries of Rashbam and Kimhi, and it is one of the directions taken by Nahmanides and Sforno.

Both of these directions find expression in the modern exegesis, as they do in the Midrash. There are those who derive from this parasha the legitimate right to demand that which is ours, and to take over the land which was promised to us, using any means available to us. Others see a perspective on proper interactions between man and his fellow, and between one nation and another in this parasha. Their conclusion is that, despite our right to the land based on the promise, and despite our being the masters of the land in reality, as descendants of Abraham, we do not have the ethical right to dispossess a member of the minority, who is dwelling in the land as a *ger toshav* (as Abraham himself was in his day), and we are obligated to bestow all privileges of citizens on the members of the minority. The dialectical dilemma between these poles is one of the characteristic tensions of our times.[138]

A Wife from the Family of Abraham – Ethical Purity

The main part of our parasha is dedicated to the journey of Abraham's slave to select a worthy wife for Isaac. It was customary in those days for parents to marry off their children, and the elderly Abraham transferred this authority to his senior slave. For the elderly Abraham, who God had blessed with long life, wealth and honor, there remained one major concern – the establishment of a worthy family by means of his son, Isaac, so that Isaac be worthy of God's blessing. It was necessary to bring an appropriate spouse from afar, to uproot her from her father's household and neighbors who were pagans, in order that she enter into the influence of the atmosphere, practices and values of the household of Abraham in the best way possible. Therefore Abraham sent his elderly slave to seek out a wife in in Aram-naharaim, which Abraham viewed as his

---

138. Concerning the first direction of the Midrash, cf. *Bereshit Rabbah*, 58:6, *Midrash Hagadol Genesis*, 23:36. Concerning the second direction in the Midrash, cf. *Bereshit Rabba*, 79:7, BT Bava Batra 15b, 16a, Sanhedrin 111a. Cf. also the discussion of N. Leibowitz, *Studies in Bereshit (Genesis)* 207-212. She prefers the second direction. Cf. further discussion on the topic in *Parashat Behar*.

land and birthplace (v. 4). Albeit the Aramites, like the Canaanites, were pagans, but the Aramite idolatry emanated from positive, albeit misguided, sources, and was, apparently, more refined than that of the Canaanite and Egyptian, which was primitive and was saturated with sexual immorality and social corruption.[139] Consequently, Abraham sent his messenger to Aram in order to take a wife for Isaac. He asked his slave to place his hand under Abraham's thigh and swear to him in that way that he would not take one of the local Canaanite women for Isaac. In response to the slave's question, Abraham said that if the woman who was chosen refused to come to Abraham's land, but rather demands that Isaac goes to dwell with her family in her land, then the slave would be freed from his oath, but he should not bring Isaac back to the place that Abraham came from under any circumstances whatsoever. Abraham hoped, based on the promises which he received from God, that God would send his angel to assist his slave in finding and bringing back the woman who was worthy, and he did not give the messenger directions in terms of the question of how to locate her.

Abraham's slave left on his journey with ten camels carrying all the finest, in order to display the wealth of the groom and his family's status to the family of the bride. He reached Haran – the city of Abraham's birth – and in the evening, he situated himself next to the well which was outside of the city; the water-drawers came there at that time from the city. After he removed his people from there, he prayed to God that He assist him in the selection, as

---

139. S. R. Hirsch, 24:4. Compare with what it says in *Derashot Haran* and the explanation of N. Leibowitz, *Studies in Bereshit (Genesis)* 214-220. Also, compare with the commentary of Luzzatto, 24:3. He maintains that Abraham didn't want to marry into the Canaanites as this kind of marriage would have prevented them from being forced out of the Land of Israel which they inhabited, and it would have run counter to the divine promise which he received.

Abraham anticipated; and in his prayer he devised a difficult ethical test for the chosen maiden: She must offer water from her jar to a thirsty and tired stranger at his request; and additionally, of her own will, without his requesting it, to give water to the thirsty, tired camels of this unknown nomad. The yardstick for the selection of a worthy wife for the heir of the divine blessings, who will establish a household based on the foundations of justice and righteousness, is not any sort of family pedigree (Abraham did not send his slave to his family, only to his land and birthplace (cf. note 144 below), and did not instruct him to seek out a wife from among the prestigious families of that land), nor intellectual ability, wealth, or outer beauty, but rather, internal ethical beauty, humanity and willingness to help another, qualities which everyone has the potential to develop.[140] These are the qualities which Abraham's slave discerned during his years of service as typifying the household of Abraham, and he saw these as necessary for someone who was to join this household and to build it. Even before he concluded his prayer, he saw a very beautiful maiden, about whom the Torah testifies that she was a single virgin, approaching the well with her jar on her shoulder, going down to the spring, filling her jar, and coming up. He swiftly turned to her and asked her to give him a bit of water from her jar. Rebecca quickly met and even exceeded all of his expectations: "'Drink, my lord,' she said, and she quickly lowered her jar upon her hand and let him drink. When she had let him drink his fill, she said, 'I will also draw for your camels, until they finish drinking.' Quickly emptying her jar into the trough, she ran back to the well to draw, and she drew for all his camels" (24:18-20). The maiden invested great effort, above and beyond the norm, in giving water to and quenching the thirst of the ten thirsty camels. This was an

---

140. Cf. S. R. Hirsch, "The Jewish Woman: Rebecca", 104, in *The Collected Writings, Vol. VIII* (Jerusalem, New York: Feldheim, 1997).

intense and exceptional act of kindness on behalf of a stranger and on behalf of his camels, without calculations concerning its practicality,[141] reminiscent of Abraham's swift and devoted actions on behalf of the three angels.

The stunned messenger, who was dumbstruck during course of the incredible watering ("The man, meanwhile, stood gazing at her, silently wondering whether the Lord had made his errand successful or not" 24:21), approaches the maiden in the end; and while adorning her with a nose ring and gold bracelets as a token of gratitude and in order to find favor in her eyes, he inquires about her family and lodging for him and his camels.[142] He was informed by her that she is the daughter of Bethuel, from the family of Abraham – evidently, hospitality was a character trait which existed in the family – and that there was both place to lodge and food for the camels in her parents home. The eagerness, diligence and dedication were authentic and impressive, and proved beyond any doubt that the hand of providence brought him to the appropriate bride. The slave thanked God for his kindness, and Rebecca ran to the tent, to her mother (and not to her father: I will show why below) to tell her about the important guest. Her brother Laban, who apparently was in his mother's tent, heard about the guest, saw the jewelry which Rebecca received, and ran to the spring and invited the man to their home. After food was placed before the camels, the excited guest asked to retell his story to the family before he himself sat down to eat what had been placed before him.

A careful analysis of the language of what the messenger says to Bethuel and Laban, compared to the language of the sequence of events as presented in the Torah, teaches the importance of

---

141. Cf. Malbim and N. Leibowitz's explanation of his words, *Studies in Bereshit (Genesis)* 224-227.

142. Luzzatto, 24:22.

parashat Hayyei Sarah

peace, for whose sake it is sometimes appropriate to alter the facts; as long as it does not harm someone else and is not at another's expense.[143] The slave wisely left out details which might embarrass his audience, or hurt them and he planted hints and details into his story which helped him to attain the goal: to convince the family to entrust their daughter to him without delay. For example: A) Despite the fact that Abraham did not request it from him, the slave told in detail of his master's great wealth and the fact that Isaac is the heir of all of this wealth (24:35-36). B) The slave was sent to the land and birthplace of Abraham – and not necessarily to his family, which he was directed to by providence;[144] yet he told that he was sent to the household of this father and family. He said this twice, both in order to flatter the members of the family, so that they see themselves as being intended for this prestigious match, and in order to add to and increase the impression that it was the hand of God which directed him to their home: Not only did the maiden meet the condition which the slave set in his heart (watering the camels), but it also turned out that she was from the family of Abraham. C) The slave adorned Rebecca with jewelry in gratitude for her kindness, and as a result of seeing that his condition had been met, and only afterwards, or as he was adorning her, he asked about her family. In his account, he reversed the order of the events: He only adorned her after he heard about the family, as – according to what he said – he was given the condition to only take someone from the family by Abraham;[145] the jewelry was meant, according to his account, specifically for a bride who was from the family

---

143. Ibn Caspi, *Tirat Keseph*, 106-107, Abravanel, Malbim, *Haamek Davar*, S. R. Hirsch, 24:35-48, and N. Leibowitz, *Studies in Bereshit (Genesis)* 234-236.

144. Rashi, 24:7.

145. Rashi and *Aqedat Yitzchak*, 24:47.

parashat Hayyei Sarah

of Abraham. D) The sign which the slave designated was that the person drawing the water would answer him, saying "Drink and I will also water your camels" (24:14). The events did not actually happen that way, but rather in two stages with an interruption between them (24:18-19). However, the man related that Rebecca responded exactly as he expected (24:46), in order to increase the impression of the miracle in the hearts of these pagans, who believe in magic.[146]

The people present were very impressed by the slave's story. Even her brother Laban – who was keen on money and known to be selfish and exploitative (24:30 and below – 29:18-27)[147] – and her father Bathuel, who never dreamed of permanently separating from Rebecca and of sending her to an unknown land, were convinced that the matter came from God. Despite the fact that they had, apparently, learned about the God of Abraham for the first time from the messenger, they were forced to admit that the truth is recognizable as such, and that a supernatural force was involved in these events, namely the God of Abraham, Who directs the future. The slave bowed once again to God, in gratitude for their consent, showered Rebecca with gifts of clothing and money, and gave treats and sweets to her brother and her mother. He did not relate to the father. The slave took note, with his discerning eye, that Bethuel was soft and weak, and that matters were determined by the brother and mother, and therefore directed his efforts of persuasion toward them.[148]

The next morning, when the initial magic had somewhat worn

---

146. N. Leibowitz, *Studies in Bereshit (Genesis)* 246-248. Cf. ad loc. 227-228, the distinction between the 'slave' who performs his master's bidding and 'the man' who acts of his own volition.

147. Rashi, ad loc.

148. Ibn Caspi, *Tirat Keseph*, 107.

parashat Hayyei Sarah

off, the family understood the implications of the decision that it had made the previous day. The mother and brother tried to push off the departure as much as possible – a year (*yamim*), or ten months (*asor*). The slave pushed them to send them off quickly, and mentioned that God was involved here ("Do not delay me, now that the Lord has made my errand successful" 24:56). They turned to Rebecca unwillingly to ask her consent (perhaps hoping that she would refuse to go with Abraham's slave), and she surprised them with her courage and determination, and her understanding that there is more here than a plot formed in the mouth of fireside storytellers. She answered in one word, which says it all: "I will go" ["אלך"] (24:58). The family, with Laban at its head, sent Rebecca and her nursemaid (personal attendant) and her maidservants with blessings, and they all followed the servant on his way back to Canaan, riding on the camels. The Torah places in the mouths of Rebecca's family the same blessing which her future father-in-law, Abraham, received from the angel after the binding of Isaac – a multitude of offspring (the blessing of progeny), victory over enemies and acquisition of their inheritance (the blessing of the Land of Israel) – almost word for word. Now Isaac and his wife were blessed with the same blessing, and it is meant to pass on to their chosen offspring.[149]

The outcome of this incredible match, which the hand of providence played a role in, was successful. The slave brought Rebecca to the inheritance of Abraham, and when they arrived, they encountered Isaac first, who was returning from his place of seclusion in the field in the vicinity of Beer-lahai-roi. Apparently, this place, where the angel appeared to Hagar and Ishmael, had become a location for Abraham's family to encounter God.[150]

---

149. Rashbam, Kimhi and Sforno, 24:60.
150. Nahmanides and Sforno, 24:62.

Rebecca lowered herself to the ground from the camel when she saw the impressive man from afar: Her heart told her that this is Isaac. Indeed, in response to her question: "Who is that man?"[151] the slave informed her that he was her future groom. She then modestly covered her head with a veil. It was customary in those days for every prestigious land-owning woman to have her own tent; and so it was in the case of the matriarch Rebecca, the wives and concubines of Abraham, and later on – the wives of Jacob.[152] Isaac brought Rebecca into the tent, which had been his mother Sarah's until her passing, transferred the tent and all of its contents to the possession of Rebecca and took her as a wife. Within a short period of time, Rebecca felt at home in Sarah's tent, and she successfully filled the void which Sarah left after her death – "Isaac loved her, and thus found comfort after his mother's death" (24:67).

After Sarah's Death

At conclusion of the parasha, after the narrative of the primary history of Abraham is completed, the Torah returns to peripheral events which occurred over the course of the first forty years of Isaac's life, presumably after the banishment of Hagar and Ishmael and the binding of Isaac, and long before the death of Sarah.

---

151. Rashbam, 24:65, 37:19, explains that the term '*halazeh*' is used for seeing from a distance, whereas the term '*hazeh*' is used for seeing up close. It would seem that this is so whether the figure is negative or positive. An example of an instance where it is negative would be in the case of Joseph, 37:19; and an example of an instance where it is positive would be in the case of Yitzchak, 24:65, and the Shunamit, 2Kings 4:25. Concerning Rivka's intuition cf. Ibn Caspi, *Tirat Keseph,* 108, *Mitzraph Lakeseph*, 24:65. According to Luzzatto 24:64, the slave had said to her that they were close to the house of Abraham, and she therefore assumed that he was Yitzchak.

152. Kimhi, 24:67. It is told concerning Rivka that after the meeting with the slave at the spring: "the maiden ran and told her mother's home (=tent)..." (24:28).

parashat Hayyei Sarah

The Torah relates that Abraham had a third wife by the name of Keturah, from whom six sons were born to him, including Midian, from whom the Midianite nation arose. They, together with other sons of concubines, were banished by Abraham before his death (the Torah notes: "And he sent them away from his son Isaac while he was still living" 25:6) eastward, to the land of the East, far from Isaac, covered in gifts. Abraham already understood well God's plan to build the family and the nation from Isaac alone, and did not find it difficult to clear his other sons out of the way, in the footsteps of Ishmael.[153] Abraham bequeathed the main portion of his possessions to Isaac, as the slave had originally told the family of Rebecca. Abraham died at a good ripe old age, when his two grandsons from Isaac were fifteen years old, and was buried by Isaac and Ishmael next to his wife in the cave of Machpelah. In order to confirm Abraham's actions prior to his death, God blessed Isaac after his father's death. Ishmael's participation in his father's funeral shows that he made peace with his father's household after God's blessing to him was fulfilled and he prospered: He fathered twelve sons who became "chieftains of their tribes" (25:16), each one having an encampment or village (an open city, without a wall – Rashi), and they ruled over large areas. Ishmael died when he was 137, having lived to an old age and succeeded materially. The Torah devotes seven verses to his genealogy, is done with him and frees itself to go on and discuss the genealogy of Isaac in great detail.

---

153. Kimhi, 25:1. Concerning the time of Abraham's marriage to Keturah cf. Luzzatto, 25:1. According to him, 1Chron. 1:32 indicates that Keturah was Abraham's concubine.

Part three- Isaac

Parashat Toldot
The Blessing of Isaac – A Guided Drama

Our parasha includes the narrative of Isaac's blessing to his two sons, Jacob and Esau. I already spoke about the significance of the blessing which Abraham received from God. In the beginning of the parasha God appears to Isaac, as well, and transmits the blessing of Abraham to him: "I will fulfill the oath that I swore to your father Abraham. I will make your heirs as numerous as the stars of heaven, and assign to your heirs all these lands, so that all the nations of the earth shall bless themselves by your heirs— Inasmuch as Abraham obeyed Me and kept My charge: My commandments, My laws, and My teachings" (26:3-5). Isaac received the promises of progeny and the land, and the promise that mankind would be blessed through his offspring.

As we continue and read the narrative of the blessing of Isaac to his sons, several fundamental questions arise. True, the Torah is a Torah of life, depicting real life characters, who are not free of errors, mistakes and sins; however, this does not free us from attempting to understand their motives. The modern commentary also wrestled with the classical questions concerning the behavior of the players in this parasha:

1) Isaac – Was one of the patriarchs of the nation actually a senile old man, unable to discern who the preferred heir to receive this important blessing was? Why did he turn to Esau and offer him the blessing?

parashat Toldot

2) Rebecca – What was she thinking, that she dared to trick her husband, let alone to include Jacob in this deception?
3) Jacob – did he actually cheat his brother?
4) Esau – ostensibly, the one who was the victim of Rebecca and Jacob's plots?!

Modern commentators developed, based on the foundations laid by the classical commentators – Kimhi (27:4; 28:3-4), Rabbenu Bahya (27:4) and Sforno (27:4, 29, 35) – a comprehensive explanation for the narrative of the blessing and the motives of its heroes.[154] According to their approach, the Torah spreads before us a complex drama, which only the narrator (i.e. the Torah) and the reader – not the players – see in its full depth and breadth. The players only know pieces of the puzzle, and therefore act as they do. We have four primary scenes and three secondary scenes before us. Two characters participate in each scene, each time at least one character switches, a third character of the four who participate in the play never joins them and the drama is thereby preserved throughout the entire length of the parasha.

Isaac and Esau participate in the first scene, Rebecca and Jacob in the second, Isaac and Jacob in the third, and Isaac and Esau in

---

154. Cf. S. R. Hirsch, 27: 1-2, Malbim, 27:1, Sefat Emet ad loc, Y. Jacobson, *Bina Bamiqra*, ad loc. Based on Benno Jacob, N. Leibowitz, *Studies in Bereshit (Genesis)* 276-278, and H. Y. Chamiel, *Maaynei Miqra (Jerusalem, 1983)*, 88-102 in the chapter on 'Isaac's blessing', and compare between them. Also, Y. Filber and Y. Medan adopt this explanation. The entire approach here, including all of its details, is based on the comprehensive commentary of H. Y. Chamiel. Cf. also H. Y. Chamiel, *Limudim BeFarashat HaShavua, Toldot*, I: 41-43, II (3):44-49, *Matot-* 273-278. Compare also Luzzatto, 27:1. According to the people who subscribe to the Documentary Hypothesis, Isaac's second blessing to Jacob is from the Priestly document whereas the first blessings to Jacob and Esau are part of a different, folk document. According to the folk source, Jacob ran away to Haran out of fear of his brother, whereas according to the Priestly document he was sent there by his father in order to marry a woman like Sarah. Cf. *Olam Hatanach, Genesis,* 168, A. Rofe, *Mavo Lesifrut Hamiqra*, 28, 36, and 97.

parashat Toldot

the fourth. The secondary scenes at the end of the parasha involve Rebecca and Jacob, Isaac and Rebecca, Isaac and Jacob. A deep and precise analysis of the text provides the reader knowledge and hints for understanding the motives and actions of the participants, and also teaches him how this narrative integrates well with everything that the Torah taught up to now.

Chapter 25:

In order to understand the circumstances of the drama, we need to begin reading from the beginning of the parasha, where it tells of the genealogy (*toldotav*=his offspring) of Isaac (from Rebecca). He married her when he was forty years old (three years after his mother died). After twenty years of barrenness in Beer-sheba and Gerar, Isaac's prayer on her behalf was answered, and Rebecca carried twins in her womb. The two sons struggled in her womb and made the pregnancy very difficult, and she asked herself: If the pain of pregnancy is so great, why do I need it? Why did I so look forward to it and hope for it? She decided to seek out God concerning this, and went, apparently to Beer-lahai-roi, which was close to where they lived, and near the well God answered those who sought him out (25:11).[155] Indeed God answered and informed her about the importance of her pregnancy and the reason for the struggle in her womb: "Two nations are in your womb, two separate peoples shall issue from your body; one people shall be mightier than the other, and the older shall serve the younger" (25:23). This prophecy was given directly and exclusively to Rebecca, and it was thereby known to Rebecca from God that the struggling foretold a future historic clash, theological and political, between the nation of the spirit and the people of the physical and of power. The nation of the physical will arise from the firstborn son, who will emerge first from her womb and will possess great physical power, and he

---

155. Ibn Caspi, *Mitzraph Lakeseph*, 25:22, Luzzatto, ad loc.

parashat Toldot

will serve his younger brother, from whom will come the nation of the spirit, the chosen one.[156] And again, of course, the relationship between the two – the two men and the two nations – will be filled with strife. She understood from the fact that this information was not given to her husband, that she should keep the information to herself. At the conclusion of the pregnancy, the first son came out, his body entirely covered with hair, and he was named Esau. The second, whose skin was hairless, emerged holding on to the heel of Esau, so they named him Jacob. Isaac was sixty years old at the time. The Torah already hinted at what became clear when the children grew up: The first became a hunter, a man of the field, wild and strong; the second became a tent dweller, introverted, calm and mild.

In the continuation of the chapter, in verse 28, we are provided with an additional piece of information accompanied by a hint: "Isaac favored Esau **because he placed game in his mouth**; but Rebecca favored Jacob." Ostensibly, we learn here of undesirable behavior in the family: Not only do the parents favor one son over the other, but there is also a difference of opinion as to who is the favored one! However, the Torah hints to us that our first impression was partially mistaken. Rebecca loves Jacob unconditionally, in light of his behavior and based on the prophecy which she received. Isaac loves both of them: Jacob completely so, in light of his level-headed behavior as a "faultless person, a tent dweller" (25:27); and Esau – "a skillful hunter, a man of the outdoors" (ibid.) – conditionally, because he brought game to his mouth, out of respect for him. It is possible that this quality is somewhat questionable, but it is sufficient to allow Isaac to also love his second son, who represents governmental, military and political power, which also

---

156. Rashbam and Hizkuni, 25:23, 27:13, Abravanel ad loc., S. R. Hirsch, 25:23.

parashat Toldot

had value in his eyes. Isaac wisely discerned that Jacob lacked the quality of self-confidence and that he tended to avoid confrontation; and thought, with a large measure of justification, that he required cooperation with Esau.

Verses 29 through 34 reveal the root of the strife between Esau and Jacob. Esau returned from the field exhausted, so hungry and thirsty that he was prepared to sell his primogeniture to Jacob in exchange for steaming lentil soup, which Jacob had placed on the fire. Esau thereby showed complete disdain for the primogeniture, the meaning of which was privilege and responsibility on behalf of the future of the family: "'I am at the point of death, so of what use is my birthright to me'… and sold his birthright to Jacob… Thus did Esau spurn the birthright." Esau will eventually discover the importance of the primogeniture and its meaning, however, by then it will be too late. His sale of the primogeniture shows his materialistic nature which was incapable of seeing beyond the here and now. From that moment on, the Torah does not recognize the primogeniture of Esau, and refers to him as the 'older' [*hagadol*] (not the firstborn [*habekhor*]), whereas Jacob, the man of vision, is, indeed the 'younger,'[*haqatan*] but he merited being the spiritual firstborn of Isaac and his successor.[157] Who then is the deceiver in our story, who presented himself before his blind father: "I am Esau, **your first born**" (27:32)? It turns out that Esau, who preferred ephemeral life, suddenly 'forgot' that he had sold his primogeniture, and presented himself as if he had a right to it. Esau, then, was the one who deceived his father and tried to steal the blessing from Jacob![158]

---

157. *Haketav Vehaqabbala*, 27:1, Cassuto, cited M. Zeidel, *Sefer Bereshit Umivnehu*, 370, in a note on 198. *Ayef*=tired, cf. Saadia Gaon, 25:29. *Ayef*= hungry and thirsty, cf. Ibn Ezra ad loc.

158. Bekhor Shor, 27:10.

parashat Toldot

Chapter 26:

The last verse in chapter 26, together with verse 9 in chapter 28, is the framework for the entire narrative. The former, verse 35, tells that Esau married two Hittite-Canaanite women, "And they were a source of bitterness to Isaac and Rebecca." What I said above now becomes clear: Isaac was also aware of the weaknesses of Esau and his unworthiness to be the spiritual heir and successor of Abraham's family. I have already shown Abraham's complete disfavor toward Canaanite women, who were corrupt pagans. This act of Esau's is, essentially an abrogation of the covenant of circumcision which God established with Abraham. By this action, Esau detached himself spiritually from the household of Abraham. Isaac agreed with Rebecca in this matter. Apparently, he was also frustrated by his inability to influence this son.[159] Of course, the idea of removing Esau from the household, the way that Ishmael and the children of Keturah and of the concubines were, was out of the question, as Esau was the product of Rebecca's womb. I will return to the concluding verse of the narrative below, but here I will note: In the final analysis, Jacob was the one to leave home, in order to continue the building of the family in Abraham's family's neighborhood – specifically that of his mother's family – in Aram, until he returned to the Land of Israel twenty years later, together with his family who bore the blessing of Abraham. At that time, Esau settled in a different land, and left the land of Canaan to Jacob.

Now that we have received the necessary background and knowledge to understand the motives of the people involved, we come to the story itself in chapter 27. Here too, the Torah plants

---

159. Rashi, S. R. Hirsch, 24:4, 26:34-35, N. Leibowitz, Studies in Bereshit (Genesis) 276-278. Unkelos, Saadia Gaon, Rashi and Rashbam explain *'morat ruah'* - disobeying the wishes of Isaac and Rebecca, meaning, disobedience to them and their path.

parashat Toldot

important clues to understanding the drama. In verse four, Isaac sends Esau, 'his elder son' to hunt game, and says to him: "Then prepare a dish for me such as I like, and bring it to me to eat, so that I may give you my innermost blessing before I die." Isaac needed a physical impetus and for Esau to fulfill a commandment of kindness, i.e. honoring one's father, in order to see fit to give a blessing to this son. The dish, and not the primogeniture, was the impetus for the giving of the blessing. In general, it appears that Isaac, who did not know about the sale of the primogeniture, and only heard of it later when Esau said "he took my primogeniture," saw Esau's primogeniture as being merely a chronological precedence and not a preeminence in worth, as we will see shortly in terms of the blessing which he prepared for each of his sons.

It is clear that Isaac was not senile and mindless, rather he was realistic and lucid; but being about a hundred years old, he was physically weak and blind. He understood that his sons had grown up to possess different, even opposite, qualities; and that Jacob was the one who was worthy of leadership, due to his superior qualities. His mistake lay in the conclusions which he drew from the situation. He believed that the attributes of both of his sons were needed in order to form a nation, and therefore they needed to cooperate down the road. Therefore, he decided to bless them himself, and thereby established a practice that would be accepted for generations to come: The blessing of the children by the father. Isaac prepared a blessing of his own for Esau, a material blessing, which dealt with possessions in this world, and this blessing required a physical impetus. The blessing of Abraham, the blessing of progeny and the Land of Israel, was intended for Jacob. He believed that Jacob was worthy of it, and that, at the appropriate time, he would also receive it from God. The Torah teaches us that this decision was a mistake, despite the logic in it. An unethical person, materialistic and lacking

parashat Toldot

in value-based direction, cannot participate in the building of the family of Abraham, which carries a special message for humanity, even if he has qualities of power and royalty, needed for the building of a family. Without ethics, there is no value to power, and true power can only emanate from an ethical source.

As was mentioned, Isaac sent Esau to prepare a dish of game in preparation for his receiving the blessing, and here Rebecca, the tool of providence to foil Isaac's plan, appears. Verse 5 explains why Rebecca did not enter into a discussion with Isaac in order to make him realize his mistake: "Rebecca had been listening ... When Esau had gone". A person who has a sensitive ear hears the tempo of the words, reflecting Rebecca's shock and the urgency which does not allow for discussion. If Rebecca does not succeed in convincing Isaac to withhold the blessing from Esau in a short span of time, he will return from the field and it will no longer be possible to repair the damage. The commentators understood the lack of dialogue between Isaac and Rebecca as symptomatic of their relationship.[160] Unlike the case of the other patriarchs and matriarchs, there was no communication between Isaac and Rebecca at the time of their marriage, nor in the period of barrenness and prayer for children, nor during pregnancy, nor concerning the upbringing of the children, nor concerning their attitude toward them, nor at the time of danger in Gerar under the patronage of Abimelech (26:6-10; the topic will be dealt with below) nor in the crisis over the blessings. It was only in the case of a life or death situation, when Esau planned to kill Jacob, that she got involved and addressed Isaac directly with an ethical argument, which is central to the narrative, and which Isaac could not reject (I will deal with its full context below): "I am disgusted with my life because of the Hittite women. If Jacob marries a Hittite woman like these, from among the native women, what good will

---
160. Cf. *Shnei Luhot Habrit* ad loc. And *Haamek Davar*, 24:64-65.

parashat Toldot

life be to me?" (27:46). The Torah hints to us that Rebecca did not understand that Isaac intended to split the blessing between the two sons. It is possible that were she to have understood, she would not have intervened; but providence desired her intervention.

Before God – Rebecca's Mistake
In verse seven, Rebecca tells Jacob about his father's conversation with Esau. She quoted Isaac as follows: "Bring me some game and prepare a dish for me to eat, that I may bless you, before the Lord, before I die." The differences between Rebecca's quote and the original words of Isaac to Esau are the root of the events which are described in this chapter. It is, therefore, important to cite the statement of Isaac again, word for word: "…"Then prepare a dish for me such as I like, and bring it to me to eat, **so that** [*ba'avur*] I may give you my innermost blessing before I die." Rebecca omitted an important word from Isaac's statement to Esau: *ba'avur* (and bring it to me to eat, **so that** [*ba'avur*] I may give you my innermost blessing). That is to say, Esau was asked to prepare a dish for his father as a prerequisite for his receiving the blessing, as Isaac assigned him: *ba'avur*, meaning 'in order,' 'so that...' (and so too in verse 25, when Isaac intended to bless Esau, not realizing that it was Jacob who stood before him, he said: "Serve me and let me eat of my son's game so that [*l'maan*] I may give you my innermost blessing"). Esau himself, when he came to receive his blessing, said: "Let my father sit up and eat of his son's game, so that you may give me your innermost blessing" (27:31). Esau's blessing was predicated on that which Isaac anticipated receiving from him.

Corresponding to this omission, Rebecca added on her own, or unaware, a highly significant addition, which reveals the reason for her actions. According to what she said, Isaac told Esau: "that I may bless you, **before the Lord**". Isaac did not intend to bless Esau

138

before the Lord, and I already discussed the nature of the blessing which he had prepared for this son. "Before the Lord" is not a casual phrase. Rather, it is a charged expression, which indicates in the Torah a person's standing in proximity to God, or a human action which is connected to divine-spiritual realm. "Before the Lord" does not only indicate a holy place in an area; rather it refers primarily to a psychological state of an ongoing experience. Adam hides "from before the Lord" and God asks him, "Where are you?" (Genesis 3:8-9). Cain leaves "from before the Lord" (ibid. 4:16), admonished after the murder; no longer worthy of closeness to God. Abraham "is still standing before the Lord" (ibid. 18:23). The construction of the Tabernacle (Exodus 27:21, passim) and the sacrifices (Leviticus 1:3 passim) were done "before the Lord," as they were means to help bring man closer to the desired state and to attachment to God. Even concerning Nadab and Abihu, who sinned out of good intentions, the verse states: "And they offered before the Lord," "died when they drew too close before the Lord" (Leviticus 10:1; 16:1). Closeness to God is subject to conditions, and is fraught with danger. In his speech to the two and a half tribes who wished to remain on the eastern bank of the Jordan, Moses wished to educate them and instill in them the mindset of standing before the Lord, and teaches them: Your promise to go to war "before the children of Israel" (Numbers 32:17) is misguided and insufficient. This is not merely the Israelites' war; it is, rather, a holy divine war. Therefore, "If you do this, if you go to battle as shock-troops, before the Lord," then I will grant your request. The tribes realized their mistake, and quickly declared: "While your servants, all those recruited for war, cross over, before the Lord, to engage in battle—as my lord orders (Ibid v. 27)." In the narrative of 'the waters of contention,' Moses took the staff "from before the Lord" (Numbers 19:9); however, he erred and gathered the entire congregation to "before the rock". Jonah ran away "from before the Lord" (Jonah 1:3) and attempted to distance himself from closeness to God, out of misguided protest against God's clemency toward sinners who repented.

Rebecca thought that Isaac had lost his mind, and that he intended to give the blessing of Abraham (the blessing of "before the Lord") to Esau! She could not accept this. After all, she had received the prophecy concerning the superiority of Jacob, and she believed that it was incumbent on her to take concrete action to actualize this prophecy, which had been told to her for this purpose. If this is Isaac's mental state, there is no point in speaking to him; as such discussion could exacerbate the situation. She, therefore, decided to force Isaac to give the blessing of the firstborn to Jacob, by means of deceit: Jacob is to appear before Isaac pretending that he is Esau. Jacob knew in the depths of his heart that he was the one who is worthy of receiving the blessing, and that when dealing with frauds such as Esau, one needs to deal with them using their methods. Also, the command of his mother, who took full responsibility upon herself, had a powerful effect on him. Even so, he carried out the deception against his father unwillingly and with a heavy heart; and even expressed to his mother the concern that even if he acted unethically this once at her request, her plan was dangerous and might bring about the opposite, bringing upon him an awful curse. Rebecca's plan to bring Jacob before Isaac wearing Esau's clothing, with goat skins on his arms, was questionable both ethically and practically. However, the surprise, time pressures and Rebecca's misunderstanding, did not allow for a better plan, and it is clear that without the intervention of providence, it would have failed.

Isaac was not convinced right away. The voice of Jacob, which entered his room with the dish which Rebecca prepared, betrayed him, but the beloved smell of the clothing and the sensation of the hairy arms did their part, together with the assistance of providence,

parashat Toldot

and Jacob received the material blessing which had been intended for his brother: "May God give you of the dew of heaven and the fat of the earth, abundance of new grain and wine ... Let peoples serve you ... Be master etc." (27:28-29) The promise of the progeny and the Land of Israel of the blessing of Abraham are not here. They were intended for Jacob. It is possible that Jacob was surprised, even disappointed by this blessing, if he had expected the more important blessing, that of primogeniture (which he thought Isaac had intended for Esau). He certainly would not have carried out this dangerous and questionable process for a 'fistful of dollars.' In any case, Isaac's plan of partnering the two brothers, the material and the spiritual, was foiled by providence.

The narrative continues in verse 30: "No sooner had Jacob left the presence of his father Isaac—after Isaac had finished blessing Jacob—than his brother Esau came back from his hunt." As soon as the blessing was completed, right after Jacob left Isaac's tent, Esau came carrying a dish for his father. A short exchange proved to Isaac that he had been misled by Jacob. Isaac's hesitations concerning the identity of the person standing before him and his anxiety over his plan's failure hints at the fact that from the outset it was important to him that the blessing which he just gave be bestowed specifically on Esau. He wisely understood right away that providence guided the events, which increased his anxiety over the fact that he erred, but compelled him to validate the process: "and I blessed him" – I have already blessed him – "now he must remain blessed": His blessing will be fulfilled! (27:33) What was done is irrevocable.[161]

161. The fact that Isaac is unable to revoke his blessing even though it was acquired through trickery is explained by Bible critics in the following way: Biblical blessings were very ancient traditions which represent belief in the potency of the irrevocable spoken word of important men. Cf. A. Rofe, *Mavo Lesifrut Hamiqra*, 306.

A painful dialogue began between the stunned father and his wounded son, Esau. Verse 34: "Bless me too, Father": At least give me the blessing which you intended for Jacob, certainly you planned something for him. The father answers in verse 35: "Your brother came with guile and took away **your blessing**." The blessing which was intended for Esau was given to Jacob, and Esau is not worthy of the other blessing. Esau understood that the sale of the primogeniture was his downfall, and he had lost his destiny. He is angry with his brother: It is not for naught that he is called Jacob [*Ya'kov*] (*a'kva*=deceit), as he deceived him twice: "First he took away my birthright and now he has taken away **my blessing**!" That is to say, he not only took the primogeniture by means of the lentil soup, and thereby the blessing of Abraham which was important to him, he also took my blessing, the material one. Isaac had no response to this, and he did not reply. Esau tried again: "Have you not reserved a blessing for me?" (27:36). Maybe you will bestow wealth and property on me, as well; as there is enough in the world for both of us! The father once again rejected him: Jacob already received complete domination over Esau, what is left for Esau? In his despair, Esau addressed his father again (verse 38): "Have you but one blessing, Father? Bless me too, Father!" It is impossible that nothing remains for you to give me of all of the possessions of this world without it being at my brother's expense! The father acquiesced to his son's tormented request in verses 39-40: "See, your abode shall enjoy the fat of the earth ... Yet by your sword you shall live." "The fat of the earth" refers to all that which is outside of the Land of Israel, here as well as in the original blessing which had been intended for Esau. Esau, therefore, received the leftovers of a material blessing, limited by the stipulation that Jacob's portion not be compromised thereby. Jacob received everything, including dominion over his brother, as long as he was worthy,

parashat Toldot

from an ethical perspective, of the primogeniture, in the full sense of the word.

The Blessing and the Flight

We now come to the conclusion of the narrative, which returns to its beginning, completing the framework. The furious Esau planned to kill his brother immediately upon the death of Isaac, and word of it reached Rebecca's ears. She warned Jacob and commanded him to flee immediately, while Isaac was still alive, to her family in Paddan-aram, and to remain there for a number of years ("a while" 27:44) until the fury passes. According to what she said, if Esau were to carry out his plan, she, "the mother of Jacob and Esau" (28:5), would lose both of them in one day, just as she gave birth to both of them in one day. Jacob would die literally, and it would be as if Esau the murderer were dead in her eyes.[162] Rebecca convinced Isaac to send Jacob to her family in Haran which is in Paddan-aram. She concealed the knowledge about Esau's plan from him, in order not to cause him pain, and instead used the strong argument: It is extremely important to prevent his marrying Hittite women of Canaan, as Esau did, which revealed his nature and the true reason for losing his primogeniture. The fact that he sold his primogeniture to begin with testifies to recklessness and an intolerable materialism; although it might have been possible to correct this deformity, his marriage to Hittite women was not rectifiable. Marriage to the corrupt Canaanite women negated the merit of the patriarchs, for their offspring are unworthy of inheriting this land, which disgorges those who are corrupt from its midst.

---

162. Cf. S. R. Hirsch, 27: 45-46. Compare N. Leibowitz, *Studies in Bereshit (Genesis)* 289-290 who brings this explanation in the name of Eliyahu ben Amozeg of Italy, a contemporary of Hirsch and Luzzatto.

Chapter 28:

Once Isaac agreed with Rebecca concerning Jacob's marriage, Isaac bestowed the coveted blessings of Abraham on Jacob, which are inextricably tied to marrying a woman who is worthy: "And blessed him. He instructed him, saying, 'You shall not take a wife from among the Canaanite women'" (28:1). He sent Jacob to Paddan-aram, in order to marry a daughter of his uncle, Laban, and to bring her with him to Canaan. Afterwards he blessed him. Abraham and Isaac received the blessing from God, and Isaac knew that God alone passed it on. Therefore, the blessing of progeny and of the Land of Israel is formulated here (28:3-4) as a prayer to God, through which he blessed Jacob: "May El Shaddai bless you, make you fertile and numerous, so that you become an assembly of peoples. May He grant the blessing of Abraham to you and your offspring, that you may possess the land where you are sojourning, which God assigned to Abraham." Isaac refers to the Land of Israel as "the land where you are sojourning" in contrast to "the fat of the earth," which refers to outside of the Land of Israel. Isaac's prayer was soon answered in Bethel.

The framework is completed in verse eight. After Jacob received the blessing of Abraham and was sent on his way by his father and mother in order to be saved from Esau and find an appropriate wife, Esau finally understood his mistake and the price he paid for it. Esau understood that his behavior was his downfall, and he attempted to appease his father (Rebecca did not count, as far as he was concerned) by marrying the daughter of Ishmael. He understood that the blessing of Abraham was connected to an appropriate marriage: "When Esau saw that Isaac had blessed Jacob and sent him off to Paddan-aram to take a wife from there, charging him, as he blessed him, 'You shall not take a wife from among the Canaanite women,' and that Jacob had obeyed his father and mother (both of them counted, as far as Jacob was concerned) and gone to Paddan-aram,

Esau realized that the Canaanite women displeased his father Isaac." He still did not understand that the hand of providence, which does not tolerate materialistic corruption, manipulated the events, and not only his parents' world view. Therefore, his repentance was only partial: He did not marry a woman from Abraham's original family, but rather a woman from the rejected son of both Abraham and the Egyptian maidservant. Nonetheless, his repentance was sincere. This is reflected in the statement of the Sages, which now makes sense to us: "And he took Mahalat – was her name actually Mahalat? But surely her name was Basemat! Rather it teaches us that all of his sins were forgiven. From here we see that a groom is forgiven for all of his sins" (PT *Bikkurim* III:3).

Thus began, according to the Torah, the historic clash between the pagan-materialistic-aggressive world view of Esau, who is Edom, and the monotheistic-ethical-spiritual world view of Jacob-Israel. It is possible to view that which is recalled in chapter 33 verse 11 as an epilogue to this narrative. Jacob returned from Aram with his wives, children and vast wealth, and addressed Esau with a request of appeasement: "'Please accept **my present [*berakhah*] which has been brought to you**, for God has favored me and I have plenty.' And when he urged him, he accepted." Take back from me the blessing [*berakhah*] which was intended for you, and which I did not need at all. Jacob said 'my present [*birkati*]' rather than 'my offering of a gift [*minhati*]', and 'has been brought to you' rather than 'I brought to you,' as he was referring to the blessing which ought to have been brought to Esau by his father. Esau accepted the blessing which had been intended for him, the blessing of worldly possessions, and the two were reconciled.[163]

---

163. Cf. N. Leibowitz, *Studies in Bereshit (Genesis)* 269,364,365 as well as H. Y. Chamiel, nt. 154, above. Compare Midrash Pesikta Rabbati 13. Compare also Y. Leibowitz, *Sheva Shanim shel Sihot*, 135. Cf. nt. 220 below.

Isaac and Abimelech – Cultural Encounters in the Second Generation

The narrative about the Isaac's dealing with Abimelech, king of the Philistines – whose land Isaac wandered to, because of drought and famine in Canaan – is inserted between the narrative about the birth of the twins and the sale of the primogeniture on the one hand, and the story of the clash over the blessings on the other. It would appear that Isaac wished to descend yet further, to Egypt, as his father did in his day, since Egypt is irrigated by the Nile and knows no drought; however, God appeared to him and instructed him not to go down to Egypt, but rather to dwell in the vicinity of Canaan, in accordance with the directions which he will receive. He was to dwell in the land of the Philistines until further notice. God once again bestowed the blessings which He had given Abraham on Isaac: The blessing of progeny and the blessing of the Land of Israel. Isaac was blessed with these – as God states explicitly (verse 5) – in the merit of his father, Abraham, who listened to God's voice and obeyed all of his instructions.[164]

It would appear that this event took place during the twenty years between the marriage of Isaac and Rebecca and the birth of the twins. Thus it was possible for Isaac, like his father before him, to pretend that the beautiful Rebecca was his sister, lest the Philistines kill him in order to take her for themselves, exactly as his father thought when he was in the same circumstances.[165] Indeed, this narrative is reminiscent of the two narratives about Abraham and Sarah – the narrative concerning Pharaoh and the one concerning

---

164. Saadia Gaon, Nahmanides, 26:2-3. According to the *peshat*, Abraham didn't observe the Torah commandments; rather, he heeded God's instructions to him – cf. Midrash Pesikta Zutrati (Lekah Tov) *Toldot* 26:5, and following him, Rashbam, Ibn Ezra and Sforno ad loc.

165. Luzzatto, 26:1.

parashat Toldot

Abimelech – although this time, Abimelech did not try to harass his guests. It could be that the memory of these events caused him to treat them respectfully;[166] perhaps it was the covenant which he, or his father, established with Abraham and his descendants.[167] In any case, one day Abimelech saw Isaac and Rebecca through his window, embracing lovingly like a young couple who were married in every sense. He understood that Isaac had lied to him, and was furious with him. Nonetheless, he permitted Isaac to dwell in Gerar, and prohibited his people from touching Isaac and Rebecca. Isaac took root there and became a wealthy landowner, evoking jealousy and ultimately xenophobia. The Philistines stopped up the wells which his father's slaves had dug, and which Isaac used to irrigate his fields and flock. In the end, Abimelech was forced, due to pressure from his people, to abrogate his covenant with Abraham; and he banished Isaac, using the argument: "For you have become far too big for us" (26:16). You are 'beyond us'. More than that, all of your wealth essentially came to you from us. You are taking advantage of us and our good heartedness, it would be better if you departed.[168] Isaac's attempt to stay in the vicinity failed, and the two wells which he dug were stopped up. He realized that he was unable to deal with the Philistines. Only in Rehobot, which was more distant, was there no fight concerning the new well. In the end, Isaac settled in Beer-sheba, outside of the borders of Philistia. God appeared to him in Beer-sheba, and

---

166. Hizkuni, 26:7. As I mentioned above in the two previous narratives, those who subscribe to the Documentary Hypothesis maintain that three separate documents are at play here. Cassuto explained that there were three different ancient traditions in Israel prior to the writing of the Torah. Cf. nt. 80 above.

167. Nahmanides, Hizkuni and Kimhi, 26:1.

168. Cf. Midrash Rabbah, 64:6. Compare S. R. Hirsch, 26:15-16, *Haamek Davar* ad loc. And N. Leibowitz, N. Leibowitz, *Studies in Bereshit (Genesis)* 260-262.

parashat Toldot

reassured him that he should not fear anyone, and blessed him with the blessing of progeny (in preparation for the recalling of his barren wife). Isaac expressed thanks, built and altar and called out in God's name [*Hashem*], just as Abraham had done there after his oath to Abimelech (21:22-34). Abraham planted a tamarisk rather than building an altar, because he did not dwell in Beer-sheba, but rather returned to Gerar, whereas Isaac remained in Beer-sheba.

To Isaac's surprise, Abimelech and Phicol, chief of his troops, decided to establish a new covenant with him. One day, they showed up accompanied by the king's entourage.[169] It would appear that the departure of the landlord, who was successful in all his endeavors, negatively impacted on the local economy and commerce. Anti-Semites throughout the generations have suffered financially from their hatred and jealousy, and realize after the fact that they harmed themselves by expelling the Jews from their midst. Abimelech and his people admitted ingratiatingly that: "We now see plainly that the Lord has been with you" (26:28) and noted in their defense, highly hypocritically, that they had not harmed any person or property of Isaac's, and therefore, he should be grateful to them, establish a covenant with them, influence his God not to harm them and to come back and be involved in their economy and commerce. Isaac did not desire conflict. He prepared a feast of appeasement for them, established a covenant with them, they swore to each other and sent them off in peace. This narrative, like that of Abraham, concludes in Beer-sheba; with once again naming it Beer-sheba, for reinforcement, after the oath with Abimelech.[170]

---

169. Onkelos. It is also possible to explain '*Ahuzat*' (26:26) as a personal name like Saadia Gaon and others, based on R. Yehuda in *Bereshit Rabbah*, 64:8.

170. Ibn Caspi, *Mitzraph Lakeseph*, 26:33, Cassuto, *Sefer Bereshit Umivnehu*, 239-240. As noted above, according to the approach of Bible criticism, we have before us three versions of the same story from three sources, or from

Part Four - Jacob

Parashat Vayetze
The Dream of the Ladder – The dream and its Meaning

Our parasha deals with Jacob's leaving from Beer-sheba to Haran when he was apparently around forty years old, and with his life there. His departure for Haran was also his departure from the life of simple (if not perfect) tent-dwelling in the household of his father, to an independent life, to an ongoing struggle for survival.

The narrative of the beginning of the journey which appears at the beginning of the parasha is characterized by the description of Jacob's dream, the dream of the ladder. This dream, whose meaning is not explained in the text, has fueled the imagination of commentators throughout the generations, and each one brought his own world to it. The Torah only describes meaningful dreams. A dream which is described in the Torah may have one of two types of content, or both of them: 1) a symbolic image, where we need to uncover what the message is for the dreamer; 2) A direct message from God to the dreamer, a message which is of immediate relevance or a vision for the future. This message may not be connected to any image, or it may serve as the interpretation of a symbolic image.[171]

---

three traditions, which is twice attributed to Abraham and once to Isaac. Cf. the discussion in *Parashat Lekh Lekha* and *Vayera*.

171. Compare Maimonides, *Hilkhot Yesodei Hatorah*, 7:3, Ibn Caspi, *Tirat Keseph*, 79-80, Benno Jacob, which is brought by N. Leibowitz, *Studies in Bereshit (Genesis)* 298. Cf. nt. 11 above.

parashat Vayetze

There are three scenes in the dream under discussion, separated by the word *vehine*.[172] The first scene is of a ladder. In the second scene, divine angels are ascending and descending the ladder. In the third scene, God was standing over the top of the ladder. There is also a direct message to Jacob in the dream: God introduces Himself: "I am the Lord [*Hashem*]," repeats the blessing of progeny and the Land of Israel which he gave to the heirs of Abraham, through whom (together with his descendants) all of the families of the earth will be blessed, and promises Jacob that He will guard him on his journey and bring him back to the Land of Israel when the time comes. There is no direct connection made between the scenes and the message in the dream. Incidentally, Jacob's second dream, which will be discussed below, is also constructed in this manner, i.e. from an image and a direct message.

The midrashic world, in general, as well as classical exegesis[173] accepted the literal meaning of the dream. In their opinion, Jacob was afraid of Esau who plotted his murder, and since he was a 'tent dweller' who was unaccustomed to dealing with the outside world, worried about his uncertain future in an unfamiliar setting, outside the warm fold of home and family. The Sages and Maimonides already established that a person sees a semblance of the aspirations and desires which occupy and disturb him during the day in his dreams.[174] Jacob himself certainly believed in the existence of divine angels (such as those who came to Abraham and Hagar. He certainly heard these stories which circulated in his family) and was convinced that he was surrounded by invisible angels who were watching over him – and perhaps over each and every person – at

---

172. Cf. nt. 11 above.
173. Bereshit Rabbah, 68:11, Rashi, 28:12.
174. "A person is only shown that which was in their thoughts", BT Berakhot, 55b, Maimonides, *Guide for the Perplexed,* 2:36.

parashat Vayetze

all times, and who switch tasks among themselves. Some of them were going up to report the actions and prayers of people in heaven, and some of them descending to carry out the tasks assigned to them from above. In his eyes, the place where he slept became the gate of heaven for the angels who were switching places in the tasks assigned to them, as God stood above them and supervised.

There is another interpretation of Jacob's dream in the Midrash: The ladder symbolizes human history which advances in stages. In each stage, a new empire rises and rules the world until it falls. According to this Midrash, God shows Jacob, who is going into exile, the future; in which the Israelites will be subjugated by various empires, however, they will all ultimately fall. In the end of days, the apex of the ladder, all of the surviving nations will be unified, led by the Israelites, under the kingdom of God.[175]

Maimonides – the rationalist philosopher, who believed that there were philosophical secrets intended for the wise hidden in the biblical text – saw a double symbol in the ladder. First – a symbol of the creation, which developed through a process of emanation of the divine profusion from the Prime Mover via the spheres to the Active Intellect and downwards, to the material, which constitutes the lower world, in which man is found. All of the stages of the emanation are important, and all of them together comprise the creation in its completeness. It is the ladder which unites them and symbolizes the unity of the creation as a whole on the one hand, and the significance of each stage on the other. Secondly, the ladder symbolizes the learning process of

---

175. Pirkei D'Rabbi Eliezer 35, Tanhuma *Vayeze* 2, Vayikra Rabbah 29:2. Nahmanides, 28:12, Maimonides, *Mishneh Torah Sefer Hamada Hilkhot Yesodei Hatorah* 7:3, *Zohar Vayeze* ad loc., and Sforno, 28:12-13, follow this Midrash. Cf. also N. Leibowitz 298-301. Compare Ibn Ezra, 27:40, who disagrees with all of this homiletic interpretation. He has his own explanation for the erroneous (in his opinion), ascribing of Christianity to Edom, and of Islam to Ishmael.

parashat Vayetze

the prophets-philosophers-leaders. Their studies begin with physics, which is the study of the material, and from there they ascend to the more exalted level of metaphysics which is the philosophical study of divinity, its ways and the knowledge of it. Thereby, the human intellect is attached to the Active Intellect, which is the lowest of the higher intellects and maintains the connection with the educated man. Ultimately, the prophet-philosopher-leader, who the profusion fills and even flows from, is required to descend to the simple people who are dependent upon him, in order to lead and guide them, and also to satisfy his aspiration and desire to share the divine emanation. He understands that he is unable to perceive the divine essence directly, and therefore he returns to the world, in which God's ways are reflected, the ways of kindness, justice and righteousness. God standing atop the ladder represents the mover and the Active Intellect and the angels are the prophets-philosophers who are exalted, and an impulse of duty to lead the world surges within them.[176]

The Kabbala, which also adopted the approach of emanations, albeit using a different system, sees in the ladder the ascent of a person who studies esotericism of the ascent of the ten *sefirot*, which are the dimensions of divinity, in order to bring the divine emanation down from them to the world, and thereby rectifies and unifies the world of the *sefirot* through his good deeds and his fulfillment of the commandments. The entire universe, including the angels, are dependent on "him [*bo*]" (28:13) i.e. man, and his ascending the ladder.[177]

---

176. Maimonides, *Guide for the Perplexed*, 1:15, 54, 3:54. Cf. A. Ravitzky, *Iyunim Maimoniyim*, (Tel Aviv, 2005), 18-25, S. Klein-Braslavi, *Halom Yaakov*, M. Halbertal, *Maimonides*, (Princeton and Woodstock, 2007), 304-311, M. Goodman, *Sodotav shel Moreh Hanevukhim*, (Or Yehuda, 2009), 119-127. Compare Ibn Ezra, 28:12: "Angels of God – thoughts of wisdom."

177. Cf. for example *"Toldot Yaakov Yoseph"*, (Jerusalem, 1972), 50, 82, Rav Haim MiVolozhin, *"Nefesh Hahaim"* 1:19, Baal Hatanya, *"Liqutei Torah"*, Num. *Naso*, 2.

Modern psychology sees dreams as a whole as a symbolic reflection of the dreamer's repressed anxieties, desires and aspirations; which he is afraid to allow to enter his consciousness. Jacob's dream is therefore interpreted as an expression of Jacob's existential anxieties in his current situation: alone, traveling to the unknown and to his peril. He is in desperate need of support and a promise that his path will be successful. The dream brings his anxieties up to his consciousness and helps him to overcome them.

However, the modern commentators generally prefer to see an ethical lesson in the dream – part of the overall message of the Torah – containing a psychological dimension. The ladder, with its legs on the ground and its head in the heaven, is therefore interpreted as a symbol for the personality and mind of the person. The meaning of the "angels" who are ascending and descending via the ladder is the movement between the two mental and spiritual poles. In the psychological sense, this refers to encompassing the contrasts between the earthly and heavenly elements in man, in a manner which I will discuss below. This is the message which Jacob received in his dream, according to this interpretation. Until now, Jacob's world was dichotomous and simple. He recognized only two mutually exclusive personality types: The crude person, the unequivocally materialistic person, hunter and man of the field, and, by contrast, the shepherd, the refined person, the unequivocally spiritual person, the simple tent dweller. Each of these personality types represents for him a completely separate system of personality and psychology, not connected to each other by means of a "ladder" containing rungs, allowing for movement between the two. Jacob identified himself with one of them. He preferred to live on the top rung of the ladder, and to be an unequivocally spiritual person. However, only a dependent person can live a purely spiritual life. An independent person faces a much more complicated challenge.

parashat Vayetze

Upon leaving for an independent life, Jacob needed to develop in himself, in his personality, the earthly element – the Esau which was latent in him – in order to take care of the material needs of his survival. This is the test of a mature person. Man is comprised of a body which has physical needs, and therefore he stands – like that ladder – with his feet on the ground. Man also has a soul, which aspires to raise him up until his head reaches heavenward. A person must both be rooted in the ground of reality and also to aspire for the sky. He must accumulate material possessions and conquer the world for his needs (as he was already commanded when he was created: "fill the earth and master it" 1:28); and, at the same time, to utilize them wisely as a winch with which to build an ethical-spiritual world for himself. If he remains attached to the ground, he will be dominated by physical sensuality, be enslaved by his impulses like an animal, and lose his life. If he disassociates himself from the physical, seeing it as a necessary evil which should be repressed, and floats to the sky by means of mortifying his body and denying it, he will lose his connection to reality and lose himself in imaginary mystical, messianic worlds. He will only be able to reach the heavens of spiritual heights with his feet on the ground and his body and soul in balance, if he knows how to integrate the worlds, if he has the wisdom to sanctify his body and possessions and use them for ethical and spiritual purposes. It is God who stands above man – represented by a ladder – and teaches him how to conduct his life, and man is given free will to utilize this guidance or ignore it. The angels ascending and descending the ladder are man's acts and actions, his conduct, thoughts, prayers and study. It is these which elevate or lower him on the rungs of the ladder, and it is these which connect his earthly body with his elevated soul.[178]

---

178. Compare with S. R. Hirsch, 28: 12-13, 17, who combines the modern and classic interpretations.

parashat Vayetze

Jacob had indeed changed. We will see below that he uses his physical prowess to roll the stone off of the well by himself, that he supports himself and even becomes wealthy, marries, fathers children, and deals with the wicked selfishness and the acts of deceit of his uncle. At the same time, he tries to maintain a lifestyle of integrity, modesty and ethics. Along the way, he avoids direct confrontations and attains what is rightfully his by means of wisdom and machinations. Jacob and his wives, as the patriarchs and matriarchs before them, are presented as men and women with weaknesses, who err and make mistakes. It is not the Torah's intention to present supernatural figures that cannot be imitated. It presents the role model as a human figure dealing with the complexity with which life confronts him, and fighting an internal struggle with the fetters of the flesh; but in all of these, aware of the goal which is found in the heavenly spirit, which can only be reached through the elevation found in an ethical life, and the sanctification of the physical sensuality. It appears that the Torah wishes to teach us that the path to election is hard and winding. Only one who passed through purgatory – the struggles with temptation and the conditions of the human environment, which opposes that elevation – and overcame it and conquered his sins and passions-- only he is worthy of leadership, which requires humility, learning from experience and understanding the soul of the sinner.[179]

The upsetting dream woke Jacob up in the middle of the night. He attributed the event to the uniqueness of the place, which he viewed as the house of God and the gate of heaven. Although this was the first revelation which the novice Jacob experienced, it made a great impression on him, and he had no doubt as to its credibility. He had always known of the destiny of the family, and the blessing

---

179. Concerning this image of Abraham, cf. S. R. Hirsch, 12:10-13. Compare with BT *Yoma* 22b.

parashat Vayetze

and promise given to Abraham, and right now, he himself received it in the dream (verses 13-14). Therefore, after he fell back asleep and then awoke in the morning, he took the rock which served him as a pillow, established it as a pillar and poured oil on it in order to sanctify it for God's name. He changed the name of the place from 'Luz' to 'Bethel,' to express its being the house of God and the gate of heaven (verse 17). He made a vow there, which is entirely one of hope and prayer: When God's promise to protect Jacob and give him success on his journey until he returns home, and it is clear that *Hashem* is his God – such that a special relationship develops between them[180] - then he will transform Bethel into a ritual location, and he will give a tithe of the possessions which God granted him to God for sacred purposes.[181] Jacob went on his way eastward with a sure step, filled with vigor and hope, in anticipation of the tasks that lay ahead.

Jacob Raises a family – Birth Pains of the Nation

The hand of providence guided Jacob straight to a well in the grazing fields near Haran where his family dwelt: That is, his uncle, Laban, the brother of his mother Rebecca (the children of Bethuel, the son of Nahor, the brother of Abraham); and his cousins, Leah and the beautiful Rachel. He encountered shepherds and asked them if they knew Laban the son of Nahor (he did not mention Bethuel, who was not a prominent person, as mentioned above; it appears that Jacob's parents had originally provided him

---

180. Saadia Gaon, Rashbam, Hizkuni, 28:21, Kimhi, 29:18.

181. Saadia Gaon, Rashi, 28:22. Modern commentators see in the story of the ladder a contrast to the Tower of Babel. The message for Jacob and his progeny is that the gate to heaven is located in the land of Israel, the locus of spirituality, and not in Babel, the locus of materialism. Cf. Yoel Elizur, *Yisrael VeHamiqra*, Genesis 11, *Olam Hatanakh,* Gen., 172, Zvi Shimon, *Daf Shvui Bar Ilan Vayeze,* 2012, no.993, nt. 2 ad loc.; also nt. 66 above.

parashat Vayetze

with information concerning the family), and they directed him to Rachel, the daughter of Laban, who shepherded her father's sheep and had reached the well at precisely that moment. Jacob asked them why they stopped tending the sheep and were all gathered next to the well long before nightfall without watering the sheep. The answer was that the stone on the well was very large and heavy, and it required the combined strength of several shepherds to roll it, and they were waiting for shepherds who had not yet arrived. It would appear that the large stone was chosen for covering the well as a result of disputes which broke out earlier between them, and the stone forced them to stand in line and wait in order until most of them had gathered, such that it was clear who was first and who was last. Another possible reason is that the heavy stone was meant to prevent strangers from using the precious water. Meanwhile, Jacob saw Rachel, he was very moved by the sudden encounter with this beautiful relative, and fell in love with her at first sight. God's promise, his love for Rachel and providence filled him with great strength, and he rolled the stone off of the well all by himself, in order to impress her. In his great excitement, he kissed Rachel, and burst out in tears of relief and joy.[182]

Jacob was invited to be a guest in the home of his uncle. Laban quickly realized the unique specialness of Jacob, who was already a professional shepherd, and suggested that he work for him in exchange for remuneration. In the course of time, Jacob discovered that Laban (=white) was, in fact, 'black' – even his name was

---

182. Concerning the lack of trust between the shepherds cf. Kimhi and S. R. Hirsh, 27:2. Concerning the xenophobia, cf. Rashbam ad loc. On the omission of Bethuel cf. Kimhi. Nahmanides, Hizkuni, 29:5. Concerning the kiss and the cry cf. Kimhi, 29:11, and Luzzatto ad loc., based on the "Biur" of Mendelsohn. Note that the expression "*ahi imo*" repeats three times in a single verse (29:10) to emphasize Jacob's emotional state at unexpectedly meeting a close relative.

parashat Vayetze

a misrepresentation.[183] Jacob asked for the hand of his younger daughter Rachel in exchange for his tending his sheep for seven years. Jacob thought that the beautiful Rachel, daughter of the wealthy lord, was not attainable for a penniless distant relative like himself. Nonetheless, he boldly proposed his offer. To his surprise, Laban agreed. Jacob was ecstatic. He had expected that Laban would reject him, or suggest a much larger number of years. He felt that these seven years were absolutely nothing compared to Rachel's worth to him.[184] To his great disappointment, at the end of this time period, it became clear that Laban had tricked him. After seven years of labor, at the age of 47, the wedding and the feast that followed took place, but Jacob (who was apparently as drunk as Lot) was shocked to discover on the day following the nuptials that they had given Leah to him in marriage, and forced Rachel to cooperate.[185] His hope of returning home with his beautiful bride, in accordance with his father's request, was dashed. In response to his rebuke 'why did you deceive me' (29:25), Laban evaded responsibility and placed it on the community: It is the local custom to first marry off the elder daughter, and he is unable to change this custom.[186] One could say

---

183. Cf. *Bereshit Rabbah*, 60:5, 6-8. According to the Midrash there, this is an ironic paradox.

184. Bekhor Shor, Hizkuni, Sforno, Luzzatto, 29:20.

185. According to Bekhor Shor 29:25 and Kimhi 29:23, Jacob didn't notice that it was Leah on account of his modesty. Rashi (29:21 and the accounting in 28:9) determines, according to the sages, that Jacob was 84 when he wed. This count is based on counting back from Jacob's death at the age of 147. The result is forced and unreasonable, as it requires that we assume Jacob to have stayed in his father's home until Ishmael's burial (when he was 63), then studied for 14 years in the study hall of Shem and Eber (as the sages teach) and only left for Haran at the age of 77. I don't think that this is the *peshat* of the text. The chronological problems can be resolved based on Cassuto, nt. 38 above.

186. Nahmanides 29:21-27, s.v. "*venitna lekha*".

in Laban's defense, that he watched out for the honor of his older and less attractive daughter, and made sure to marry her off – albeit in this devious way – and to spare her from embarrassment. Jacob was forced to agree to marriage with Leah, to complete the seven days of the feast, to marry Rachel at their conclusion, and to work an additional seven years in exchange for her. Laban gave each of his daughters a maidservant, Zilpah for Leah and Bilhah for Rachel.

Providence hinted to Jacob that his deceit toward his father ("Your brother came with guile" – 27:35), for the purpose of advancing the younger at the expense of the firstborn (the justifications for it, which I described in Parashat Toldot, notwithstanding), resulted in a punishment which was poetic justice: The switching of the younger Rachel with the firstborn Leah,[187] accompanied by fourteen years of exile and servitude. Jacob, who had been an accomplice to an act of deceit, was turned into the victim of a similar act. In this way, his sense of justice and integrity was sharpened. God has his own plan, and life is much more complicated and challenging than the idyllic image which Jacob envisioned until he awoke the day after the first night of his nuptials.

The Torah now begins to relate the narrative of the raising of Jacob's family, which the Israelite nation came from. Abraham and Isaac may be defined as the roots of the family; Jacob may be viewed as the trunk, and his sons as the branches: the primary branches from which the secondary branches in the lineage of the Israelite nation grew. The Torah also recounts the creation of the family's wealth; to teach us that, in addition to the importance of

---

187. Compare *Maasei Hashem* of R. Eliezer Harofe, Hatam Sofer on the Torah and Rosenzweig, *Naharaim*, 13. According to them Laban spoke cynically to Jacob when he said that while it might be acceptable where Jacob came from to place the younger ahead of the elder, here it was not. In *Midrash Tanhuma* Buber *Vayeze* 11, the source for this notion, this accusation is placed in the mouth of Leah that morning.

parashat Vayetze

the fertility, motherhood and family, accumulation of wealth is also important, as it allows the family to serve God comfortably and with peace of mind, and about the importance of using them to fulfill the will of God, expressed through the commandments he gave to man.

In the beginning of the narrative, God saw Leah's suffering, i.e. that Jacob loved her less than he loved Rachel ("The Lord saw that Leah was unloved" – v. 31)[188] and compensated her. Jacob loved Leah less, both because he found her less beautiful than Rachel, and because she had deceived him (at her father's command) on the night of the nuptials. Leah turned out to be a fertile woman, she bore Jacob four sons: Reuben ("The Lord has seen my affliction"), Simeon ("The Lord heard that I was unloved"), Levi ("This time my husband will become attached to me") and Judah ("This time I will praise the Lord"). It would appear that Rachel harbored a certain feeling of superiority toward her sister due to love that Jacob showed her. She was punished for this by being barren, while the rejected Leah was granted children. Rachel was struck with jealousy, and she complained to Jacob: "Give me children, or I shall die," (30:1) meaning there is no point to my life. Jacob responded insensitively. He became angry at her and rejected her request, saying that it was the hand of God: it is not in his power to take God's place and remove her infertility.[189] In his defense, the possibility exists that his comments were directed against the pagan notion – which was apparently accepted in her father's household – that certain people can influence God by means such as through *teraphim* (household idols - which I will discuss below). A person who is in distress must pray to God, do all that he can and hope

---

188. Ibn Caspi, *Mitzraph Lakeseph*, Kimhi, Bahya ben Asher, Luzzatto and S. R. Hirsch, 29: 30-31.

189. According to Bereshit Rabbah, 71:10.

parashat Vayetze

for divine assistance.[190] Rachel offered that Jacob marry Bilhah (as Sarah offered Hagar to Abraham) in the hope that forgoing of her direct and natural motherhood would help her to conceive in the future. Bilhah bore Jacob two sons: Dan (this name was given by Rachel, signifying God's answering her request, as the children of Bilhah were considered like her own: "God has vindicated me; indeed, He has heeded my plea and given me a son.") and Naphtali (a sign of Rachel's successfully struggling with her sister: "A fateful contest I waged with my sister; yes, and I have prevailed"). Leah, who had ceased bearing children, offered Zilpah to Jacob, for the same reason which motivated Rachel in the case of Bilhah. Zilpah bore Jacob two sons: Gad ("What luck!" – Leah was the one who named these sons)[191] and Asher ("What fortune! Women will deem me fortunate").[192] Leah strained to win Jacob's attention in order to bear more children. Reuben found fine, fragrant and rare mandrakes, to which people attributed supernatural powers relating to conception. Leah offered them to Rachel in exchange for a night with Jacob, who normally preferred the tent of Rachel, both because he loved her more, and because of the hope that she would finally conceive. God once again listened to Leah, who did not eat from the mandrakes, and she bore two more sons and a daughter: Issachar ("God has given me my reward"), Zebulun ("this time my husband will exalt me"[193]) and Dinah. The downtrodden and forlorn Rachel finally merited and bore Joseph ("May the Lord add another son for me").

---

190. Nahmanides, Kimhi, 30:2 and N. Leibowitz, *Studies in Genesis (Bereshit)*, 331-335

191. Compare Saadia Gaon with Rashi, Rashbam and Kimhi.

192. Compare Saadia Gaon and Rashbam with Ibn Ezra, Kimhi and Sforno.

193. Meaning that he will dwell with me, from the word *mishkan* - a place of dwelling, in accordance with most of the commentators.

parashat Vayetze

It would appear that Jacob's seven years of work on behalf of Rachel came to an end at this point, and he was finally able to return home, as he had promised his parents, together with his two wives who were also his relatives, and many offspring. He hoped that in the meantime Esau had calmed down.[194] Rachel's giving birth at that point seemed to Jacob to be an additional sign of the conclusion of the first stage of raising a family. The children grew up and were educated – at least in their infancy – in the environment of the family of Abraham, outside the land of the Canaanites, the significance of which I have already discussed. The time had come to go home – to the land promised to his ancestors, for him and his progeny, in order to build a permanent home and settle down.[195] The raising of the family took place in the context of the tragedy of the sisters. One--favored and winning the love of the man – was punished with infertility for her pride and became bitter due to her infertility. The other, the "unloved" in her words, had children; yet despite her hopes, which she expressed through the names of her first three children, she did not capture the man's love, and she too turned into a burnt-out woman. This situation was the source of clashes between the brothers and between their offspring, clashes which accompanied the Israelite nation throughout many generations.[196]

---

194. Bekhor Shor, Rashbam and Hizkuni, 30:25.

195. Compare Kimhi, 30:25. Jacob fathered twelve children within a span of seven years, albeit with four wives, of whom Leah alone bore seven. This figure includes the interruptions described in the text. Cassuto explains in *Sefer Bereshit Umivnehu*, 318-321, that the traditions concerning the birth of Jacob's sons were consolidated together with other chronological traditions, which were at the disposal of the redactor. This constricts the births into a period of seven years, which is theoretically possible. Cf. notes. 38 and 185 above. It may be possible to alleviate this tight clustering by assuming that Rachel didn't wait until the birth of Judah, and gave her handmaiden to Jacob earlier and Leah acted similarly after seeing that Bilhah became pregnant.

196. N. Leibowitz, Studies in Genesis (Bereshit), 324

parashat Vayetze

Jacob tried, with a lack of sensitivity, to maneuver in this thicket, but did not succeed in resolving it. He therefore devoted himself to his work and the building up the material acquisitions of the family.

The Clash between Jacob and Laban – Transformation from Naiveté

Jacob surprised Laban with his request to leave Haran with his wives and children and return to his family in Canaan. Laban, cognizant of the blessing which he received in Jacob's merit, and Jacob's high standard of work ethic, did not want to lose this outstanding servant. Being a selfish and crafty individual, he interpreted Jacob's request as a plot, as a pretext for demanding a raise, and he offered it to him. Jacob was persuaded and agreed, as he wished to also establish wealth for his household, and asked that his salary going forward would be all the sheep born with dark speckles or spots, and the white ones which are born will be Laban's. In order to prevent any possible claims by Laban, he suggested that all sheep which were speckled and spotted be removed from the flock.[197] Laban agreed. Soon, with the assistance of his sons and people, he removed all of the speckled and spotted male and female animals from the flock, He took these for himself and distanced them three days journey, in the hope that the white females in Jacob's custody would conceive from the white males and give birth to white young exclusively. Jacob ingeniously placed rods in which he had peeled white stripes in the sheep's watering troughs. Jacob was familiar with the ancient theory, according to which pregnant females are affected by what they see, and give birth according to this influence. He designed it such that when the sheep came to drink, they would see the peeled rods, and it would influence them to give birth to speckled and spotted

---
197. Rashi, 30:32.

parashat Vayetze

young. Although Jacob knew (as did Laban) that the rods had no actual influence, he did so to put Laban's mind at ease, that he had no plot hidden up his sleeve.

After fourteen years of experience managing flocks at close quarters, in addition to his experience as a shepherd in his father's household, Jacob could have anticipated the results of the step which he took from the outset. (Laban was also certainly no less experienced than Jacob, but it is possible that he did not take note of the phenomenon which Jacob noticed). According to the laws of genetics (Mendel's laws; Jacob, of course, was not familiar with them, but he knew their practical consequences), those white animals who had spotted animals among their parents or grandparents gave birth to a certain percentage of spotted young. Therefore, even after the white animals were separated from the spotted ones, it was possible for the white male and female parents to produce spotted young. Jacob also learned from experience that those white animals which have the genetic characteristics (in modern terminology) of a mix of different colors possess a stronger sexual potency, and therefore it is worthwhile to only allow those to mate. ("Moreover, when the sturdier animals were mating [those who would become aroused quicker], Jacob would place the rods in the troughs, in full view of the animals, so that they mated by the rods; but with the feebler animals [it would take longer for the feebler ones to become aroused and they would bear fewer young] he would not place them there. Thus the feeble ones went to Laban and the sturdy to Jacob." 30:41-42). In the following stage, Jacob wisely took the sheep which were born spotted and removed them from the rest of the flock when they matured, together with the males which were spotted, and greatly increased the amount of spotted young through the following litters. According to his testimony in his speech to his wives (31:7) Laban attempted periodically to change the terms

parashat Vayetze

of the deal, in light of Jacob's successes, and Jacob accommodated him, however his success continued. According to that testimony (31:10), God showed him in a dream speckled and spotted males impregnating the sheep. It thereby became clear to him that God helped him. This approach succeeded and his flock gave birth to streaked, speckled, and mottled animals in large quantities, despite the fact that he started off with only white ones.[198]

In the final analysis, Jacob gathered for himself a huge flock of spotted, streaked, speckled, and mottled animals, and became very wealthy. Laban and his sons looked with frustration at the success of Jacob – who they viewed as a lowly foreigner – who succeeded in overcoming their plots, by means of his wisdom and God's assistance. Like the Philistines and Abimelech, and like anti-Semites of all generations, they were jealous of the successful Israelite, who they view as if he acquired all of his wealth thanks to them, and developed hatred toward him.[199] Jacob heard the words of the sons of Laban, and saw Laban's angry face. God allayed his fears, and commanded him to return to the land of his birth. When he was in Aram, Jacob became immersed in the desire for accumulating property and enjoyment of the pleasant, tranquil material life; just as his descendants tripped up in this way in their time, when they became attached to Egypt because of the

---

198. This explanation is based on Yehuda Feliks, *Olam Hatanakh,* Genesis, 180-182. Meir Bar Ilan adds regarding Jacob's plan that he apparently separated the flocks into smaller flocks from the beginning, such that each one contained a single stud, in order to be able to observe and determine which ones begat spotted sheep. The white sheep lacking the genetic potential to produce spotted sheep were consumed by Jacob and his children. In this way the spotted flock increased exponentially. Cf. the *Parasha* sheet of Bar Ilan on *Vayetze,* 2011 no. 943. Compare BT Gittin 58a, Bava Meziah 84a, Bekhor Shor, 30:33 and Luzzatto, 30:39, who accept the erroneous, ancient theory of the peeled rods, as being scientifically accurate.

199. Cf. Hatam Sofer and Hafetz Haim on the Torah, ad loc.

parashat Vayetze

abundance of goodness there. Only the hatred of the gentile, and the explicit command of God (as He promised him in the dream of the ladder – "I will return you to this land," 28:15) - succeeded in awakening Jacob and prodding him to leave the exile when he was 67 years old, after twenty years spent in the company of Laban.

Jacob summoned Rachel and Leah to the field for a secret discussion, and clarified the situation for them: Laban is jealous and is trying repeatedly to exploit and deceive him. Only God is helping him, and quashes Laban's attempts and saves the flock which Jacob is entitled to in lieu of his work from his hands. God, who promised him in Bethel protection and success – and he, Jacob made an oath to Him there – commanded him now in a dream to return to the land of his birth and revealed to him that He would help him to increase his flock in spite of Laban's plotting. Rachel and Leah agreed to go on the journey with Jacob as God commanded, and affirmed every word that he said. In a unique feminist expression they expressed their anger at their father's cold, chauvinist behavior toward them; for in his greed, he sold them like objects, in exchange for Jacob's work. They confirmed that all of their family's wealth was attained justly and with integrity. They claimed that Laban dropped all of the wealth which he attained through Jacob's outstanding work into his pocket, rather than paying him properly and thereby seeing to the support of his daughters and grandchildren. At that time, Laban was far away, having left to shear his sheep. Jacob took advantage of the situation and ran away with his family and property to Mount Gilead, on the way to his parents in Canaan. Rachel stole her father's *teraphim*, idols which were part of his collection of pagan ritual objects, for - as I explained above – it was believed that it was possible to influence God by means of these objects, and that God's decree could be changed using them.[200] She was concerned,

---

200. Luzzatto, 31:19.

parashat Vayetze

that using the *teraphim*, Laban would find out too quickly about Jacob's running away and where he was located, and thereby harm the escapees.[201] Rachel did so without informing Jacob; who, of course, did not attribute any significance to *teraphim*.

Laban learned of their running away after three days, and he left with his people to run after Jacob, who Laban accused of stealing his gods and abducting his daughters and grandchildren. After seven days of searching and chasing, Laban overtook Jacob at Mount Gilead. On the night before the encounter, God appeared to Laban in a dream (as He appeared to Abimelech in a similar situation), and warned him not to harm Jacob. Laban was therefore forced to have a discussion with his son-in-law. He presented his accusations to Jacob and attacked him verbally with great hypocrisy. Making himself out to be righteous, like Abimelech, he complained about Jacob's running away like a thief in the night, about his abducting his daughters and not letting him, their father, kiss them and his grandchildren, and part from them "with festive music, with timbrel and lyre" (31:27). About the theft of the *teraphim*. Laban asked: "but why did you steal my gods?" (31:30). He was totally unaware of the ironic absurdity of this question – what sort of god is it, if it can be stolen?[202] He declared aggressively, that he intended to harm Jacob and his people, but God prevented him from doing so. Jacob answered that he ran away because he was afraid, based on past experience, that Laban would not permit him to take his daughters with him, and he denied taking the *teraphim*. Confident of the integrity of

---

201. Rashbam, Ibn Ezra, 31:19, based on *Tanhuma Vayetze* 12, *and Pirkei D'Rabbi Eliezer* 36.

202. Bereshit Rabbah 74:8. An additional irony may be suggested; that Laban's gods, the *teraphim*, were hidden in Rachel's *makom turpah*, private place.

parashat Vayetze

the members of his family and his people, Jacob decreed capital punishment for the thief, permitting Laban to put anyone found in possession of the stolen item to death. Rachel concealed the *teraphim* in the cushion (saddle) of the camel, and sat on it inside the tent. Jacob anxiously watched Laban's actions, as he searched in every tent and groped in every corner. When he came to Rachel's tent, she explained to him that it was difficult for her to stand up in his honor, as she was having her menstrual period. Laban checked everywhere, but did not find what he sought.

After the failure of the search, Jacob felt calm and protected by God; and out of this sense of security he gave free rein to his feelings toward his father-in-law. All of the anger which had been restrained in the course of the twenty years during which Jacob worked for Laban now burst forth. He described all of the acts of deceit, fraud and exploitation inflicted on him by Laban. He rebuked him for his ungratefulness for Jacob's faithfulness, dedication and industriousness, and that for the fact that only God protected him, and saw to it that he receive proper compensation. Were it not for that protection, Jacob argued, Laban would not have seen him off, as he put it, "with festive music" (31:27), but rather "empty-handed" (31:42).[203] Laban played innocent and said that everything which Jacob amassed came from Laban's possessions, and that he only wanted to ensure the welfare of his daughters – that Jacob not attack them sexually[204] and not marry other wives in addition to them – and the welfare of his grandchildren and his property. However, he finally understood deep down that for the welfare of his daughters and grandchildren it was best that he be an ally of Jacob, God's protégé, rather than his enemy. He offered him, exactly as Abimelech had offered Isaac, to establish a

---

203. Rashbam, 31:42.
204. Ibn Ezra, 31:50.

covenant with him. Jacob agreed to his request, his people set up a mound of rocks, which was a monument to their covenant. The two of them named the monument using two names: '*Gal-ed*' (or '*Yegar-sahadutha*' in Aramaic, Laban's language), indicating that this mound of rocks would serve as testament to their covenant, and as a demarcation of the separation between their forces; and 'the Mizpah,' indicating that God was watching to see if they were plotting against each other even after separating from each other. Jacob offered up a sacrifice and prepared a feast for Laban and his people as is customary when establishing a covenant, and as Isaac and Abimelech had done (26:30).[205] Each swore by their gods that they would not cross this border in order to attack the other. Laban asked Jacob to swear that he would not harm his daughters, and not marry other women in addition to them. Laban swore by the gods of the brothers Nahor and Abraham (rather than Betuel and Isaac who were not important in his view),[206] that they judge anyone who abrogates the covenant. Jacob, on the other hand, swore by the God ('Fear' – 31:53) of his father Isaac. The next morning, Laban took leave of his daughters and grandchildren, blessed them and returned home. Jacob continued on his way to Canaan, until he reached the east bank of the Jordan, where he, once again, encountered divine angels; this time awake, rather than in a dream. He understood that a circle had closed when he returned home to the borders of the Land of Israel. For that reason he found himself once again in a special place, like Bethel. He called the location of the new encounter with the angels Mahanaim – a contraction of '*Mahaneh Elohim*' [God's camp] (32:2), or named for the two camps which met here – God's camp and his own.[207]

---

205. Bekhor Shor, 32:54.
206. Kimhi, 31:53.
207. Ibn Ezra, Kimhi, Bekhor Shor, Nahmanides, 32:3.

Parashat Vayishlah
Encountering Esau – the Characteristic of Faith and the Return of the Blessing

This parasha describes that which transpired concerning Jacob and his family when he returned to the Land of Israel which was promised to his progeny. He knew the prophecy which his mother received when she was pregnant, and remembered the struggle over the primogeniture and the blessings. He understood that the struggle between him and his offspring on the one hand and Esau and his progeny on the other was approaching, but he had to try and reach a compromise at that time. His desire to make peace with his brother was strengthened by feelings of guilt for stealing Esau's blessing. He attempted to meet him as soon as possible, so that he could prepare for his life in the Land of Israel in accordance with Esau's reaction.[208] Therefore, despite the fact that Mount Seir – Esau's dwelling – was out of the way for Jacob as he headed for his father's home, he sent agents of appeasement to Esau, to inform him of his return. These messengers – who were unaware of the old fight and Jacob's concern – returned from their journey and informed him that they met with Esau and he was going out to meet him with four hundred of his men. Jacob could not tell whether Esau was heading for appeasement or war.[209]

The two brothers had grown up, raised families and accumulated wealth, and it appears that the time of personal clash between them

---

208. Y. Leibowitz, *Sheva Shanim shel Sihot al Parashat HaShavua*, 134-135.
209. Bekhor Shor, 32:7-8. His explanation appears more compelling than that of the other commentators, who are divided regarding the message that Jacob received from his messengers. Cf. on the one hand, Rashi, Kimhi and Sforno, 32:7 and Nahmanides, 32:8, and on the other hand, Rashbam, Hizkuni and Luzzatto, 32:7.

parashat Vayishlah

had passed. However, in this parasha their personal story evolves into the narrative of the historic-worldwide clash between Edom – representing national materialistic power, containing a pagan element – and the Israelites, representing the spiritual, ethical power of the individual and family, whose freedom emanates from the freedom of the transcendent God, who is free of the matter which He created. In Edom's world, the individual is a tool in the hands of the government's materialistic power. In the world of the Israelites, political power is a tool for the spiritual elevation of the individual and of the community.[210]

Jacob acted quickly to protect himself, as any person immersed in uncertainty and existential danger would do.[211] His fear is particularly understandable in light of his temperament; as by nature, he was fearful of confrontation. Although he was cognizant of the divine promise, he did not allow himself to remain passive, expecting that the promise would be fulfilled by means of God's intervention in events. His taking action was not purely the result of his natural fear; it was also due to his recognition that he had to do everything in his power, with initiative, wisdom and judgment, as he did in Paddan-aram. He knew that the realization of the promise depended on his being worthy of it in an ethical sense; but that it also depended on his actualizing his intellectual potential and the initiative with which God endowed him. Jacob teaches us what the proper attribute of faith is. A person may not, regardless of his righteousness, rely on miracles and sit idly by, self-righteously

---

210. Nahmanides, 32:26, S. R. Hirsch, 32:8.

211. Contrary to Rashi, Ibn Ezra, Hizkuni, Rashbam, and Maimonides, who each in his own way follows in the path of the Midrash, and says that Jacob was concerned lest the promise not be fulfilled because of his sins, and that he would be killed. Rather, according to Kimhi on 1Sam. 16:2 and Abravanel 32:8, quoted by Nechama Leibowitz, *Studies in Bereshit (Genesis)* 354-355. Compare Kimhi 12:12.

parashat Vayishlah

and haughtily, as if everything were guaranteed to him. He is also expected to not give in to fear, not run away from the battle, and not leave those relying on him unprotected from danger. True heroes are afraid, but they overcome the fear and do everything in their power to extricate themselves from the crisis, while still hoping for divine salvation. Only such people stand a chance at meriting divine assistance.[212]

Jacob did not know what Esau had in store for him, war or brotherhood.[213] He, therefore, prepared himself for all eventualities: A) He divided his small camp in two, in preparation for a possible war, with the slaves (the soldiers), the maidservants and cattle in one camp, and the nuclear family in a separate camp. If one of the camps is attacked, the other could escape. B) He prayed to God. In his prayer, Jacob emphasized that he did not know how someone as insignificant as himself merited all of the kindness and goodness which God had performed for him until now,[214] from the time when he crossed the Jordan possessing nothing more than his staff, until now when he is returning with great wealth. Nonetheless, he dared to remind God of His promise, and prayed to be saved from the hand of his brother Esau. C) He once again sent messengers, carrying precious gifts, to greet his brother. He gathered together hundreds of animals from his flock for this purpose, organized them into several herds, and instructed his messengers to bring them to Esau one herd after another, in order to slowly cool down his wrath, if

---

212. Cf. Kimhi, 32:14, Abravanel ad loc. and *Aqedat Yitzchak*, in his introduction to his commentary. Compare *Tosefet Beracha*, beginning of Parashat Miketz.

213. Bekhor Shor, 32:8.

214. Saadia Gaon, Ibn Ezra, Ibn Caspi, *Mitzraph Lakeseph*, Nahmanides, Kimhi and Sforno, 32:11, in the footsteps of the opinion of Rav Abba in *Bereshit Rabbah*, 76:5, contrary to Rashi who follows the opinion of Rabbi Levi ad loc.

parashat Vayishlah

it had not yet abated.[215] Jacob wanted to let his brother know that he has no designs on Esau's possessions, or on that of the family which had been promised to him, as he had enough of his own. He hoped that the gifts would soothe Esau's anger, and smooth over that which Jacob wronged him.[216] The worried Jacob waited through the night (one night or two) together with his people and his cattle, and personally supervised the sending of the gift (over the course of one day or two).

Providence presented Jacob with another challenge on the eve of the fateful encounter with Esau, in order to clarify for him the task which was incumbent on him and his progeny, and to demonstrate to him that he was capable of dealing with fears, dangers and threats face to face. Jacob was unable to sleep during the night before the encounter because of his extreme apprehension. He got up in the middle of the night having decided out of tactical considerations to move his nuclear family from Mahanaim to the north, to the other side of the ford of the Jabbok, in order to further distance them from the other camp. Perhaps he was overcome by fear and decided to run away with them. After he brought his family across, together with most of its possessions, he remained alone and fought with a mysterious man for the remainder of the night. This man symbolized the forces of darkness: the forces that oppose light, which is represented by the image of Jacob. The purpose of the clash was to strengthen Jacob in preparation for his encounter with his brother, and the narrative of the clash is to strengthen the descendants of Jacob throughout the generations in their clashes with other cultures. The clash and its recounting contain an educational dimension – teaching to dare to cope and not to

---

215. S. R. Hirsch, 32:19-21.
216. According to *Midrash Qohelet Rabbah* 9:28, cf. Rashi, 32:9.

parashat Vayishlah

run away. The clash symbolizes the struggle of the Israelites throughout human history, which was a period of the darkness of a long exile for them.

The clash, during which opponents clung to each other in a wrestlers' embrace was not decisive, despite the fact that Jacob's strength was less than the superhuman strength of his opponent. As in the case of his rolling the stone, Jacob discovered tremendous inner strength which prevented a resolution of this struggle. However, Jacob was injured bodily, and at the conclusion of the battle he was unable to stand up, and instead was limping on his hip, which was strained because that person tore a tendon there. Jacob was, therefore, unable to run away from dealing with his brother. On the other hand, the man discovered that he was unable to defeat Jacob. He requested from the mortal that he release him from his grasp, "for dawn is breaking" (32:27). Toward the end of the exile – as occurred toward the conclusion of Jacob's exile in Aram – the spiritual-ethical strength will gradually increase. The Torah does not indicate when we will know that the time of dawn has arrived. Did the voices of equality, freedom and brotherhood, which began to overcome the forces of subjugation and discrimination in the nineteenth century, signal its arrival? We saw that they were followed by the Holocaust. Is the rise of the Jewish people in the twentieth century, and their return to their land, sovereign in their own state, the indication? For now, we cannot know. It is possible that the dawn depends on us ourselves. In any case, Jacob demanded a blessing from the man before he would allow him to disappear. Why exactly did he demand this? According to our approach, this blessing indicates that only the nations of the world's recognition of the superiority of the ethical-monotheistic position of the Jewish people, and their recruitment on behalf of this position, can free the world from the grasp of the

parashat Vayishlah

forces of darkness. Such recognition was given to Jacob, upon his return to Canaan, only in the merit of his preserving his uniqueness, not assimilating into the general culture which surrounded him in the exile of Padan-aram. His descendants learned this lesson in their exiles. According to the biblical viewpoint (as we see in the narratives concerning the subjugation in Egypt, concerning the attempts made by Balak and Balaam and concerning the Babylonian exile), the nations want the Israelite spirit to become assimilated in their midst, so that they can dominate the entire human culture; however, the Israelites – by means of their will and power – will struggle and preserve their uniqueness, and the nations will accept their path upon themselves and thereby be blessed, in accordance with God's promise to Abraham. The tendon which the man tore in Jacob's thigh symbolizes the vulnerability and weakness of the physical. Jacob's body was injured, and the Israelites will always remember that its strength is not in its body, but in its spirit, and they will thereby preserve their uniqueness and might. The prohibition against eating the thigh tendon is a reminder of this.[217] The person informed Jacob that he is going to receive an additional, worthier name: Israel, "for you have striven with beings divine (in the form of the man who he fought) and human (Laban), and have prevailed," (32:29), and he blessed him. The mysterious man disappeared with the sunrise, and Jacob named the place Peniel, marking being saved from the face to face clash with a representative from the divine realm.

---

217. *Sefer Hahinukh*, 3, Kimhi, 32:25-26, 34:30, S. R. Hirsch, 32:25-27. Compare Rashbam, 32:21-29, Nahmanides, 32:25-26, and Abravanel ad loc. The source for this approach to the clash is *Midrash Lekah Tov*, which is quoted by N. Leibowitz, *Studies in Bereshit (Genesis)* 368-369. The idea concerning the educational lesson that Jacob received from the struggle to be strong and persevere comes from my cousin, Avishai Eilat. Regarding the meaning of the names Jacob and Israel, cf. further S. R. Hirsch, 43:6.

parashat Vayishlah

As we recall from Parashat Vayera, Maimonides holds that angels only exist in dreams and prophecy is glimpsing into the mind of the prophet. According to this explanation, the clash with the mysterious man took place in Jacob's dream, or in his mind, and the limp was psychosomatic, or the result of the exertion of bringing the family across the Jabbok in a hurry at night. Jacob's fear of Esau together with his guilt feelings spurred an awareness of his weakness. He aspired to be as self-confident as Esau, and in his dream he accomplished this, and attained the promise that his name would be changed to Israel, a name which indicates coping and success.[218]

The next day, when the brothers finally met, it turned out that the nocturnal lesson bore no immediate practical fruit. Jacob was not yet deserving of the name Israel. After he fawningly greeted Esau, he presented the two maidservants – together with their children – to him first, to be on the safe side, and then Leah and her children, and finally Rachel and Joseph, who were most precious of all to him. It appears that the Bible does not neglect to address this flawed behavior. Jacob paid dearly for showing preference to Rachel and Joseph in this way, a fact which did not escape the notice of his other sons. The jealousy and conflicts within the family – and later between the tribes which came from it – continued until the exile of the ten tribes.

Jacob was profuse in denigrating himself as subservient to Esau – the work of an astute politician interacting with someone who is more

---

218. Maimonides, *Guide for the Perplexed*, 2:42, and Y. Leibowitz, *Sheva Shanim shel Sihot al Parashat HaShavua*, 140, based on Rav Avraham ben HaRambam, and Gersonides, quoted by Abravanel ad loc. Cf. also Ibn Caspi, *Tirat Keseph*, 116-117, and *Mitzraph Lakeseph*, 32:4. Regarding Jacob's feelings of guilt cf. Benno Jacob ad loc. Concerning the possibility that Jacob tried to escape cf. Rashbam, 32:23. Concerning the clash as an embrace cf. Rashi, Nahmanides, Luzzatto, 32:25. Regarding the keyword '*panim*' in the story cf. H. Y. Chamiel, *Limudim BeFarashat HaShavua*, 58.

parashat Vayishlah

powerful, forgoing illusory honor, hoping that the more powerful person will be won over by flattery. Jacob therefore called his brother "my master," and referred to himself as his "slave." He bowed to him seven times, and his wives and children bowed, as well. Jacob thereby demonstrated that the material blessing which he took away from his brother had not been fulfilled. In actuality, it was Jacob who bowed to Esau and gave him gifts, as a subject would act toward his master in ancient times.[219] Esau also did not know what to expect. It is reasonable to assume that his anger had long ago abated. He remembered that Jacob was cunning and competitive, and doubted that his character had changed. He was flattered by his brother's behavior. He referred to Jacob as "my brother," and refused to accept the gifts; claiming that his own wealth was sufficient. However, Jacob urged him again to accept them as a token of good will and appeasement. Jacob was prepared to willingly and officially return the material blessing, which he mistakenly took from him: "Take my present [*birkhati*=my blessing] which has been brought to you" (33:11).[220]

This time as well, Jacob's initiative and wisdom stood him in good stead. New strengths were revealed in Esau – Jacob's twin brother, whose descendants are partners in the development of human culture – which were concealed from us until now. Kisses, hugs and tears replaced hatred, jealousy and desire for revenge. Esau was shown to be humane, considerate of those who are weaker than him, and respectful of their rights. Jacob's love for his brother was aroused, and they both cried.[221] After much pressure from

---

219. Sforno, 33:4.
220. Midrash Bereshit Rabbati based on Moshe Hadarshan, ad loc., Martin Buber, *Darko Shel Miqra*, 291-292, N. Leibowitz, *Studies in Bereshit (Genesis)* 268-269, 347-348, 364-365 Y. Leibowitz, *Hearot Leparashiyot Hashavua*, 28-29, H. Y. Chamiel, *Meiynei Miqra*, 102. Cf. nt.163 above.
221. S. R. Hirsch and *Haamek Davar*, 33:4.

parashat Vayishlah

Jacob, Esau agreed to accept the gifts, and the appeasement became a fait accompli. Esau suggested that the two of them continue on the journey together, but Jacob wanted to separate from Esau and even declined the soldiers who Esau's wanted to leave with Jacob to protect his camp. He said that he did not want to detain Esau, due to the slow pace of the children and the sheep; and promised that he would join him in Seir. The brothers parted, and Jacob traveled on until he found, east of the Jordan and north of the ford of Jabbok, a comfortable place to encamp, and built a house for his family and booths for his cattle. He named the place Succoth.

Lethal Zealotry

After Jacob recuperated, he continued on his journey westward to Canaan and reached Shechem unharmed, as per God's promise, and purchased land there from the sons of Hamor, who was the prince of the area of the city Shechem. 'Shechem' was also the name of Hamor's son, the youth who plays a significant role in this parasha. Jacob established a tent and built an altar in accordance with the practice of his ancestors, and named it "El-elohei-Yisrael [God, the God of Israel]" (33:20).[222] The young and inquisitive Dinah left to the city to make the acquaintance of the local women, and Shechem the son of Hamor saw her there, desired her, enticed her to come to his house, and raped her there. He fell in love with her and attempted to persuade her to marry him by means of flattery, went through the motions of asking her forgiveness, and asked his father, the prince of Shechem, to acquire her from her father, while still holding her captive.[223] Jacob heard about the incident and

---

222. Cf. Y. Knohl's interesting commentary, *Meayin Banu*, 2008, 69-72.

223. The postmodern commentary suggests a feminist reading of the incident involving Dina. The text is silent regarding her perspective, in line with ancient texts' treatment of women. This explanation suggests that the latter

chose to remain silent until his sons returned from the field, where they were grazing their sheep. Somebody hastened to inform the brothers of the incident and they rushed home. Hamor (discerning Jacob's weakness), instead of punishing his criminal son, addressed Jacob's sons cajolingly and offered them commercial cooperation, permission to acquire land, marital ties with the local inhabitants and whatever dowry they demanded, all in exchange for Dinah.

The Torah wishes to teach us here when and in what fashion one should break the boundaries of restraint and choose to use physical force. Until this point, Jacob and his sons, who faced Laban and Esau, learned that it is possible to win by means of spiritual strength. Now the sons learned that their father's way was not always appropriate, and that there are situations in which they are required to unsheathe the sword. Shechem and Hamor crudely trampled all human and ethical values, and the dignity of man was lowered by them merely because they considered Dinah – as a woman and as the daughter of a foreign family – inferior to themselves, and therefore exploitable. Her brothers had every right to kill the criminal rapists and their associates who collaborated in the act, whose ethical corruption brought them to the lowest rung.[224] Jacob, by contrast, remained as he was. He was helplessly silent, not fulfilling his paternal obligation to his daughter, just as he had not properly fulfilled his

---

part of the incident was consensual, and that Dina, who had experienced her mother's being unloved, fell in love with Shechem and had no desire to return to Leah's tent.

224. Maimonides, *hilkhot Melakhim*, 9:14, (as per the obligation of the Noahide commandment to establish an ethical judicial system), Kimhi, 34:27, Nahmanides, 34:13 (as per the rational obligation to establish laws which regulate interpersonal interactions and to prevent abduction and rape). According to Maimonides, all of the residents of Shechem were deserving of the death penalty. According to Nahmanides, only the rapist and his close accomplices were liable.

parashat Vayishlah

obligation as a husband to her mother, Leah. He did not take part in the plan to rise up against the rapist and his accomplices. Jacob's sons deceived Shechem and all of his people; claiming that anyone who was not circumcised could not marry into their family, they caused all of the males of Shechem to be circumcised. It makes sense to assume that the brothers hoped that the people of Shechem would refuse this condition and that they would thereby be able to recover Dinah without having to resort to violence, but their hopes were dashed. Shechem's desire to marry Dinah got the better of them. The alternate plan of Jacob's sons was to take advantage of the third day from the time of the circumcision in order to enter Shechem, punish the criminals and rescue Dinah. Simeon and Levi (the sons of Leah, and therefore Dinah's brothers through both parents) thought otherwise. In their fury over the affront against their family's honor and in their zeal for their sister's honor they crossed the boundaries which the Torah is trying to teach us about. The two of them went through the city of Shechem like a storm, its males falling into the trap which Dinah's brothers set for them: The men of the city circumcised themselves in order to enter into the dubious covenant with Jacob's family, and therefore had no strength to fight for their lives. Simeon and Levi killed all of the males in the city, and freed Dinah from the household of Shechem.

The people of Shechem agreed to circumcise themselves, as Jacob's sons suggested, because they were convinced that Shechem's marrying a woman from Jacob's family would be worthwhile, and benefit all of them (verse 23). (At the same time, Hamor and his son suggested to Jacob's sons possible benefits that could result from the connection between the two families).[225] The greed of the people

---

225. N. Leibowitz, *Studies in Bereshit (Genesis)* 382-385. Regarding the distinction between the intentions of the brothers and the intentions of Simeon and Levi, cf. Nahmanides and Luzzatto, 34:13.

of Shechem and their cooperation with the rapist-kidnapper – a modus operandi adopted by anti-Semites throughout the generations – justifies the plunder of the city and the capture of the women and children carried out by all of the brothers. However, in no way does it justify collective capital punishment for those who were not directly involved in the crime. Simeon and Levi acted with extreme zealotry and took into their own hands, the unauthorized role of prosecutor, judge and executioner in contravention of every compelling legal practice. The other brothers did not join them in this act of killing.

Jacob, who, as usual, feared conflict, was angry at the two of them and scolded them for endangering the camp by their actions, rendering it vulnerable now to acts of revenge. His words are revolting. He should have responded with pride both to the crime of the people of Shechem and to the excessive punishment which Simeon and Levi imposed for it. There is another aspect to the weakness of Jacob. It was clear to Jacob that a person who wants all of humanity to be blessed through him cannot exhibit unbounded zealotry, which places a collective punishment – of capital punishment – upon the innocent and the guilty alike. This is not the way of divine ethics. However, Jacob did not say so at this time, rather he was silent in response to their answer, which was critical of his reply: "Should our sister be treated like a whore?" (34:31). Being aware of his own weakness, he absorbed the personal affront; he also restrained himself concerning the act of zealotry which was severe in an ethical sense and delayed his response in this matter. In the meantime, he concerned himself with survival. However, the actions of Simeon and Levi were neither forgiven not forgotten, as it is embedded in the soul of the nation which will arise. When the time comes for Jacob to take leave of his children, to bless them before his death and to reveal to them the future that awaits them (49:1), he saw fit to exact retribution from the two

parashat Vayishlah

wayward sons and put them in their places. He directed that the tribes who come from them be scattered and that they be spread out among the other tribes (49:5); out of concern for the tranquility of the future nation and in order to remove the influence of hotheaded zealotry. Therefore, these two tribes did not receive inheritances at the time of the division of the Land of Israel to the Israelites: Simeon was absorbed within Judah and Levi was scattered among the tribes throughout the entire Land of Israel. Thereby, zealotry was meant to strengthen the entire nation; and in the absence of a concentration of zealots, the breaking down of boundaries would be prevented.[226]

Just as Esau was capable of also revealing his inner humanity and set aside his sword (which is his means of existence, as Isaac said to Esau: "you will live by your sword," 27:40); so too, Jacob is capable, when facing the epitome of corruption, to be Israel, to draw his sword and to stand up for his rights against the evildoer. The boundaries of zealotry are thin and fragile. Only wise and cautious leadership knows how to confidently navigate between invalid zealotry and appropriate zealotry, between fawning and diplomatic resourcefulness, between properly standing up for legitimate rights and an unbounded revolt, between collective punishment and a determined ethical stance, between an exile mentality and a redemption mentality. The nation which came from Jacob-Israel, had to – and will have to – steer itself between the diplomacy of Jacob – "the art of the possible" – and the fighting pride and love of freedom of Israel. In the course of the generations, there has been an ongoing disagreement among the Jewish people between the rational moderates and the romantic and mystical freedom fighters

---

226. The commentary regarding the incident at Shechem is according to Nahmanides, Luzzatto and S. R. Hirsch, ch.34, especially 25-34. Regarding the zealotry cf. *Haamek Davar* ad loc., and the discussion on *Parashat Pinhas*.

as to the appropriate means to use in order to advance the interests of the nation and its values. The two entities – Jacob and Israel – struggled and continue to struggle within the nation. The decisions are entrusted to the leadership of each generation, which did not always succeed in its execution. In the beginning of the nation's journey, Jacob entrusted Judah with leadership (49:8-10), and I will show that he had good reasons for doing so.

Balancing Between Subservience and Zealotry
God instructed Jacob to leave Shechem, to go up to Bethel and to build an altar there. Jacob instructed the members of his family and all of his people to remove all of the foreign gods which remained in their possession from Padan-aram – including the *teraphim* and the spoils of Shechem--from their domain, to purify themselves using water, and to wear clean clothing in preparation for the ascent to Bethel and the ritual service that they would perform there in honor of God, who fulfilled all that He promised Jacob when he was running away from Esau. All of the pagan accoutrements were handed over to Jacob, who buried them, thereby fulfilling the final component of Jacob's requests of God in the oath which he took at Bethel: "… and the Lord [*Hashem*] shall be my God" (28:21). The Lord [*Hashem*] became the God and sole highest leader for the household of Israel. The camp of Jacob left Shechem and no one dared attack it, due to the great fear which fell on the residents as a result of the slaughter carried out by Simeon and Levi. When they arrived at Bethel, Jacob fulfilled his part of the oath (28:22). He immediately built an altar at that place, and named it "El-Bethel". Deborah, the nursemaid of Rebecca, died nearby. It would appear that Deborah, who went with Rebecca and Abraham's slave in order to assist the young bride, returned to Haran after she carried out her task. It is possible that she returned there at Rebecca's behest,

parashat Vayishlah

having heard about Jacob's wives giving birth and wishing to assist them, and perhaps also to urge Jacob to return home, as she had promised him before he left on his journey. Now, in her old age, she joined Jacob on his journey to the Land of Israel, both because of her attachment to Jacob's wives and children, and because of her yearnings for Rebecca; however, she did not succeed in meeting her.[227] This greatly distressed Jacob's people, who buried her under the oak in Bethel; and named it Allon-bacuth (the weeping oak).

The Torah hints to us time and again that Jacob's fawning approach (possibly, as opposed to other non-violent political conduct) is not appropriate. Jacob is confronted with his failing (the name connoting 'retreating' or 'crooked') to adopt some of Esau's strength and to be worthy of the name Israel (connoting 'straight', 'upright'), once again, this time by God. God appears to Jacob again at Bethel, this time as "El Shaddai." He officially added the name 'Israel' for Jacob, which will now become his preferred name, as the mysterious man promised him; and repeated the blessing of progeny and the blessing of the Land of Israel. God thereby emphasized to him that the submissive and fawning Jacobean conduct is invalid, just as murderous zealotry is invalid; and the Israelite behavior is superior to it, and is meant to serve as a balance between them. I will return to this blessing and to the events that occurred afterwards in Bethel in the discussion of Parashat Vayehi.

After the repetition of the blessings of progeny and the Land of Israel in that same revelation, Jacob fulfilled the third part of his vow. He established a pillar next to the altar, poured wine on it and anointed it with oil and conducted a ceremony for the official

---

227. Nahmanides, Luzzatto, 35:8. Rashi, 35:8, based on Rabbi Moshe Hadarshan, and Bekhor Shor, based on *Midrash Hagadol,* 597, suggest that Rebecca sent Deborah to Haran in order to instruct Jacob to return home, as she had promised him that she would at the time of his escape from Esau, 27:45. This explanation is also accepted by Kimhi and Hizkuni.

naming of the place, Bethel: "And this stone, which I have set up as a pillar, shall be God's abode" (28:22). Like Beer-sheba, whose name was reinforced by Abraham and Isaac, Bethel received its name from Jacob three times. Jacob continued slowly on his way southward to his father's home. When he reached the road to Ephrath (the road to Bethlehem) Rachel went into labor. There were complications in the labor, and Rachel died in childbirth. On death's doorstep, she heard that the child was a male son, and she gave him a name with a dual meaning: Ben-onni (child of my strength or child of my suffering; son of my mourning). Jacob changed the name to Benjamin, in order to negate the dual meaning and affirm the positive meaning: 'child of my strength.' Jacob was shocked and grief-stricken having lost his beloved wife, it possibly having been his fault.[228] Rachel was buried right there, on the crossroads to Ephrath, and Jacob placed a monument at her grave, which was extant and known when these words were transcribed.[229] Jacob continued on his way, and paused at Migdal-eder. It was there that Reuben slept with Bilhah, his father's concubine; whether in order to bring Jacob back to the tent of Leah, the mother of Reuben,[230] or to assert his future dominance as the first born.[231] The matter became known to Jacob. Jacob decided not to have any further children as a result of this event,[232] and the number of his sons – twelve – was

---

228. According to *Bereshit Rabba*, 74:4, Rachel dies as a result of the curse which Jacob places upon the thief of the *teraphim*, "whoever your gods are found in their possession will not live", 31:32. Regarding the naming of Benjamin by Jacob cf. Ibn Caspi, *Mitzraph Lakeseph*, 35:18.

229. Regarding the location of Rachel's tomb cf. Luzzatto, 34:16, Hagi Ben Artzi, *Daf Shvui shel Bar Ilan*, no.893, *Vayehi*, 2010.

230. Rashi, 35:22.

231. Cf. *Daat Miqra*, 35:22.

232. Kimhi, Bekhor Shor, Nahmanides according to the peshat, Hizkuni, 35:22.

parashat Vayishlah

sealed. Jacob's journey concluded in his father's home in Mamre, at Kiriath-arba – now Hebron. When Isaac passed away, at the age of 180, Jacob and Esau (who were 120) buried him, as Isaac and Ishmael had done for Abraham. The death of the fathers enabled an expression of appeasement on the part of the sons.

The genealogy of Ishmael was briefly surveyed at the end of Parashat Hayyei Sarah in order to move on to the genealogy of Isaac. This Parasha similarly concludes with a brief survey of the genealogy of "Esau being Edom" (36:1). Esau, who until now divided his time between Hebron and Seir, chose to settle in the hill country of Seir the Horite, far from Jacob who lived in Hebron, because "the land where they sojourned could not support them because of their livestock" (36:7). The brothers, neither of whom got the better of the other, separated. Esau's household, which grew into a power, which from now on would be engaged in an ongoing confrontation with the Israelites, as promised in the prophecy "one people shall be mightier than the other" (25:23). The Torah briefly enumerates the descendants of Esau and their generals, the descendants of Seir the Horite and their generals, and the kings who reigned in Edom even before the Israelites were consolidated as a nation headed by a leader.[233] Among the descendants of Esau, it is worth noting Teiman (Yemen), the son of Eliphaz, who was the son of Esau, and his stepbrother Amalek, the son of Eliphaz and his concubine Timna. The name Amalek is familiar to us from the history of our nation, as is the name Teiman from the atlas. Esau and Amalek represent the absolute antithesis of the Israelites. It is interesting that here too, similar to previous genealogical lists, that certain names are repeated two or three times.

---

233. Compare Ibn Ezra, Rashbam, Sforno, Luzzatto, 36:31, *Torah Nidreshet* ch.24. Bible critics bring this vs. as a proof for the late redaction of the Pentateuch in the monarchic period at the earliest. Cf. A. Rofe, *Mavo Lesifrut Hamiqra,* 24.

Part five – Joseph and his Brothers

Parashat Vayeshev
Do Dreams, in fact, Speak Lies?
In this parasha the narrative of the lives of Joseph and Judah– Jacob's genealogy (toldot=his offspring) – and their relationship with each other and the other sons begins. In this narrative, we are introduced to the beginning of the process of the fulfillment of the prophecy given to Abraham at the 'covenant between the pieces.' We are once again presented with a drama, which takes place on two planes: The plane of father-son relationships (as there had been between Isaac and Jacob and Esau, and perhaps between Abraham and Ishmael and Isaac) and the plane of the relationships among the brothers themselves. The current drama is broader in scope than the previous one, both in terms of the number of players active in it, and in terms of the ramifications for the future, as it lays the foundation for the history of the tribes and the kingdoms which came from the family of Abraham, as related throughout the length of the Bible.

This time, of course, all of the brothers belong to the family and all have a share in the blessing given to Abraham, Isaac and Jacob; however, the following drama develops due to feelings of jealousy and competition between the brothers, involving lack of communication and misunderstandings: A rift between Joseph and the other brothers, Joseph's removal from the family by the brothers without their father's knowledge (in a more violent and shameless way than that which was done to Ishmael and Esau), and

parashat Vayeshev

then – after many vicissitudes and surprises-- the reunification of Jacob's family. However, this unification rests on a duality. Jacob divided the inheritance of the primogeniture between two of his children, in accordance with their talents, rather than their birth order. The leadership of the **family** in his old age and after his death was given to a brother, Joseph, Rachel's firstborn son, who was initially removed by his brothers; and the leadership of the **nation,** which will eventually develop from the family, was given to another brother, Judah, the fourth son of Leah. Eventually, after the house of Judah received the leadership of the nation by means of the kings David and Solomon, the nation again split into two camps, reflecting the two who Jacob chose for the primogeniture: The Kingdom of Judah on the one hand, and the Kingdom of the children of Joseph – the Kingdom of Israel – on the other.

This split reflects the tension between two forces – represented by Joseph and Judah: Joseph, the classical rationalist survivor, the son of **Jacob** (although the kingdom which came from his is called 'Ephraim' or 'Israel'), and Judah, the romantic fighter, the son of **Israel.** The struggle between these two forces finds expression in history and beyond it; and, according to tradition it will be resolved in the end of days when the Messiah who is the descendant of Joseph and the Messiah who is the descendant of Judah unite the nation once and for all. At that point, the vision of Isaac and Jacob concerning the unification of the material and spiritual in the Jewish people will be realized with the complete balance of its components. Every individual Jew and each group of people contain a measure of materialism and spirit, rationalism and romanticism; the vision for the future of the Jewish people is the unification of all of these forces for the building of the nation.[234]

---

234. Compare S. R. Hirsch, 48:19, 49:26, 28, Rav Kook, *Hamisped BeYerushalayim*, 1904.

parashat Vayeshev

We derive several further lessons from the drama before us. The first lesson is the Torah's viewpoint that God controls historical events and directs them. It is possible for a person to make a choice based on personality, conscience and the norms which he has accepted upon himself, and he is responsible for his choices and actions; however, the ultimate plan cannot be stopped, and "it is the Lord's plan that is accomplished" (Proverbs 19:21).[235] The second lesson concerns the criteria for leadership. Although all twelve brothers comprised the future Israelite nation, they were in need of leadership. The brothers were examined one after the other toward this end, and, as mentioned, Joseph and Judah were chosen for this role. The third lesson concerns sin and the proper means of repentance. The father erred in showing preference to his son, Joseph, the brothers erred in their understanding of their father's actions, and were afflicted with wanton hatred, wronged their brother, and the path to repentance is long and winding. The Bible typically presents the patriarchs as mortals with weaknesses who err and sin, in order to teach us not to repeat their mistakes, and in order to teach us the concept of repentance, as well as to teach us that each of us has the potential to advance and improve, and that a person who was tested by sin and repented, has priority in terms of leadership. In the earlier generations, a true sinner was banished from the family. However, from the generation of Jacob's sons and on, repentance atones completely and all of the brothers joined together to build the household of Jacob.

The plot of the story rests on two central motifs: the father's love for one of his sons and meaningful-prophetic dreams. Like

---

235. Ps. 105:16-23, *Midrash Bereshit Rabbah*, 4:33, Nahmanides, 37:15, *Aqedat Yitzchak* 28, and the commentary of Abravanel ad loc. on the topic of divine decree and free choice. Compare Y. Leibowitz, *Hearot Leparashiyot Hashavua*, 31-32.

parashat Vayeshev

Abraham who did not want to part from Ishmael, and Isaac who loved Esau because he provided him with game, Jacob showed his primary love for Joseph. Joseph was the firstborn of his beloved wife, who was cut down in her prime. Like her, he was comely and good looking, and after he was orphaned from his mother, his father pampered him quite a bit.[236] Jacob's mistake was that he showed Joseph favoritism, giving him an expensive, unique ornamented tunic. The brothers interpreted this as conferring the primogeniture on Joseph; that is to say, choosing him to be the exclusive heir of Abraham's blessing, and thereby their disinheritance from participation in the blessing, and giving their younger brother dominance over them.[237] They viewed Joseph, to a large degree with justification, as a spoiled, arrogant, contentious and flattering youth, who was unworthy of this inheritance. Would the "offspring of Jacob [indeed consist only of] Joseph" (37:2)? In this family, where standing was established based on the mothers, cracks formed between the sons of the matron Leah and the sons of the maidservants. The young Joseph, Rachel's son, went to the grazing fields with the sons of Leah, and assisted the sons of the maidservants with their work ("And he served as a helper to the sons of his father's wives Bilhah and Zilpah" 37:2). He brought negative reports concerning both groups, which were fighting with each other, to his father, in order to find favor in his eyes. All of this led to the development of the brothers' hidden hatred toward him.

Joseph's dreams were the straw that broke the camel's back. Joseph dreamed two dreams. (Pairs of dreams also appear in the subsequent parashas, in the case of the dreams of the officials and of Pharaoh.) He understood that if he told them the dreams,

---

236. Rashbam, Abravanel, Luzzatto, 37:3.

237. Hizkuni, 37:2, Sforno, 37:18, Abravanel, S. R. Hirsch, 37:11-12, 18, and the commentary of *Aqedat Yitzchak* ad loc.

parashat Vayeshev

it would only increase the tension, but he was unable to restrain himself and keep them inside of himself. The first dream, the dream of the sheaves, reflects his aspiration to be the leader of the family.[238] The second dream, containing thirteen celestial objects bowing down to Joseph, reinforces the first. More so, in this dream the parents bow down to Joseph in addition to the brothers, and the event is cosmic, not merely local. Thirdly, the stars, sun and moon, being the brothers and parents, bowed directly to him, as opposed to their sheaves bowing to his. Fourthly, in this dream, unlike its predecessor, there is a number. As I already showed in the dream of 'the covenant between the pieces,' this signifies time. Therefore, the prophecy in this dream gains greater validity.

The Torah informs us that Joseph was seventeen when he had his dreams and thirty when he stood before Pharaoh and became viceroy in Egypt. The mention of his age is only significant in the context of the dream which foretold that Joseph would be ruler within thirteen years from the time of the dream. After telling of his fateful dream, Joseph was sold into slavery and was a slave in Egypt; and in the end, he spent time in prison. These thirteen years can be divided into two periods: The first eleven years, symbolized by the eleven stars, are those that passed until the dreams of the officials in the Egyptian jail. During these years, Joseph temporarily lost his faith in himself and in the divine presence, and relied on human assistance.[239] After these comes the second stage of the thirteen years mentioned in the dream; the sun and moon represent an additional two years of waiting ("After two years' time," 41:1), which were decreed against Joseph, until Pharaoh's dreams.

The second dream, in which the number appears, stirred the anticipation in Jacob for the time of its actualization (although

---

238. Bekhor Shor, 37:8.
239. Rashi, 40:23.

he kept this to himself) and moved the brothers from hatred to jealousy. Jacob berated Joseph, in order to calm the brothers down. He said to him that his mother had already died and, therefore, the dream could not reach fruition: "Are we to come, I and your mother and your brothers, and bow low to you to the ground?" (37:10).[240] However, the brothers perceived the way Jacob actually related to the dreams, and they – after what happened to Ishmael and Esau – worried about another selection of one unique son to receive the blessing of the patriarchs. They were unaware of what providence had decreed in the divine plan – as Jacob knew, as well – "Now the sons of Jacob were twelve in number" (35:22). The stage of 'selection', the "purification and consolidation of the family" had passed; from now on the family would grow and strengthen and become a nation, whose size was meant to protect it from negative external influences. However, providence hid its intention from the brothers. The matter developed into an unavoidable crisis.[241]

The Selling of Joseph – Clashes of Leadership and Domination

Jacob was unaware of the tension between the brothers and its dangers. He sent Joseph to check on the welfare of his brothers, who had already been shepherding for an extended period of time in the portions of the field which their father had acquired in Shechem. Perhaps Jacob was concerned that the fear which his sons had instilled in the inhabitants of the area had dissipated, and they would now begin to harass them as revenge for the slaughter in Shechem.[242] Joseph was aware of the brothers' reservations concerning his

---

240. Bekhor Shor, 37:10, 11.

241. The explanation of Joseph's dreams is based on H. Y. Chamiel, *Maaynei Miqra* (Jerusalem, 1992), 116-123, *Limudim BeFarashat HaShavua*, *Vayeshev* 2, 59-62.

242. Targum Johnathan, Rashbam, Bekhor Shor, Hizkuni, 37:13.

parashat Vayeshev

behavior and actions, but since he did not for a moment think of banishing his brothers from the family and disinheriting them from participation in the blessing, he did not realize the intensity of their hatred and jealousy. He, therefore, accepted the task which his father assigned him. When he arrived at Shechem, he did not find them, but he did not take advantage of this as an excuse for getting out of this unpleasant encounter with them. Faithful to the promise that he made to his father – who he loved and respected – he wandered to and fro searching for them, until a man (apparently an agent of providence – like the person who Jacob wrestled with) addressed him and asked him what the purpose of his wandering was and directed him to the place, which he had heard the brothers say among themselves that they were going to, namely, Dothan.[243] When he arrived, his brothers saw him from afar, and they plotted to kill him, to cast him into one of the pits and to tell their father that he had been devoured. Like Cain in his day, they lost their self-control, and sought an aggressive, quick and lethal solution, without considering its consequences. It would seem that the initiative for murder came from the pair of hot heads – the zealous sons of Leah, who we already met in the incident of Dinah – namely, Simeon and Levi. Apparently, they were the ones who said "They said to one another… 'Come now, let us kill him'" (37:19-20).[244] Invalid zealotry knows no bounds, and here it pops up within the family, but there was someone there who stopped it. Reuben took responsibility – as is fitting for the firstborn – for preventing the crime.[245] He tried to save Joseph and bring him back to their father, opposed their plan to kill Joseph, or to perpetrate any act of violence against him. As he later testifies (42:21), he said to them: "Do no

---

243. Rashbam, Nahmanides, and Sforno, 37:15-17. Compare Ibn Ezra ad loc.

244. Bereshit Rabbah, 84:16, *Tanhuma Vayehi* 9, Pseudo-Johnathan, 37:19, Rashi and Rashbam, 42:24, Kimhi, 37:24, 42:24.

245. *Rashi, 37:22, based on Midrash* Bereshit Rabbah, 4:15.

parashat Vayeshev

wrong to the boy," as if to explain to them that Joseph's behavior was merely forgivable, youthful folly. However, they did not listen to him or answer him. He therefore suggested a 'compromise' between killing Joseph and saving him, which was acceptable to them. They stripped Joseph of his ornamented tunic, the symbol of leadership, and threw him in a deep pit which contained no water, so that he should die there. Reuben refrained from direct confrontation with them, and planned on returning to the pit to rescue Joseph.[246]

The brothers closed their ears and hearts to Joseph's pleas and cries (42:21) and departed from there in order to eat their meal.[247] However their agitation and conflict continued. They noticed a caravan of Ishmaelites at a great distance coming toward them, and Judah affected a further clever retreat from the plan of killing Joseph. While he wanted to banish Joseph, he nonetheless understood that causing their brother's death by means of depriving food and drink was an extreme and invalid act, which would be considered murder, even though done passively. He, therefore, made the case to his brothers that there was no reason for or benefit in the death of Joseph, reminded them that he was their brother and flesh and blood and that God is a witness and knows all that transpires, and, therefore, this action will haunt them for the rest of their lives. He, therefore, suggested that they sell Joseph as a slave to the Ishmaelites, and thereby remove him from their household. The brothers heard his words, but continued to be conflicted.[248] Judah's suggestion spared them from the

---

246. This interpretation by Bekhor Shor, Luzzatto and D. Z. Hoffmann explains Reuben's two consecutive statements (37:21-22). Compare Nahmanides ad loc., especially 37:22, 26, 42: 21-22.

247. Compare Abravanel ad loc.

248. Abravanel and Luzzatto, 37:26. Compare N. Leibowitz, *Studies in Bereshit (Genesis)* 406-407.

parashat Vayeshev

murder of their brother, while satisfying their need to banish him and degrade him, transforming him from a king, who everyone bows to, into a slave.[249] However, they did not rush to carry out this suggestion. It is possible that some of them held that a life of slavery as a stranger among pagans was worse than death. While they were still eating, uncertain and waiting for the Ishmaelites to approach them, a caravan of Midianite traders approached from the opposite direction and passed by the pit: hearing Joseph's cries, they extricated him from the pit and took him with them in captivity. They were the ones who met the Ishmaelites and sold him to them. The Ishmaelites brought him to Egypt to sell him as a slave there.[250] These events were not observed by the brothers. Joseph had every reason to think that the brothers were the ones who sent the Midianite traders to the pit in lieu of payment. The alternative possibility, that his removal from the pit was a coincidence, and that the brothers wanted him to die in the pit, was even more terrifying. I will later return (in the discussion of Parashat Miketz) to Joseph's thoughts about his brothers.

Reuben returned to the pit in order to save him and bring him home, in accordance with his original plan; but finding an empty

---

249. Sforno, 37:27.

250. Rashbam, Bahya ben Asher, Hizkuni, *Biur*, Malbim, Luzzatto, 37:28, S. R. Hirsch, Benno Jacob, Buber and Rosenzweig, 37:25. The explanation of Saadia Gaon, Ibn Ezra and Kimhi, 37:28, is also possible. They explain that the Midianites are also referred to as Ishmaelites, and that it was the brothers who pulled Joseph out of the pit and sold him to them. According to Rashi the brothers sold to the Ishamaelites who in turn sold him to the Midianites, who sold him to the Egyptians. According to Bible critics, two version of the event are before us: According to the first, Reuben saved Joseph from death, and the Midianites were the ones who pulled him out of the pit and that is how he was kidnapped; and according to the second, Judah saved Joseph from death, and the brothers sold him to the Ishmaelites. Cf. *Olam Hatanakh*, Genesis, 207, A. Rofe, *Mavo Lesifrut Hamiqra*, 84-85.

parashat Vayeshev

pit, he was terrified to find that he had missed the opportunity. Once again, Reuben's good intentions ended in disaster (see above, the incident of Bilhah 35:22). He told his shocked brothers about Joseph's disappearance from the pit, and they assumed that he was either kidnapped or devoured. There was nothing they could do. One may assume that they were happy to be rid of him, without having to be directly involved with his disappearance. As per their original plan (37:20), they slaughtered a kid, dipped Joseph's tunic in its blood, and sent it to their father by means of messengers. The messengers told Jacob that they found the tunic in the field, and asked him to identify it: "Please examine it; is it your son's tunic or not?" (37:32). He identified it and concluded that Joseph, his beloved son, was devoured by a wild animal.[251] Jacob rent his clothes and sunk into extended mourning. His grief over the loss of his beloved son was intensified by his feelings of guilt[252] over sending Joseph on the journey, a mission which ended in tragedy, and he refused to be consoled. The sons returned home and tried, together with their wives, to console him, but to no avail.

God's control over events, referring to Jacob and his family's descent to Egypt, is evident in the narrative: Jacob's preferential treatment of Joseph, Joseph's dreams, Jacob's decision to send Joseph to his brothers in the distant location of Shechem, the person who chanced upon Joseph and directed him to his brothers in Dothan, the merchants who passed by the pit and extricated Joseph without the brothers' knowledge such that the brothers did not know his fate, Joseph's success in Egypt, the official's wife's lust and deceit which sent him to prison, where he met the wayward officials, the officials' dreams, Pharaoh's dreams, the official who returned to Pharaoh's service remembering Joseph,

---

251. Bekhor Shor, 37:32.
252. Kimhi and Hizkuni, 37:34-35.

Joseph's finding favor in Pharaoh's eyes despite being a Hebrew slave, the extended famine which strengthened Joseph's rule and forced Jacob to send a delegation to Egypt, which led to the entire family's being sheltered there by Joseph.[253]

Selected for Primogeniture

In this parasha, the selection from among the brothers for the spiritual primogeniture of the nuclear family continues, to determine which of the tribes that came from the chosen sons will be destined to lead the nation. The candidates were the sons of Leah – Reuben, Simeon, Levi and Judah – as well as Rachel's first born, Joseph. The sons of the maidservants - the maidservants not being from Abraham's family – were not in the running. The tribe of Levi, by means of Moses and Aaron, led the nation at the time of the exodus; from the time of the entry into the Land of Israel it was left with only the religious leadership. The tribe which came from Jacob and Rachel's child of their old age, Benjamin, received a short period of leadership, during the kingship of Saul (see I Samuel 9 and on); however, this kingship failed and was taken from him. The Torah therefore only recalls in detail the events concerning the household of Judah and the household of Joseph, because of their significance to the nuclear family and to the Israelite nation. The narrative of Judah explains why he was not chosen to be the firstborn of the **family,** and connects us to his primogeniture as king among the tribes of Israel, with the establishment of the monarchy by the household of David. The narrative of Joseph explains his selection to be the firstborn of the family, as well as the addition of his first two sons – Manasseh and Ephraim – to the tribes of Israel, despite the fact that they were almost completely assimilated in

---

253. *Bereshit Rabbah*, 86:5, *Tanhuma Vayeshev*,4, ed. Buber, 15, Bekhor Shor and Hizkuni, 39:2, Kimhi, 39:7.

parashat Vayeshev

Egypt. As was mentioned, the first sons of Leah – Reuben, Simeon and Levi – had already been disqualified. Reuben, the biological firstborn, always had good intentions (as was mentioned), but his actions were not acceptable. He was zealous on behalf of his mother, Leah, wanting to prevent his father's new relationship with Bilhah, Rachel's maidservant, and slept with Bilhah, to his father's chagrin. He thereby demonstrated hasty thoughtlessness, and defective sexual morals, characteristics which are not befitting the head of a household. The author of Chronicles says of this: "The sons of Reuben the first born of Israel. He was the first born; but when he defiled his father's bed, his birthright was given to the sons of Joseph son of Israel, so he is not reckoned as first born in the genealogy" (I Chronicles 5:1). In the incident of Shechem, Simeon and Levi exhibited dark zealotry, lack of proportionality and defective social ethics.[254] A narrative is now told, concerning the next candidate, the fourth son of Leah – Judah. As is typical of the Bible's presentation of leaders, here too it reveals unworthy aspects of the future leader (I have shown that the Torah does not spare Joseph from a similar presentation). However, as in the narrative concerning Judah's role in the process of the brothers' plotting against Joseph, we also see here the first indications of signs of leadership and taking responsibility on the part of Judah.

Let's examine this narrative in greater detail. Long before the selling of Joseph, Judah departed from his father and brothers and moved to the area of the plain, where he saw a beautiful Canaanite woman, was enticed and married her. She bore Judah a son, Er, his firstborn, who he married to Tamar. Her origins are not mentioned, but her father's household was apparently from the neighborhood. She found favor in the eyes of providence, which manipulated events such that she ultimately bore Perez and Zerah from Judah,

---
254. Bekhor Shor, 49:3-7.

parashat Vayeshev

and Boaz descended from Perez. Boaz in turn married Ruth, the Moabite, and King David descended from them. Tamar apparently found favor in the eyes of all who knew her, due to her fine character and her charisma. In this narrative the Torah once again teaches us what the yardstick is for determining who is worthy of leadership: Primogeniture does not necessarily lead to election. Er followed in the Canaanite footsteps of his mother: "But Er, Judah's first born, was displeasing to the Lord, and the Lord took his life" (38:7). Tamar, the wife of Er, was given to the second son, Onan, as per the customs of levirate marriage. However, he refused to impregnate Tamar and let his seed go to waste so that she should not bear him a child. This was due to the fact that he knew that according to the practices of levirate marriage, their firstborn would be considered the child of his deceased brother, and his brother's inheritance would go to that son. He had expected to inherit that inheritance together with his younger brother, Shelah. This greed, which was accompanied by sexual immorality, letting his seed go to waste, was wicked in God's sight, and Onan was also put to death by God.[255] Tamar was, therefore, a virgin; although Judah was notaware of this fact, nor did he know that two of his sons were killed by God because of their sins. He thought that Tamar caused the deaths of his older sons, and was concerned lest his third son also die because of her. He therefore pushed off their marriage with a claim that was not serious, namely that Shelah was still young. Judah left Tamar husbandless, but did not cast her out, as he considered himself responsible for her living with dignity. For her part, she did not seek a husband from another family. She remained husbandless for a long time, until the death of Judah's wife, Shua's daughter.

Tamar saw that her intended husband, Shelah, had grown up, and that Judah was deceiving her with false pretenses, and did not

---

255. BT Yevamot, 34b, Luzzatto, 38:1, 9.

actually plan on marrying her to anyone. She took the initiative, aspiring to free herself from being husbandless and to build a perpetuation for herself and for the household of Judah.[256] She held that Judah was the next in line for levirate marriage, and she looked for an opportunity to take advantage of the loneliness of the wifeless widower. When one of her relatives saw fit to inform her that Judah was going up to Timnah to his sheepshearers, together with his friend Hirah the Adullamite to celebrate with his sheepshearers, she understood that Judah was consoled about his loss. She removed her widow's clothing, dressed up as a prostitute, covered her face with a scarf and situated herself at the crossroads, where Judah was expected to pass through, a place visible to all who passed by, or next to the well. Judah's inclination got the better of him, and he slept with her. At her request, he gave her a security until he paid the prostitute's fee: his staff, seal, and cord (the identity card of ancient times). Judah later sent his Canaanite friend, Hirah, to pay the prostitute's fee – a kid – but Tamar had disappeared. She took off her veil and again put on her widow's garb. Hirah tried to locate her; however the local residents claimed that they did not know of any cult prostitute in their area. Judah was afraid of conducting an organized search for her, lest he become a laughingstock for his very involvement with a prostitute, as well as for his negligence in leaving his seal in her possession. He gave up on the attempt to pay the prostitute's fee and to reclaim his seal, cord and staff. After about three months, one of her associates made sure, possibly according to her own plan, to inform Judah that his daughter-in-law Tamar had been unfaithful (she was intended for his younger son) and that she was pregnant. Judah saw this as a good opportunity to rid himself of this 'dangerous' woman. He, therefore – as the head of the household – sentenced his son's widow, who ostensibly

---

256. S. R. Hirsch, 38:1.

parashat Vayeshev

defiled his honor and that of the family, to death by burning, as was the custom in ancient times. Due to her nobility and morality, Tamar was careful for Judah's honor, and while she was being brought out to be burned, she sent his seal and cord to him via a messenger, saying: "I am with child by the man to whom these belong" (38:25). She placed her trust in Judah's integrity. Hearing her words and seeing the signs, Judah underwent an incredible metamorphosis, and rose from the lowly state to which he had sunk. He proved that he was worthy of leadership by means of the mental powers which he recruited. He publically identified the signs, and admitted that they were his. Despite the shame and embarrassment, he publicly acknowledged both her innocence and his error, not giving her to his son, Shelah; he confirmed his paternity of the twins, Perez and Zerah, who he fathered through her. Judah, who was in the forefront of the initiators of the goat trick against his father, after his messengers said to Jacob, "please examine" (37:32) the ornamented tunic which had been dipped in blood; was now subject to the poetic justice of a goat trick – the prostitute's fee – of Tamar's, who said to him, "please examine" (38:25).[257]

Judah's leadership was intended for a time later than the events of this parasha. Here, after the failure of Leah's sons (and their brothers, the maidservants' sons) in their behavior toward Joseph, Joseph himself stood out as being worthy for primogeniture and being the head of the family. His juvenile, arrogant and perverse behavior toward his brothers in his father's household, which

---

257. BT Sota, 10b, *Bereshit Rabbah*, 85:9, 11. The story of Yehuda and the daughter of Shua began long before the sale of Joseph, according to Ibn Ezra, Gersonides and Luzzatto, 38:1. The sale of Joseph took place simultaneously with the events that transpired with Judah and his family, and Judah, according to Luzzatto, would 'come and go'. The incident involving Tamar was, according to the explanation of 'poetic justice'- subsequent to the sale of Joseph. Regarding divine providence in the story, cf. *Aqedat Yitzchak*, 28.

parashat Vayeshev

brought slavery and imprisonment in Egypt upon him, may now be viewed as putting his brothers to the test – a test of their dealing with him – which they failed. However, their failure enabled his maturation. He advanced and overtook them, and ultimately attained the primogeniture. They unknowingly sentenced him to thirteen years of suffering as a slave and prisoner in Egypt. These years correspond to the years of maturation in Judaism ("A son, from birth until he is thirteen years old – is called a minor, and is called a child... if he is thirteen years and a day, or older – he is called an adult, and he is called a man": Maimonides, Mishneh Torah, *Hilkhot Ishut* 2:11). Joseph matured over the course of these years emotionally and intellectually, psychologically and ethically; and then he was given the opportunity to prove himself. Indeed, once he grew up in Egypt, he showed faith in God, good judgment, ability to plan (as opposed to Reuben), practical intelligence, personal charisma, exalted sexual ethics (as opposed to Judah) and faithfulness to his family (again, as opposed to Judah, who went down to dwell with the Canaanites). His faith in God did not lead him to inaction; on the contrary, Joseph – following in his father's footsteps – took initiative, acted, planned and dared. He, thereby, fully actualized the potential which God instilled in him. His path to success – both in Egypt and in his family, in preparation for inheriting the primogeniture – integrated personal initiative with divine blessing. Therefore, the time had come for him, as the intended head of the family, to test his brothers in order to choose from among them – and not necessarily from his offspring – his heir in the leadership of the nation which will eventually emerge from the family: "By this you shall be put to the test..." (42:15) This test was the basis for Jacob's decision, as he remained the 'official' head of the family, to declare Judah the future leader, as I will soon show.

In this test, which will be described in detail during the discussion of the next parashot, Reuben once again fails, as usual, unwittingly (42:22-23), while Judah – who had undergone a transformation – demonstrated outstanding leadership, took full responsibility for his failures and those of his brothers; and repented, atoned for his flaws and attained royalty, as it says in I Chronicles 5:2: "Though Judah became more powerful than his brothers and a leader came from him, yet the birthright belonged to Joseph." It appears that it was as a result of the strength and pride which he demonstrated in that test which flowed from moral strength which had developed within him, that Jacob chose him, rather than Joseph, for the future monarchy of Israel, especially since his brothers preferred him and his leadership to that of Joseph – "You, O Judah, your brothers shall praise…Your father's sons shall bow low to you…The scepter shall not depart from Judah" (49:8, 10). We repeatedly encounter in the narratives of Genesis that the leadership in Israel is not acquired through the natural primogeniture, but rather by means of attachment to ethics, which flows – as clarified above – from monotheism.[258]

Joseph's Servitude in Egypt – a Spark Among the Shells

After the Torah concludes the narrative of the family of Judah, it resumes the narrative of Joseph, which took place concurrently. Joseph was brought to Egypt by the caravan of the Ishmaelites, who purchased him from the Midianites, who extracted him from the pit.[259] Joseph was sold in the Egyptian slave market to Potiphar, the chief steward (the chief butcher-chef, or the chief of the army

---

258. Cf. *Aqedat Yitzchak*, 23, S. R. Hirsch, 48:19. Compare H. Y. Chamiel, *Limudim BeFarashat HaShavua, Vayehi* 2, (3), 74.

259. There is an inconsistency between this vs. and 37:28 on the one hand, and 37:36 on the other. It isn't clear in the final analysis who exactly sold Joseph to the Egyptians, the Midianites or the Ishmaelites. Cf. nt. 250.

parashat Vayeshev

who slaughters the enemies) of Pharaoh. We are shown, for the first time, the ugly side of slavery, in which a person loses his freedom and his independence and is subject to exploitation, arbitrary rule and oppression by his master. The exile of the family and the nation begins here, and the narrative of the exodus from Egypt – redemption from exile and freedom from slavery – essentially begins. We have before us two narratives of the exodus from Egypt, one historical and the other ethical. The historical narrative: We sold Joseph, we went down to Egypt and settled there, we became a nation of slaves, God redeemed us and took us out, took us as his nation, gave us his commandments, led us through the desert and brought us to the Land of Israel. The ethical narrative is the story of the 'other:' the weak – the slave, the convert, the orphan, the widow, the poor and the Levite--and in our day, immigrants (to Israel) from underdeveloped countries, single mothers and contract workers. The litmus test of a society is the way in which it relates to its weaker members. The Torah never ceases to show us, in light of the subjugation in Egypt, how awful subjugation is, and how great freedom is; and, based on this, how to relate to the weak 'other' lacking in inheritance or property and wealth, lacking in roots and connections or family support: "For you were strangers in the land of Egypt" (Exodus 22:20), "for the land is Mine" (Leviticus 25:23), "for it is to Me that the Israelites are servants: they are My servants, whom I freed from the land of Egypt, I the Lord your God." (Leviticus 25:55) The patriarchs already owned slaves and maidservants: Eliezer, Hagar, Abraham's slave, Bilhah and Zilpah; but except for the harsh incident concerning Hagar and Sarah, this was a 'deluxe' form of slavery, in which Abraham and his descendants were commanded to circumcise these slaves, and they became part of the extended family. In the narrative of Joseph we encounter slavery which was part of the social fabric of human

parashat Vayeshev

society in that era, with all of its ugliness and cruelty. Joseph succeeded in coping even with this. Below, we will again encounter slavery, which Joseph could have imposed on the entire Egyptian nation, but he restricted and limited it. Of course, the subjugation of the Israelites in Egypt is a classical and extreme case of mass subjugation. The Torah provides alternatives to slavery in the Ten Commandments and in various other commandments.

Joseph quickly captured his master's heart through his wisdom and his charisma. He succeeded in all of his endeavors, was appointed to be the estate manager, and became the official's confidant, whom he relied on in all matters except for his own meals, which were his top priority. Joseph attributed his success to divine assistance, and told this to whoever was willing to listen. This is how Potiphar and his wife first heard of Hashem, who caused Joseph to succeed. Potiphar's wife fell in love with the handsome and successful Joseph and tried to seduce him. Joseph evaded her time and again, using the argument that he could not possibly betray the trust of his master who had been so good to him; and even if they were to succeed in concealing their sexual relationship from him, he was not willing to sin to God, who sees everything. Joseph, thereby, preserved his moral purity, and, at the same time, delicately refrained from reproaching her, in order to retain his position. On her final attempt, when they were alone together in the mansion, she grabbed him by his garment and asked him to sleep with her, and he was forced to disrobe and leave his garment **in her hand** in order to quickly escape from her, although when he exited the house, he walked calmly, in order not raise suspicion. The woman understood that there was no chance that her plan would succeed, and that it is possible that her servants saw Joseph flee from the house without his outer garment, and that the matter might thereby be revealed to her husband.[260] With feelings of humiliation and embarrassment of a woman of standing who is unaccustomed to rejection, and certainly from a slave; she decided to proactively make a move to protect herself and to take revenge on Joseph.[261] She raised her voice, alerted certain servants who were in the courtyard or garden[262] at the time, and accused Joseph of attempted rape. His garment – which, according to her account, he took off in preparation for rape and left **with her** (not **in her hand**) when he was forced to flee when she screamed for help[263] – served as evidence for her claim. She described to the servants, with anti-Semitic contemptibleness, about the ethnic thread shared common to her and them. She told about **the man**, (and not **the slave**, as she noted in her presentation to her husband) **a Hebrew** – of an inferior nation – who her husband brought into the household as the head of the servants, and who did everything possible to dominate them, to demean them and to be involved sexually with the women of the household – "to dally **with us**" (39:24) – and thus she incited them against Joseph, and even denigrated her husband, by revealing his flawed judgment.[264] When speaking to her husband, she complained about Joseph's ungratefulness and his disloyalty. She thereby attacked his male pride – "The Hebrew **slave** whom you brought into our house came to me to dally **with me**" and "Thus and so **your slave did to me**" (39:17-19), and provoked his jealousy and anger. It is uncertain whether he was angry at Joseph or at his unfaithful wife. It is reasonable

---

260. Bekhor Shor, 39:14, Nahmanides, 39:12-13, Sforno, 39:12, Abravanel, ad loc. S. R. Hirsch, 39:12-15.

261. Cf. *Daat Miqra*, 39:13 and compare N. Leibowitz, 417-418.

262. Rashbam, Kimhi, 39:14, Luzzatto, 39:11.

263. Luzzatto, 39:18.

264. Luzzatto, Sforno, 39:14, N. Leibowitz, 418-419.

parashat Vayeshev

to assume that knowing both of them well, he believed Joseph; however, he had no choice, out of embarrassment, other than to pretend, cover up for his wife and punish Joseph. Joseph once again found himself in a pit, namely the prison that was the responsibility of his master, the chief steward. It is interesting to note that the ornamented tunic caused him to be cast into the first pit, and the current garment caused him to be cast into this pit.[265]

Even in prison, Joseph was able, by virtue of his wisdom and with the help of providence, to stand out and succeed. He found favor in the eyes of the chief jailer, who was subservient to the chief steward, and won his total confidence. Joseph was placed in charge of the prisoners. Later, Pharaoh's chief cupbearer and the chief baker were placed in the prison of the chief steward; apparently because of their negligence in the preparations for the great feast in honor of Pharaoh's birthday. They were imprisoned until Pharaoh decided their fate. The chief steward put Joseph in charge of dealing with these important prisoners. Joseph's ongoing contact with all of these officials, who providence provided for him in prison, prepared him well for the royal position which awaited him; in addition to his learning matters of finance and administration in the household of Potiphar.[266] One morning, at the end of a year of the chief cupbearer and the chief baker's incarceration, Joseph noticed that their faces were pouty. In response to his questioning, they answered that they each had a dream, and no one was able to interpret it. Joseph asked them to tell him their dreams, in the hope that God would help him interpret them. The chief cupbearer told

---

265. U. Simon, "Yoseph V'ehav- Sipur Shel Hishtanut," *Baqesh Shalom Verodfehu*, (Tel Aviv, 2002), 60-87. Cf. Ibn Ezra, Nahmanides and Sforno, 39:19, Hizkuni, Luzzatto, 39:20, who explain based on *Midrash Rabbah* 87:9, that the official who had loved and appreciated Joseph didn't kill him on account of doubt, as he was well aware of his wife's character.

266. *Meshekh Hokhma* ad loc. And *Daat Miqra*, 40:23, towards the end.

parashat Vayeshev

him that in his dream, he saw a fine vine containing three branches, bearing clusters of grapes. He saw himself pressing juice from the grapes into Pharaoh's cup and placing it into Pharaoh's hand. Like everyone else, Joseph knew that the major annual feast in honor of Pharaoh's birthday would take place in three days.[267] The number appearing in the dream referred to a unit of time, as mentioned above, and it transforms an ordinary dream into a prophetic one. The squeezing of the grapes into Pharaoh's cup by the dreamer himself pointed the direction. Jacob's heartening interpretation was that the three branches were three days, "In three more days," he told the chief cupbearer, "Pharaoh will remember you and return you to your exalted post." Joseph utilized this propitious moment to ask the official to mention him favorably to Pharaoh, and to say that he, Joseph, was not born a slave. Rather, he was unjustly kidnapped from his land and is currently in prison, having done nothing wrong. The chief baker was impressed by the compelling interpretation of the dream[268] and he also told his dream. He saw three interwoven straw baskets on his head, one on top of the other, containing loaves of bread and cookies, and the birds of the sky were eating fearlessly from the top basket. In opposition to the dream of the chief cupbearer, in which the official was active and served Pharaoh, the chief baker was passive in his dream, he did not even attempt to remove the birds from their prey, and Pharaoh did not appear in it. Here too, the picture pointed the direction. Joseph's sad interpretation was that the three baskets, like the three vine branches in the chief cupbearer's dream, were three days. After three days, Pharaoh would also recall the chief baker, and hang him on a tree, as prey for the birds of the sky.

---

267. Ibn Ezra, Bekhor Shor, 40:12. Luzzatto, 40:1, 4, 13, 19.
268. Unkelos, Rashmbam, Bekhor Shor, S. R. Hirsch, 40:16. Saadia Gaon explains *"vayar sar haofim, ki tov patar,"* (40:16) - Joseph interpreted it favorably.

After three days, on Pharaoh's birthday, the king made a feast for all of his people and passed sentence on the two officials. The chief cupbearer was shown mercy and was returned to his post, participated in the feast and fulfilled his function in it. The chief baker was sentenced to death, and was hung on a tree. Even so, Joseph's hope to be helped by flesh and blood, instead of by means of his own efforts and help from the Divine Presence, were dashed.[269] The agitated chief cupbearer suppressed the traumatic event and forgot it and Joseph's request. Joseph sat in prison for an additional two years, in accordance with the dream of the stars.

Parashat Miketz
Pharaoh's Dreams – Joseph's Opportunity

After two years passed, the course of Joseph's dramatic life took a turn for the better through the intervention of providence. The chief cup bearer remembered Joseph, as this remembrance served his purposes. Pharaoh's bizarre dreams are recounted in the beginning of the parasha. None of the king's wise men were able to find an interpretation for them which satisfied the agitated king. In his first dream, he saw seven fat cows rising from the Nile and grazing in the reed grass. Seven scrawny cows then rose out of the Nile after them. They stood next to the fat cows, but did not graze, and then they swallowed the fat cows, but one could not tell that they had consumed them. Pharaoh woke up as a result of the force of the dream, fell back asleep and had a second dream. In the second

---

269. Rashi, 40:23. It is interesting that Luzzatto suggests the possibility, that the first appearance of the word *"mealekha"* in vs.19 is a scribal error. In any event, he explains that apparently it doesn't refer to decapitation, which there is no need to mention, nor does it appear in the actualization, (40:22), or again in the words of the chief cup bearer to Pharaoh (41:13), according to the second explanation of Ibn Ezra, 40:19.

parashat Miketz

dream he saw seven full ears of grain growing, and after them seven scorched ears sprouted, which swallowed the full ears. Based on the recommendation of the chief cup bearer, who dared to mention his wrongdoing and the dreams of the officials and Joseph's accurate interpretation to the king; Joseph was summoned from prison, dressed in new clothing and placed before Pharaoh. Joseph stated that he was not a professional interpreter of dreams; rather God had helped him in interpreting the dreams. Pharaoh told him the details of his dreams, and Joseph interpreted them properly. Joseph wisely understood that the dreams were not personal ones, relating to the fate of the dreamer. Joseph's dreams, and those of the officials, were personal dreams, in which providence revealed its plans for the dreamer. (It was forbidden for Joseph's brothers to try and foil this plan, and to scheme against Joseph. The chief baker may have been permitted to attempt to work against that which was decreed against him, but it was not in his power to do so.) On the other hand, Pharaoh did not see something in his dream concerning his personal fate. What is more, the dreamer was a king, and therefore the dream related to his responsibility toward his nation. God showed Pharaoh (through the medium of Joseph) that which He intended to do to Egypt over the coming years, thereby honoring Pharaoh and giving Joseph the opportunity to escape his captivity and to rise to a very high position. But – I would point out at this stage – Joseph did not view his 'career' as the goal. He viewed himself as an agent of providence in assisting, to the best of his ability, and at the same time to instill knowledge of God in Pharaoh, his courtiers and the Egyptian nation.[270]

Joseph interpreted the two dreams as one dual dream, containing an important message for Pharaoh and the Egyptian nation.[271]

---

270. Cf. H. Y. Chamiel, *Limudim BeFarashat HaShavua*, Miketz 1, 62-64.
271. *Bereshit Rabbah*, 80:4.

parashat Miketz

This message was given with a time frame; I have already shown repeatedly that numbers in dreams indicate units of time. The seven cows and the seven ears of grain represent seven years. Seven years of abundance will soon commence, followed by seven years of severe drought, during which the residents and their animals will perish as a result of famine. It was clear to Joseph that the purpose of the dreams was to rouse Pharaoh – by means of Joseph – to take initiative in order to prevent the tragedy which was about to occur, and to save his nation.[272] Driven by providence,[273] and recognizing that he should no longer rely on others, but rather take initiative and act daringly, Joseph suggested a course of action to the ruler, one which would save Egypt from the serious consequences of the dream's fulfillment. He suggested that he appoint a man of discernment and wisdom, a capable administrator, to prepare systematically for the famine. The ruler should authorize the person who he chooses for this to appoint a network of officials and - with their assistance - store up food and grain from all over the kingdom in the king's warehouses during the years of abundance, to be eaten during the years of famine. Pharaoh was impressed by Joseph's words and by the fact that the dream is a revelation of the divine plan, and that the God who plans and carries out was assisting Joseph. The political perspective on the dream as revealed in Joseph's interpretation, i.e. basing the interpretation on the fact that it was the dream of a king and not a personal dream – all of this convinced Pharaoh of the power of this interpretation and of the wisdom, or divine inspiration, of the interpreter.[274] Pharaoh addressed his advisers, Joseph's interpretation having found favor in their eyes, with a rhetorical question: Is there such a man of

---

272. Bekhor Shor, 41:25, 27, 33, Sforno, 41:33.
273. Abravanel, ad loc.
274. Luzzatto, 41:8. Cf. N. Leibowitz, *Studies in Bereshit (Genesis)* 453-455.

parashat Miketz

discernment and wisdom, who fits the criteria suggested by the interpreter of the dreams? Can we locate him immediately? He informed everyone present of his decision: Since God assists Joseph and bestows wisdom on him, there is no one worthier to be appointed for the proposed task. The people will act in accordance with his directives, and all of the officials will obey him.[275] In order that he successfully carry out this complex task, Pharaoh appointed Joseph to be his viceroy, responsible for all of the kingdom of Egypt, which from now on will be run purely according to his instructions. Joseph received Pharaoh's ring, was clothed once more in royal garments – clothing of fine linen, and a gold chain – and he received a special chariot for his use, the spare chariot of the ruler.[276] Servants ran before it announcing his arrival by calling out *'avrekh,'* [אברך] to ensure that everyone bent their knee (*berekh*-ברך) as a sign of respect.[277] Pharaoh nicknamed him 'Zaphenat-paneah' [צפנת פענח], in recognition of revealing that which is hidden (*mepaneah zephunoth*- מפענח צפונות),[278] and gave him Asenat, daughter of Poti-phera, priest of On, as a wife.

The continuation of the parasha is devoted to Joseph's rise to greatness, and his success in the provisions plan: To scrimp and save in terms of current consumption, to accumulate

---

275. Onkelos, Saadia Gaon, Rashi, 41:40. Compare Gen. 3:15, 15:2. "*Hanimtza*" serves both of Pharaoh's rhetorical questions.

276. Onkelos, Saadia Gaon, 41:43. Similarly, *Mishneh Torah*- a second copy of the Torah.

277. Regarding the chariot cf. Saadia Gaon, 41:43. Regarding *'avrekh'* cf. Bekhor Shor, 43:41 and Ibn Janah, *Sefer Hariqma*, 105.

278. The commentators differ as to whether this is an Egyptian name which later entered the Hebrew language, or if it is a Hebrew translation of an Egyptian name. Cf. Rashi, Rashbam, Kimhi, Ibn Ezra, 41:45, *Olam Hatanakh, Genesis*, 228. There are other commentators who maintain that Pharaoh understood Hebrew (Nahmanides and Rabbenu Bahya).

surplus grain and food in Pharaoh's warehouses throughout all of the cities of Egypt and to see to their preservation. Due to providence, these were seven years of exceptional prosperity exclusively in Egypt, and thanks to Joseph's wisdom, Egypt succeeded in properly preparing for the drought which followed them. It would appear that aside from the total cessation of rain in the region, the sources of the Nile atypically consistently decreased, and only small quantities of water, insufficient for sustenance, reached Egypt. The drought and famine prevailed over the entire region; and Egypt, which was the only place where it was possible to acquire food, became a pilgrimage site for all of the Near East (41:29-30, 53, and 56).[279] The food which Joseph collected was sold to both the nation and to foreigners, under the supervision of Joseph and his people. Asenat bore two sons for Joseph before the onset of the famine. He named the first born Manasseh, referring to the past, meaning, 'God has helped me forget my parental home and all of my hardships', and to come to terms with the fact that I myself need to build my life. He named the second Ephraim, referring to the present and future, indicating the fertility, births, prosperity, success and honor which he attained in Egypt, after his period of suffering there. Thus Joseph's assimilation into Egypt was complete, and it appeared that his separation from his father's household was final. The turning point came in the course of the drought, which continually intensified. In the course of events, Joseph discovered that not only were Pharaoh's dreams being actualized, his dreams were as well, and his role in the establishment of the household of Israel was only beginning.

---

279. N. Leibowitz, *Studies in Bereshit (Genesis)* 521-522.

parashat Miketz

Joseph and his Brothers – Spy Stories

The knowledge that it was possible to purchase food and grain in Egypt reached Jacob, and he instructed his sons not to sink into inaction,[280] but rather go down to Egypt to purchase food for the family, to save them from the famine. Ten brothers (Benjamin remained with Jacob) arrived in Egypt, came before Joseph and bowed down to him. They did not recognize him, but Joseph recognized them, remembered the dreams which he dreamed about them – dreams which came true at that point – he acted like a stranger toward them and accused them of spying. All of their claims of innocence did not help. When they mentioned their father and their brother, Benjamin;, Joseph, who wished to intimidate them, informed them that they had to prove their innocence and honesty by one of them bringing Benjamin to Egypt, while the others were imprisoned until Joseph saw Benjamin. It appears that the brothers refused this draconian suggestion. None of them agreed to be the agent, and therefore Joseph imprisoned all of them until they reached a decision among themselves.[281] After three days, Joseph informed them that he changed his mind. He told them that since he was God-fearing, he had no intention of harming them or their family remaining in Canaan without food.[282] He allowed them to return home with the food, and to bring Benjamin with them on their next trip. He informed them that until then, one of them would remain imprisoned in Egypt as a hostage. The brothers had no choice but to agree to this proposal. The situation brought back difficult memories for them: Once again, they would have to appear before their father and explain the absence of one of the brothers. This event from the past cropping up awakened their

---

280. Saadia Gaon, Luzzatto, 42:1. Compare *Haamek Davar*, ad loc.
281. Cf. Yitzchak Samuel Reggio, ad loc. cited by Luzzatto, 42:17.
282. Bekhor Shor, Nahmanides, Sforno, 42:17-18.

parashat Miketz

guilt feelings.[283] Even though they were not the ones who sold Joseph or harmed him bodily, the brothers blamed themselves in the midst of this new crisis for ignoring Joseph's screams in the pit, thereby indirectly causing him to be lost. The only thing Reuben was capable of doing at this time was to say to them: 'I told you'! Showing extreme insensitivity, he saw fit, in this difficult moments, to rebuke them for not listening to him at the outset; this, instead of taking the leadership role, reassuring them and trying to consult with his brothers. All of these things were said in Joseph's presence. The brothers did not know that he understood their language, as he made use of a translator ("an interpreter", 42:23) in order to communicate with them. Hearing their words, Joseph felt like crying, but restrained himself. He imprisoned Simeon, the second son of Leah after Reuben, as he now knew, based on what he heard from Reuben's own mouth, that he, Rueben, did not participate in the crime and even tried to prevent it. Joseph understood that the hotheaded zealots, Simeon and Levi, were the ones who plotted the scheme against him.[284] He ordered his confidants to give his brothers provisions for the journey and to secretly return the money which they paid for the grain and pack the money at the bottom of each of their sacks, except for one, where the money was packed at the mouth of the sack. Perhaps this one was Levi's sack – he being Simeon's partner – in order to cause him distress. On the way, when the brothers opened their sacks, that same brother discovered his money near the mouth of his sack. This terrified the brothers, as Joseph had intended. They were concerned that this would end up harming them, and saw it as divine punishment: "What is this

---

283. *Aqedat Yitzchak* ad loc.
284. Rashi, Rashbam, Ibn Ezra, Bekhor Shor, Luzzatto, 42:24, based on Bereshit Rabbah 97. *Targum Yerushalmi*, 42:24, 27. Cf. nt. 244 above.

parashat Miketz

that God has done to us?" (42:28).[285] Apparently, they were afraid of going back and returning the money which they found, lest they be interrogated further.

When the brothers returned home, they told their father what happened to them in detail. They opened their sacks to empty them out into storage vessels, and to their horror, they each found their money in the bottom of their sack (except for the one whose money was already found in the inn). When they reported the sequence of events to Jacob, the brothers softened the story so as not to overly frighten their elderly father. They did not tell him about their three day incarceration, or the fact that Simeon was in prison, rather than in the inn. In the end, they did not tell about Joseph's threat that they would die (apparently by means of the famine, not having the opportunity to purchase more food in Egypt, and if they, nonetheless reached him – he would execute them) if they did not listen to him and thereby prove that they had not come to spy on Egypt. They fabricated a positive motive for returning to Egypt with Benjamin; that Joseph promised to enable them to establish commercial ties with Egypt.

Jacob was shocked to hear the ruler's request that they bring Benjamin to him. He blamed the brothers for the loss of his sons one after the other, because of their fights and their jealousy: Joseph was missing, Simeon was detained and Benjamin was sought, and

285. Kimhi, *Daat Miqra*, 42:27, *Haketav Vehaqabbala*, 42:28. Mordecai Luzzatto suggests that the brothers received provisions for the way for their donkeys in small bags as well, with the exception of Simeon's donkey. Therefore, Levi opened his bag at the inn in order to feed his (Simeon's) donkey, and found the money. Cf. the *parasha* sheet of Bar Ilan no.946. The difficulty remains, according to this interpretation: When Levi found the money, why didn't the brothers hurry to search their bags and to check them? It is also possible to say that the money was at the opening of all of the bags, hidden beneath the top layer of food. However, Levi needed to remove a double portion, for Simeon's donkey as well; and was, therefore, the only one to find his money.

parashat Miketz

all of the tragedies are piling up on him.[286] Reuben proposed that Jacob place Benjamin in his care and that he would be responsible for him; and if he did not return him, Jacob could punish him by killing two of his sons. He thereby implicitly conceded the double portion he was entitled to as a firstborn (I will return to this). Jacob and Judah listened with revulsion to Reuben's foolish and horrible offer. Judah already knew the meaning of bereavement, as he had lost his wife and two of his sons. Jacob viewed this suggestion as further confirmation of the fact that Reuben was unfit to be the firstborn. He did not respond to the offer, which invited the possibility of further death in his family – the death of the sons of Reuben.[287] Jacob ruled: "My son will not go down with you" (42:38).

The drought continued. The inevitable moment arrived when Jacob was forced to ask his sons to go down to Egypt again, as if he had forgotten the demand of the Egyptian ruler. Judah rose up yet another level in his development as a leader. He took responsibility, and asked his father to place Benjamin in his care, in order to save the entire family, especially the children, from death: "I myself will be surety for him; you may hold me responsible: if I do not bring him back to you and set him before you, I shall stand guilty before you forever" (43:9). The words 'I shall stand guilty before you forever' imply that Judah took the risk of a rupture between him and Jacob and the family. As a person who is guilty to Jacob – if he failed to return Benjamin – he would permanently be distanced from the family, or at least lowered to an inferior position in it. His offer is very different than that of Reuben, who did not offer to sacrifice himself, but rather his two sons, on behalf of Benjamin.

---
286. Kimhi, Sforno and Saadia Gaon, 42:36.
287. *Bereshit Rabbah*, 91:12. Cf. also H. Y. Chamiel, *Limudim BeFarashat HaShavua*, 64-66.

parashat Miketz

Jacob tried to delay the inevitable by complaining about his sons: Why did they mention Benjamin in the man's presence? They explained that he inquired about their family, and specifically asked whether they had a father or brother; and they had no way of knowing that he would ask them to bring that brother, Benjamin, to him. In reality, Joseph had not directly asked that question. The brothers altered the story from the actual events, to avoid being blamed by Jacob for revealing Benjamin's existence, in order to evade the charge of spying. Their father had no choice but to accept Judah's offer, in order to save their lives. Jacob preferred to place the responsibility on a person who already lost two sons, rather than on a person who offered to kill two more. He instructed the brothers to take with them the money which was returned to them – perhaps it was returned by mistake – in addition to money for that which they would purchase, and to bring some of the choice products and delicacies of the land as a gift for the ruler: Balm, honey (fruit nectar), nuts (Semitic pistachios) and almonds. Jacob concluded his words with a prayer to God that they succeed in their mission, and that they bring home both Simeon and Benjamin. He did not mention Simeon by name, as he was angry at him because of the incident of Shechem, and referred to him as "your other brother" (43:14).

The brothers went down to Egypt and stood before Joseph's people. When they arrived, Joseph saw from afar that they had brought Benjamin. He instructed that they be invited to his house, and he prepared lunch for them. The brothers were afraid that they had been summoned to the ruler's house in order to resume the accusation that they had stolen the money that was found in their bags. Before the meal, they explained to the steward that there had been a mistake: They discovered in the inn (they were imprecise here, so as not to complicate the story) that their money was found in their sacks, and they now want him to accept it from them. The man reassured them, telling them that their God had apparently put treasure in their bags for them, as he personally received the payment and was not missing any money from his register. He released Simeon, and sent him to them.

The brothers bowed to Joseph when they came before him, and presented him with their offering. Even before the meal, Joseph inquired as to Jacob's wellbeing. The brothers responded to his question, and placed Benjamin before him, and he blessed him: "May God be gracious to you, my boy" (43:29). Joseph was much moved, went off to his room for a short while and cried. It is worth noting that Joseph cried before and would cry again a number of times; however this was not crying out of pain, suffering or distress. Joseph overcame those. His crying occurred when he could not contain his emotions, when he was under tremendous psychological tension, or when this tension was released, and it always revolved around the family from which Joseph was forcibly separated from for many years. It would appear that behind the tough, rational mask, there was a sensitive and sentimental soul. The brothers were surprised, as three sets of food were served. Joseph ate different food than the Egyptians, and they ate different food than the Hebrew brothers, whose food was an abomination to the Egyptians. Their surprise intensified further when they were seated at the table according to their ages ("from the oldest in the order of his seniority to the youngest in the order of his youth," verse 33), despite the fact that they had never told Joseph their ages. The meal turned into a feast, which continued until the wee hours of the morning, and everyone got drunk.

Joseph invited his brothers into his house, prepared a banquet for them, permitted them freedom of movement in his domain, and deliberately caused them to get drunk, in order to be able to accuse

parashat Miketz

them later of theft:[288] The next morning he ordered his confidants to fill his brothers bags with grain, to once again secretly return their money – each one's money at the mouth of his sack – and to place Joseph's silver goblet in Benjamin's bag. The brothers went on their way, and did not have a chance to go far out of the city before the steward chased after them and overtook them. He accused them, in accordance with Joseph's orders, of being ungrateful and of stealing the important goblet, which his master used for divining the future.[289] The brothers denied the charge, stated that they were honest people and reminded him, in their defense, of the fact that they had offered to return the money which had been returned to them by mistake. They declared (as Jacob did when Laban accused him of stealing the *teraphim*), that if one of them is found to be a thief, he would be put to death, and all of them would be slaves to Joseph. The man corrected their offer: He said that he believed that most of them were honest men, and therefore, justice dictates that the thief should be a slave, and the others would be free to go on their way. The search began in Reuben's sack, and continued sequentially. No one got excited when each one's money was found in the mouth of his bag; but the goblet, which was the object of the search, was found in the end of the search in the bag of the youngest, Benjamin. The brothers rent their garments as a sign of

---

288. Luzzatto, 43:34. Regarding Jacob's alias for Simeon above - '*aher*'- cf. Nahmanides, 43:14.

289. An ancient rite for divining the future was the swearing of demons through smooth vessels that were mirror-like, such as burnished copper or silver vessels, which were rubbed with oil, and which the demons were reflected in and communicated with the wizard (cup demons). Alternatively, vessels were filled with water, upon which drops of oil were poured, and the future was divined according to the image which formed in the Cf. Ibn Caspi, *Mitzraph Lakeseph*, 44:5, Lev. 19:26, Yoseph Dan, *Torat Hasod shel Hasidut Ashkenaz*, 190-194. Compare *Olam Hatanakh*, Genesis, 234, Leviticus, 136.

mourning, loaded their donkeys, and returned to Joseph. Joseph reproached them for their actions, and Judah, who, like the rest of the brothers, already knew and understood that they had fallen prey to libel, accepted the divine sentence for the sale of Joseph, conceded that his claims had been dispelled, and once again declared that they would all be slaves to Joseph as a punishment for the theft. Of course, he did not bring up the previous suggestion that the thief himself should die.[290] Joseph reiterated his steward's statement: The thief will be a slave, and they are free to return to their father. Judah's role in the parasha is already hinted at in verse 14, which tells of the brothers' return to the house of Joseph after the discovery of the 'theft': "When Judah and his brothers reentered the house of Joseph…" not "and [they all] reentered". I will elaborate on Judah's behavior in the continuation of the narrative below.

Joseph's Treatment of his Father and Brothers – the Psychological Aspect

The commentators struggled with two fundamental questions. A) Why did Joseph not take his father's difficult situation into account and – after he was appointed to his lofty position – contact his father, to let him know that he was all right? B) Why did Joseph pretend to be a stranger to his brothers and systematically abuse them time and again? Was he guided by feelings of revenge? Granted, the hand of providence directs from above, but this does not explain a person's personal motivations, whose free will is not taken from him. Did the twenty years that passed and the positive outcome, in retrospect, of the brothers' actions not blunt Joseph's anger? Philo already addressed the second question, and Bekhor

---

290. Kimhi, Gersonides, in his father's name, 44:10, Ibn Caspi and Hizkuni, 44:16.

parashat Miketz

Shor already addressed the first. Many commentators after them, both classical and modern, also dealt with these questions, and there is a very broad range of answers. Some simply claim that indeed Joseph wished to punish them and to make them suffer for their actions.[291] Others suggest that Joseph took upon himself to see to it that his dreams were fulfilled in all of their details, in order to actualize providence's plan; and he wanted to bring both Jacob and Benjamin to Egypt so that they bow down to him, before he revealed himself to them. This stance also invites critique of Joseph.[292]

Granted, the Torah does not hide the negative aspects of the patriarch's behavior from us. However, it seems to me that the spirit of the presentation in this parasha is not directed toward displaying Joseph's shortcomings; on the contrary, it aims at showing the path of proper behavior, which explains Joseph's being chosen for the leadership of the family. Joseph is presented as righteous, wise, sensitive, possessing long-term vision and a wily tactician. Revenge and the fulfillment of dreams overriding the suffering of the elderly man, even if they are wrapped in the intent of providing food for the family in conditions of plenty in Egypt, do not fit an image which is meant to serve as an ethical role model. Therefore, other commentators[293] tried to delve into Joseph's mind

---

291. Kimhi, Abravanel and Kli Yakar.

292. Nahmanides, *Haketav Vehaqabbala, Haamek Davar*, 22:9; Y. Medan concurs with this explanation. Cf. also *Aqedat Yitzchak* ad loc., who attacks the suggestion of Nahmanides, arguing that "the one who generated the dreams shall provide its solution", waiting for the fulfillment of the dreams does not justify making his father suffer.

293. Cf. Philo, *On Joseph*, 232-236; Gersonides, the eighth telos, R. Isaac Arama, author of the *Aqedat Yitzchak*, Abravanel, 42:7, 43:15, 44:1-2, Alshikh, 44:1; *Ohr Hahaim*, 45:26; S. R. Hirsch, 42:9, N. Leibowitz, *Studies in Bereshit (Genesis)* 459-461, 466-469, whose explanations serve as the basis for the

parashat Miketz

and understand this wise man's psychological motivations. During his years of servitude and incarceration, Joseph had plenty of time to think about his family. The fissures that developed between its different factions when he was still a youth were well known to him. He gave much thought to the hatred and jealousy which led to his being lowered into the pit, and in his imagination he recreated the chain of events: the deal they made with the merchants to sell him as a slave. He did not know that such a deal never actually took place, and that the merchants actually found him and took him without the brothers' knowledge. In any case, it was clear to him that his brothers did not know his character and motives, and they did not know that he never intended to rule over them and to disinherit them from participation in the building of the family's future. Therefore, he must have asked himself repeatedly, what did they tell their father when they returned without him? Did they regret their actions? Did his father know about their involvement in his disappearance and come to terms with it, or did he think that his beloved son disappeared through no fault of his brothers? How is the family functioning after the tragedy? He asked himself again and again, why didn't anyone – especially his father – try to look for him? (There is even someone who takes this to an extreme and built his entire interpretation of these events on the supposition that Joseph thought that his brothers had succeeded in turning Jacob against him, and that their father cooperated with them in the goal of ridding themselves of him, as his forefathers had rid themselves of members of the family who were unworthy in their day.[294])

interpretations below. There are those who explain that Joseph was concerned about those in Pharaoh's court who were jealous of him, and therefore refrained from sending a secret delegation to Canaan, lest he be accused of treason, nor did Joseph desire to tell his whole sordid tale to Pharaoh.

294. Cf. Y. Ben-Nun, *"Hapilug VeHaahdut," Megadim* 1, 1986. It is hard to accept Ben-Nun's explanation in its entirety. The spirit of the text doesn't

parashat Miketz

His being freed from slavery and imprisonment and his rise to power afforded him the opportunity to make contact. However, what will happen in the family – assuming they are still unified – when the details of the event and the malice of the brothers becomes known to their father? And if, God forbid, the father knew and did not search for him, is there anywhere for Joseph to return to? Won't his return to the family as viceroy of Egypt intensify his brothers' hatred for him and their jealousy of him? In any case, the chances that the family would remain united were zero, and revealing the events of the past would only exacerbate the situation. Joseph has seven years from the time when he was appointed to his task by Pharaoh to plan his approach in fine detail. He knew that representatives of the family would come to him to purchase food after the outbreak of the famine. His plan aimed at achieving the following goals:

A) To find out what his father knew, and to check his wellbeing.

B) To find out if his brothers repented and regretted their plotting against him.

C) To make sure that his brothers understand his aspirations and motives.

D) To make sure of the unity of the family, to assure its welfare and to do his best to see to it that all of its members are worthy of the blessing of Abraham.

E) To instill an awareness in the family's consciousness that the hand of providence directed and directs events.

Joseph decided to put the brothers through a test – or more accurately, through a series of tests – both in order to see whether they would be tempted to sin again in order to escape from distress,

---

allow for the supposition that Joseph believed that his brothers had turned their father against him, and that he was an accessory to the plot to get rid of Joseph, and built his entire plan based on this belief.

parashat Miketz

and also to prove to them what his true self was like; not only as it was in his youth, when his brothers referred to him derisively as "the master of the dreams" (37:19), but also now, **after both of his dreams were fulfilled.** Joseph could have acquired the primogeniture and disinherit his brothers from the family inheritance, primarily, the blessing of the patriarchs. In other words, he could have lowered them to the standing of Ishmael and Esau (or worse) and to cause – with the consent of providence, of course – that his progeny alone would become a great nation, through whom the families of the earth would be blessed, and would inherit the land of Canaan. He had very good reason to believe that providence was acting on his behalf, and perhaps even wished to cause the brothers to receive their punishment at his hands. However, Joseph viewed the divine blessing as the heritage of the entire family, and therefore wanted to reunite it, or at least to give it the opportunity for unification, if it passes the test. This, of course, is after he sees to their survival during the years of famine.

According to Maimonides' doctrine of repentance, true repentance consists of the sinner being placed in a similar situation to the one in which he previously sinned – and his overcoming his inclination, or impulse, to sin again. This overcoming is associated with the transformation of the personality. The personality who reacted to the previous situation the way that it did, must be replaced with a new system of responses and relationships, conscious and unconscious, to the same situation (this sort of change took place in the case of Judah, as I showed, and as I will show further, below). This doctrine is already expressed in Joseph's plan: To place the brothers in a situation in which they will be forced to once again choose one of two reactions to their distress concerning their younger brother, who is from a different mother – this time it was Benjamin. Joseph could have hidden the goblet in another brother's

parashat Miketz

bag and to see if they were prepared to support the accused and pay the price for their faithfulness to their brother, but he specifically wanted to test how they related to Rachel's son. It should be noted further that Jacob had been, and he is liable to be, an additional victim of their response. They harmed him when they caused Joseph to be lost to him (and as a result –Simeon, as well) and are liable to harm him again if they cause Benjamin to be lost to him.

Let's examine the test with which Joseph tested his brothers. In the previous situation, they saw Joseph as a threat, and they chose to dispose of him violently. Now, Joseph (as Zaphenat-paneah, the viceroy of Egypt) deliberately placed them in a crisis. In this situation, the choice that was given to them was not that of saving themselves at the cost of sacrificing Benjamin; as they were not being threatened. Rather, they were given the option of accepting Joseph's words: "Only the one with whom it is found shall be my slave; but the rest of you shall go free" (44:10); i.e. they could have decided that if Benjamin was unlucky and the goblet was found in his articles, it is his problem. However, as I will show below, Joseph made the decision difficult for them. On the other hand, they could try to protect Benjamin to the best of their ability, or to join in that which was decreed about him. Will they once again chose to leave their younger brother to his fate and thereby harm their father again?

The test was therefore conducted in two stages. The first aimed at bringing Benjamin to Egypt, while the second was directed toward the brothers' treatment of Benjamin in Joseph's presence. Had the brothers failed the test, Joseph would have protected Benjamin and heard from him what transpired in the household during the years when he, Joseph, was missing from it. If the brothers were willing to sacrifice themselves in Benjamin's place, Joseph would then know that they repented, and that there was a chance of healing the

parashat Miketz

rift. Therefore, in the beginning he accused the brothers of spying, extracted information from them regarding the wellbeing of his father, and demanded that they bring Benjamin with them when they return to Egypt as proof of the truth of their claim that they were not spies, and also hid the money in their sacks. I will deal with the meaning of this action presently. When Benjamin was brought, the second phase of the test took place. In preparation for this phase – in order to make it more difficult for them to write off their brother in whose possessions the goblet was found and to leave him to his fate – Joseph repeatedly hid their money in their bags. This intensified their fear and their feeling and understanding that, on the one hand, a malicious governmental force was plotting against them, and on the other hand, they were receiving their punishment from God for the awful act which they perpetrated. The situations which Joseph wisely placed them in, led them to a complete process of repentance: Acknowledgment of their guilt (42:21), regret, confession and commitment to refrain from this sin in the future. The brothers passed the test. When the goblet was found, it was clear to them that Benjamin was innocent. Therefore, their decision not to abandon him, and to have compassion on their father, testified to the fact that they had repented fully. They all rent their garments, and returned to Joseph without hesitation. Judah proposed to Joseph that they all share in the punishment. They thereby demonstrated both the unity which now existed in the family – all of the brothers bear that which was decreed against one of them – and the acceptance of the sentence for the sin which they performed in the past. The theft, which Benjamin was accused of, represents the actual sin, the plotting against Joseph, which the brothers admitted to, regretted and were willing to accept the punishment for.

Once again Judah is shown to be a leader. He addressed Joseph representing the family and he presented their position in two stages. First, in the first stage he refrained from blaming anyone and set aside any excuses or justifications: "What can we say to my lord? How can we plead, how can we prove our innocence? **God has uncovered the crime of your servants;**" again, the fabricated crime represents the actual sin. Secondly, all of the brothers are guilty of the actual sin, and they are now all willing to accept the sentence: "Here we are, then, slaves of my lord, the rest of us as much as he in whose possession the goblet was found" (44:16). Joseph rejected the offer, demanded that Benjamin remain with him as a slave, and informed the other brothers that they were released.

Would the family have been unified like this – and have found the candidates to lead it after Jacob – had Joseph not put them to the test? In this parasha I have again shown Reuben's unfitness to be the head of the family, the strengthening of the figure of Joseph as not only responsible for the physical existence of the family, but also its unity; and Judah, who, underwent a tremendous personal transformation since his confession in the incident concerning Tamar. Once the food which was acquired during the first trip to Egypt ran out, and the lives of the family members were again in danger, he took upon himself the leadership role and personal responsibility, as I have shown: He informed his father that logic had to overcome emotion, hope had to overcome worry, and they had to go down to Egypt with Benjamin so that they do not perish. He guaranteed Benjamin's return, and saw himself as a sinner to his father for the rest of his life, if he did not fulfill this task. So far, he had not accomplished this task. In this speech to Joseph, he did not raise the possibility of Benjamin's return to Jacob. It would appear from what he said that he preferred to remain a slave to Joseph, together with his brothers, rather than to be forced to return to Jacob without Benjamin. Joseph blocked this possibility: He held on to Benjamin and freed the others to go on their way. He did this with noteworthy courtesy: "Far be it from me ... the rest of you go back in peace to your father" (44:17). Judah was therefore forced to surpass himself, in order to accomplish the seemingly impossible. Joseph, for his part, waited to hear what this man – who had suggested with calculated cynicism that they sell him as a slave for profit in order to distance him from the arena of competition for the inheritance, without compassion for their father and without taking into account the completeness of the family – had to say.

Parashat Vayigash
The Speech of Judah's Life

In this parasha, the narrative of Joseph and his brothers reaches its climax and its happy ending. Judah made the speech of his life to Joseph. This is a masterpiece by a man who understood that his life and that of his family depends on the impact of the words which he will say to the foreign ruler. Judah – who caused Joseph's sale and began to rectify his error when he took responsibility for Benjamin – saw it as his responsibility to rise, recruit all of his intellectual and spiritual powers and put his life on the line in order to save Benjamin, Jacob (from the loss of another son) and, essentially, the entire family, as it was unclear how and if it would survive Benjamin's separation from it under such circumstances. At this point, Judah demonstrated his full abilities as a leader and a responsible individual. He undertook a complex and dangerous mission. His failure could have provoked the ruler's wrath and brought disaster on him and his family. He decided to tug at his interlocutor's heartstrings, while demonstrating humility and self-deprecation on the one hand, and sophistication on the other. Since Joseph asserted that he was God-fearing and since Judah saw the concern which Joseph expressed for their father, and the closeness which he showed toward the brothers; Judah understood that this is not some heartless tyrant, but rather a person of significant human sensitivity. Nonetheless, the complex plot by means of which Joseph framed the brothers – and whose purposes were not known to Judah at this point--indicated sophistication and skillful plotting.

Judah exhibited sophistication of his own in countering Joseph's sophistication. This can be seen in what he omitted from his presentation, as well as from what he added to it. He omitted the accusation of spying and the theft of the goblet, in order not to make waves. He added the question, which he and his brothers invented when they repeated the story to their father (prior to their second descent to Egypt) regarding their encounter with Joseph, pretending he had asked them, "Do you have a father or brother?" (44:19 compare 43:7. As was mentioned, they told Jacob this so that he would not blame them for needlessly revealing the family's Achilles' heel). Joseph knew exactly what had been said, but, nonetheless, Judah repeated it and presented the question as if it had been asked by Joseph. He then placed entire sentences into Jacob's mouth – which it would seem Jacob never said to his children (44:26-29) – concerning Rachel and her children, Joseph and Benjamin. This addition was meant to move the ruler, and to evoke his mercy. It would appear that Judah intended to hint strongly to Joseph, by means of his presentation, that it was clear to everyone present in the room that the accusations of spying and of stealing the goblet were a plot, which there was no point in discussing. Judah essentially told Joseph that it is clear to us that you were not motivated by security concerns – protecting Egypt from spies – in your actions toward us. You led us, for some reason which is not clear to us, to speak about our family, our father and younger brother. The question, "do you have a father or brother?" was at the top of your agenda, even if it was not asked directly. Your actions will unjustly bring disaster on our elderly father. You must reveal your intentions to us, because we understand that there is more to this than you are telling us, and you are only pretending.[295]

Judah utilized keywords which convey ethical and emotional messages. In the opening of his speech (44:18-19), he addresses Joseph as the 'master' and refers to himself and to the members of his family as 'slaves'. The word 'slave' appears thirteen times in the speech[296] and 'master' – seven times. Judah ascribed inferiority to all those who stood before Joseph, to demonstrate that he, Judah, is cognizant of the ruler's unlimited power, as he has authority over the attributes of justice and compassion, as well as forgiveness. A person who portrays himself as a slave and his interlocutor as master demonstrates self-deprecation. One can assume that self-deprecation on the part of Judah – who his father described as "Judah is a lion cub" (49:9) – was particularly meaningful to Joseph. (Of course, Judah was unaware of this significance. He did not know that his interlocutor recognized him and was aware of the characteristics which Jacob would ultimately ascribe to him in that blessing. It would appear that Judah himself was not entirely aware of his being a "lion cub".) In general, slavery between people is strongly looked down on in the book of Genesis. Man is created unique, in the divine image. His being lowered to the state of being a slave is therefore a denigration of the divine image. In terms of relationships between people, a slave is on the bottom rung of

---

295. Bekhor Shor, 44:18-32, esp. 18, 19, 21, 22; also N. Leibowitz, 484-485 and E. Samet, *Iyunim BeFarashat HaShavua*, (Jerusalem: 2008), ad loc., based on Bereshit Rabbah, 93:8, *Tanhuma Vayigash* 5: "from the outset you approached us scheming". Cf. also Rashi, 44:19 and Kimhi, 44:18. This sheds light on Nahmanides 44:19, '*al derekh raboteinu*'.

296. N. Leibowitz 487-488.

society, and slavery is the most demeaning punishment imaginable. And yet, Judah – who had suggested that Joseph be sold as a slave – is prepared to sacrifice himself and accept slavery on himself, in order to save his brother (44:33).

Other keywords in this speech are 'father', which appears there fourteen times,[297] – as Judah already discerned that the ruler exhibited inexplicable sensitivity toward their father – and 'lad' (seven times), 'brother' (six times), 'younger' (four times) and 'child' (once). These words are meant to evoke feelings of compassion in the ruler's heart. Judah depicts a difficult situation of an elderly father, who lost his beloved son and is about to lose the lone son who remains from his beloved wife. Judah pretends to quote his father (44:27-29) as saying things which are meant to shock the ruler.[298] Judah acknowledges the specialness of Rachel and her sons' to Jacob; only Rachel is referred to as Jacob's wife in Judah's speech.

Hearing Judah's words, Joseph learned for the first time what it was that his father understood from his brother's words when they returned without him. He discovered that his father mourned for him this entire time, and did not send people to search for him because he thought that he had been devoured.[299] Judah repented fully, and once again took personal responsibility: Once again, he presented himself as Benjamin's guarantor and offered himself as a slave in place of his brother, both in order to save Benjamin, and in order to prevent his elderly father's heartbreak.[300]

---

297. N. Leibowitz, 484. *Daat Miqra*, 189-190.
298. Ibid., 486-487. Cf. also Kimhi and Nahmanides, *'al derekh hapeshat'*, 44:19.
299. Based on Y. Ben-Nun, nt. 294 above.
300. Bekhor Shor, 44:32.

Salvation and Confession

All of Joseph's goals were achieved. Judah struck his heartstrings accurately and answered all of his questions and doubts, which were like an open wound in Joseph's heart. He was shocked to hear that his father thought that he has been devoured, and was happy to know with certainty that his father had not stop loving him. He learned that his brothers repented fully. His excitement peaked. All of the pieces of the puzzle came together at once, and the divine plan for the fulfillment of the 'covenant between the pieces' stood before him with the utmost clarity. One task remained: To reveal himself to his brothers, to allay their fears and prove to them that they were mistaken when they ascribed to him the desire to control the family inheritance. Joseph could no longer restrain himself, but as a ruler, he was not prepared to be seen publicly as an emotional person. He, therefore, instructed his people to leave him alone with his guests. He thereby also insured that the family's secrets would not become known to strangers. He then burst out in cathartic crying, revealed himself to his brothers and allayed their guilt feelings and fears. He informed them that he had no feelings of vengeance, as he attributes his being sold to Egypt to the will of providence, which sent him there – through them – in order to place him in the position of viceroy so that he could ensure the survival of the family and its prosperity during the years of famine. Joseph did not ignore his brothers' guilt, but maintained that their punishment was in the hands of God, and not in his hands.[301] The

---

301. Regarding the desire to remain secretive, cf. Rashi, Nahmanides, 45:1. Joseph was careful not to disclose details of his difficult personal story to strangers. The commentators see two stages in Joseph's words to his brothers. Following the first occasion upon which Joseph spoke to his brothers, they were extremely scared. There are those who think that when Joseph said – "*I am Joseph, does my father yet live?*" - he was rebuking them by asking Judah: 'You are requesting compassion for your father?! You yourself, as

parashat Vayigash

brothers discovered that their perception of Joseph was mistaken. He had the ability to harm them without having to answer to anyone, yet he used his position of power to benefit, rather than harm, them.

The time had come to inform their father about the incredible salvation of his beloved son, about the dreams' fulfillment, providence's involvement in guiding the events and the need to unite the family in Egypt for the duration of the further five years of famine which were anticipated. After lengthy explanations and persuasion, the brothers digested the new situation. Joseph and Benjamin each wept on the other's neck, Joseph wept on all of his brothers' shoulders and then the brothers (who in the past were unable to speak to him peacefully) gathered up the courage to speak to him. All of the members of Joseph's household heard his cries, and from there the word spread quickly to the household of Pharaoh and his officials. The leaders of Egypt, led by Pharaoh, accepted the news regarding Joseph's brothers who arrived in their land from Canaan approvingly. Pharaoh invited (via Joseph) the entire family to live in Egypt in conditions of prosperity. He commanded that the brothers be given wagons with which to bring all of the people of Jacob's household to his country. Pharaoh also suggested that they not bother to bring all of their personal belongings from Canaan, as all of Egypt's finest awaited them.

Descent to Egypt and Settling there – a Symptom of the Exile

Joseph sent his brothers to inform his father of the news, and to bring the family to Egypt. He supplied them very well with provisions, and even gave them gifts and requested that they not quarrel or

well as all of your brothers, caused him terrible suffering, which it is difficult to believe that he survived.' Joseph didn't present himself as their brother, nor did he speak of 'our father'. Only once he perceived their stress did he try to calm them as their brother. Cf. regarding this BT Hagiga, 4b, Sforno, Malbim, *Torah Temimah*, *Beit Halevi* (Joseph Dov Soloveitchik) 45: 3.

parashat Vayigash

assign blame among themselves. The brothers no longer viewed the fact that Benjamin received three hundred pieces of silver and five changes of clothing, while they only received one garment to replace their ripped clothing, with a jaundiced eye.[302]

When the brothers returned home, they informed their elderly father of the news: Joseph is alive and he is the ruler of Egypt. Jacob's heart skipped a beat because he was so overwhelmed emotionally, and it was difficult for him to believe it. After they went over all of the events in detail, and conveyed Joseph's words to him, and after he saw the splendid wagons,[303] he was convinced and said that it sufficed for him that Joseph was still alive, even if he were not ruler in Egypt.[304] He wanted to leave and go meet his lost son, at the end of his life. It seems that the brothers, including Joseph, did not tell him about the sale of Joseph. Jacob, therefore, thought that Joseph wandered in the field, was abducted by bandits, beaten, stripped of his tunic which was ripped in the process of his being abducted and beaten, and was sold as a slave in Egypt.[305]

After a few days journey, the family stopped in Beer-sheba, the southern tip of the Land of Israel. Jacob sacrificed an offering there, in thanksgiving for God's kindness and as appeasement for the fact that he was going down to Egypt in opposition to God's explicit instructions to Isaac not to go down to Egypt despite the famine, and despite his own misgivings about doing so.[306] God appeared to him in a dream at night and called to him, using language of

---

302. Rashi, 45:24, Hizkuni, 45:22.
303. Rashbam, 45:19, 27. Ibn Caspi, *Tirat Keseph*, 132, *Mitzraph Lakeseph*, 45:18.
304. Rashbam (ms.) and Ibn Caspi, *Tirat Keseph*, 132, *Mitzraph Lakeseph*, 45: 28.
305. Nahmanides, 45:27
306. Kimhi, 46:1, Abravanel, ad loc.

parashat Vayigash

affection and closeness, "Jacob, Jacob" (46:2), approved his going down to Egypt, allayed his concerns about it, and promised him that He would support him and assist him in all situations and in all places, not only in the Land of Israel. Jacob received a promise that he would meet Joseph, and that his family would grow in Egypt and become a nation, and that he himself would be well cared for by Joseph, die in Egypt with Joseph by his side, but be buried in the Land of Israel under Joseph's supervision. Several commentators interpreted Jacob's concerns as concern for the future of his family, and the nation which would emerge from it, in exile; and not merely as concern for his personal situation, and modern commentaries have expanded on this approach. Will his descendants succeed in preserving their uniqueness and culture? Will they become immersed in the prosperity of Egypt and forget about their land, as he had forgotten about it when he was with Laban? Of course, the great subjugation which was promised in the 'covenant between the pieces' was also a significant reason for worry and fear.[307] It seems that the family's descent into exile, where the nation would ultimately come into being, was the reason for God's referring to him by his exilic name – Jacob. These commentators viewed God's words to Jacob in that dream – "and I will also bring you up" (46:4) – as not only a promise to bring him to an Israelite burial with his ancestors in Canaan, but also as an allusion to the return of the entire nation to the Land of Israel, as promised in the 'covenant between the pieces.'[308]

---

307. N. Leibowitz, *Studies in Bereshit (Genesis)* 501-502, based on Hizkuni (and Bekhor Shor), 46:3. Compare *Haamek Davar* and *Meshekh Hokhma* ad loc. It is interesting that God calls out to people twice in order to allay their fears. This is in this case, as well as in those of Abraham at the binding of Isaac and Moses at the bush. Cf. H. Y. Chamiel, *Limudim BeFarashat HaShavua*, 66-68.

308. Ibid. 508-509., based on *Mekhilta Beshalah* 3, and *Shemot Rabbah*, 3:3.

parashat Vayigash

Jacob sent Judah ahead to prepare Joseph for the family's arrival, and to coordinate their arrival in Goshen, as Joseph planned. He did not merely rely on Joseph, as he did not know to what degree Joseph had been influenced by the Egyptian culture, after all of the years that he lived in it. He preferred to have the foundation in preparation of their coming – a separate place which is free of idolatry and its influence – be shared by Joseph and Judah, who he knew well and relied on. All of the members of the family arrived in Egypt, together with their livestock and possessions, and Joseph left his palace in his chariot to go out and meet them in Goshen and appeared to Jacob. Joseph wept (again) on his father's neck, and Jacob declared before everyone that now, having seen Joseph, he was ready to die; as now death would be at a good old age, and not as going "mourning to Sheol" (37:35).[309] The arrivals numbered seventy (not including the brothers' wives). Joseph and his sons, Manasseh and Ephraim (3), who were already in Egypt,[310] were counted among the members of the family:

Jacob – 1

The offspring of Leah – 32

The offspring of Zilpah - 16

The offspring of Rachel – 14

The offspring of Bilhah – 7

Nechama also brings the explanation of M. Buber on God's words here (also in *Darko Shel Miqra*, 95), which is identical to her explanation. Compare *Haamek Davar*, 46:3.

309. Luzzatto, 46:30. In the dispute between Rashi and Nahmanides concerning who cried on whose shoulder, Rashi's explanation is the most convincing. Cf. H. Y. Chamiel, *Limudim BeFarashat HaShavua*, 68-69.

310. Rashbam, 46:8, 26; Bekhor Shor, Ibn Ezra, 46:27, Abravanel, Luzzatto, 46:8. The Torah doesn't provide any details about slaves, miadservants or any others who were attached to Jacob's household, who may have gone down to Egypt with them. Cf. *Haamek Davar*, 46:7, regarding this.

parashat Vayigash

The total for persons being Jacob's own issue (not including Jacob, Joseph, Manasseh and Ephraim) who came down to Egypt – 66.

The total of Jacob's household who came to Egypt (not including the brothers' wives, as mentioned above) – 70.[311]

Joseph prepared his father and brothers for their first encounter with Pharaoh. He directed them to present themselves as shepherds and cattlemen. The Egyptians, whose economy was based on irrigated agriculture, despised shepherds and cattlemen. These occupations were inferior and degraded, and only the lower

---

311. Four comments regarding the census of the family that went down to Egypt. A) *Haketav Vehaqabbala*, 46:18, brings to our attention, in the name of the Vilna Gaon, that the descendants of the matrons were double that of the descendants of the maidservants. B) Simeon married a Canaanite woman and fathered a son with her - Saul, (Judah also married a Canaanite woman who died, whose son was among those who went down to Egypt; although this story is already known to us as is Judah's metamorphosis, in contradistinction to Simeon). The Torah emphasizes this in order to imply that the rest of the brothers remained loyal to the instructions of Abraham and Isaac (cf. Kimhi and Ibn Ezra, 46:10). C) Only Asher, from amongst all of the brothers, had a daughter - Serah. D) *Ohr Hahaim*, 46:12, explains that Hezron and Hamul, Judah's grandsons, through Peretz, were born in Egypt, and were not among those who went down. The Torah enumerates them here as replacements for Er and Onan (the sons of the Canaanite woman and the brothers of Shelah), as per the laws of Levirate marriage, to ensure that Judah have five portions amongst the seventy who went down. The Levirate marriage took effect with respect to the children of Peretz, the firstborn, for his deceased brother. See further details of this explanation in Cassuto, *Sefer Bereshit Umivnehu* (Jerusalem: 1990), 321-327, *Sifrut Miqrait Vesifrut Canaanit I*, (Jerusalem: 1972), 108-117. According to this, only two great-grandchildren of Jacob's were amongst the people who went down to Egypt: Heber and Malchiel, the grandchildren of Asher through Beriah. May friend Daniel Malakh explains the Sifrei on Moses's blessing to Asher, "blessed with children is Asher," which Rashi cites but finds no explanation for, based on this fact. I would add that he is the only one blessed with a daughter.

classes were involved in them. However, since it was a required economic sector (animals for agricultural work, sheep and cattle for meat, milk, wool and skins), officials were placed in charge of these occupations. Jacob and Joseph decided to emphasize to Pharaoh that they were shepherds, and thereby – ensure their separation from the Egyptians and protection from their influences, and their acquisition of the land of Goshen which is in the vicinity of Ramses, a bit distant from the main population centers, which contained suitable grazing land for their abundant cattle. Joseph could have certainly arranged senior positions in the Egyptian government apparatus, as Pharaoh himself offered; however, Joseph and his father did not want that, since Joseph was aware of the corruption in the Egyptian governmental system and was concerned about the destructive influence that it could have on the family.[312] After Joseph informed Pharaoh of their arrival and their having settled for the time being in Goshen, he brought five of his brothers to meet the king. He picked the brothers who were the least powerful and the least impressive, so that Pharaoh would not recruit them for his army.[313] In answer to Pharaoh's question, the brothers said that they were shepherds and that they came to Egypt to tarry ("to sojourn [*lagur* לָגוּר]" 47:4: In the Bible, this word connotes transiency) in Egypt due to the drought in Canaan. They asked to sojourn in Goshen. Pharaoh accepted their request and instructed Joseph to settle his family there on a permanent basis. Afterwards, Joseph brought his father for a courtesy visit with Pharaoh. Pharaoh, seeing before him and elderly man, stooped

---

312. Cf. Abravanel ad loc., *Aqedat Yitzchak* and *Haamek Davar*, 46:34; S. R. Hirsch, 46:33, N. Leibowitz, *Studies in Bereshit (Genesis)* 516-518. Fill in with the words of Abravanel which are quoted by N. Leibowitz, ad loc. 18.

313. Rashi, 47:2, based on *Bereshit Rabbah*, 95:4. According to Bible critics, based on the LXX, there are two versions of the story. Cf. *Olam Hatanakh*, 241-242.

and wrinkled, the ongoing mourning for his beloved son and the other troubles which befell him having left their mark on him, was surprised by his appearance and asked him with wonder what his age was. Jacob answered that he is only 130 years old, but he was prematurely old because he had such a difficult life. He was still far from the age at which his ancestors died, but he appears old for his age.[314] Jacob blessed Pharaoh with peace when he came to the encounter, and he gave him another blessing before he departed, as befits a king and in appreciation of his favorable relationship to his family. Joseph happily fulfilled Pharaoh's instructions, and provided his brothers with property in the choice lands of Egypt. He made sure that his family was treated demonstrably favorably, providing them with the choicest produce of the land gratis, while the Egyptian nation groaned from the difficulties of the drought and famine and paying their prime possessions for the food which Joseph provided them with.

Jacob's sons' temporary sojourn in Egypt turned into permanent dwelling in prosperity and all of the finest: "Thus Israel settled in the country of Egypt, in the region of Goshen; they settled in it, and were fertile and increased greatly" (47:27). The word 'settled' can be interpreted pejoratively: One can infer that the Israelites forgot their destiny – to settle in the Promised Land (where God, Himself, was meant to dwell in their midst: See, e.g., I Kings 6:11-13) – and became addicted to the pleasures of the exile. This process, unfortunately, seems to be typical of the Jewish people, from then to the present. Jacob himself acted this way in his last six years in Haran. It is possible that if they had internalized the fact that their life in Egypt was supposed to be transient, and if they had not settled in the exile, but rather in anticipation of the future which

---

314. Rashbam, 47:9, Bekhor Shor, Ibn Caspi and Hizkuni, 47:8, Nahmanides and Luzzatto, 47:9.

was promised to them in their land, it would have been easier for them to bear the servitude which was decreed on them from the beginning in the 'covenant between the pieces': "... your offspring shall be strangers in a land not theirs, and they shall be enslaved and oppressed four hundred years" (15:13).[315]

The Strengthening of Joseph

The Torah tells us of the solidification of Joseph's position in Egypt, while also strengthening Pharaoh's power: He worked at saving the Egyptian nation from starvation; while also taking over all of the Egyptian nation's means of payment for the food which he sold them. He thereby collected all of the money in the kingdom, and then – the cattle of the Egyptians, and then – all of the land that was fit to be worked; and he transferred all of them to Pharaoh for posterity. The famine continued and the Egyptians offered to be sold as slaves to Pharaoh in exchange for food. However, Joseph the Hebrew, who was opposed to slavery, especially having experienced it personally, preferred not to totally steal their freedom, and saw to it that they retained some measure of control over their affairs. He turned the members of the nation into sharecroppers of the king's land, and required them to give Pharaoh a fifth of the produce grown from the seeds which he sold to them. He relocated the nation group by group from one settlement to another in order to disassociate them from their land[316] and integrated them into the work on the governmental lands, in accordance with the needs and

---

315. S. R. Hirsch, 47:27, 29, *Kli Yakar*, 47:27. Cf. also *Meshekh Hokhma* Lev. 26:44, H. Y. Chamiel, *Limudim BeFarashat HaShavua*, 71-72, B. Lau, *Etnahta*, 120-123.

316. Regarding the transfer of the populations Cf. Rashi, Rashbam, Kimhi, Bekhor Shor, Hizkuni, Luzzatto, *Haamek Davar*, 47:21; concerning only purchasing the properties cf. Nahmanides, Abravanel, *Meshekh Hokhma*, 47:19. Compare U. Simon, *Bakesh Shalom Verodfehu* (Tel Aviv, 2002), 90-92.

with the flow of the Nile, which the agriculture of Egypt is based on. In the years of drought, when the flow of the Nile was weak, and did not provide for even minimal needs after the payment for sharecropping, Joseph supplemented the produce with grain from his storehouses, to meet their needs. After the drought, the Egyptians supported themselves from the four-fifths of the produce which they produced, while a fifth was collected as a tax, as was mentioned, for Pharaoh.

It is interesting that the laws of ownership of land in Egypt were the opposite of those which were instituted later, based on the Torah, in the Hebrew state in the Land of Israel. Egypt's economy is entirely dependent on the Nile, and its complete utilization requires centralized planning. The economy of the Land of Israel is dependent on rain and the initiative and diligence of farmers (Deuteronomy 11:10-11). In the absence of control over the natural and human resources, there is no room for a centralized economy. Furthermore, according to the viewpoint of the Torah, the Land of Israel and its citizens belong to their creator, God, and not to a king of flesh and blood. Therefore, in the Land of Israel, the property is divided among the families: One can not acquire land of a family inheritance permanently, and it reverts back to the original owner in the Jubilee year, even if the one who purchased it was the king. I will mention three other topics in this context: The laws of slavery, the status of the king and the status of the priests. According to the Torah's laws, a Hebrew man may only be sold as a slave under narrowly defined conditions and for a limited time. In Egypt, by contrast, slavery was the foundation of the social and political system. The Israelite king is limited in terms of silver, gold, property and wives; and he is subservient to the divine law of the Torah (Deuteronomy 17:14-20). By contrast, the Egyptian king was a deity, controlling unlimited powers. In the Land of Israel, in the Torah state, the priests and Levites, the members of the tribe of Levi, did not receive an inheritance for working the land, or for grazing, as the other tribes did. They only received residential houses and courtyards for housekeeping. Nor did they receive a salary, and they had to rely on the good will of citizens to observe God's commandments concerning the gifts of the priests and Levites. By contrast, in Egypt, even the king was not allowed to acquire the land of the priests, in addition to which they benefited from a fixed income which they received for their livelihood from the governmental budget.[317]

Parashat Vayehi
Jacob's Departure from Joseph – the Actualization of the Primogeniture

This parasha describes events which took place during the time when Jacob was in Egypt, where he spent the last seventeen years of his life, his blessings to his children and grandchildren before his death and his burial in the Land of Israel when he was 147 years old. The conclusion of the parasha is devoted to the period between the death of Jacob and the death of Joseph and his burial in Egypt. The parasha opens with two emotionally charged meetings between Joseph and his father. In the first encounter, when Jacob felt that his time to die was approaching, Jacob invited Joseph to come to him, and had him swear that he would not bury him in Egypt. He asked Joseph to place his hand under his thigh and to swear that he will bring his body up from Egypt for burial in his ancestors' grave, in the cave of the field of Machpelah. Joseph promised that he would do so, but Jacob pressed him to swear, fearing that Pharaoh might

---

317. S. R. Hirsch, 47:22, Y. Leibowitz, *Sheva Shanim shel Sihot al Parashat HaShavua*, 171.

parashat Vayehi

prevent him from carrying out his promise. Joseph swore, and Jacob bowed to God as a sign of thanksgiving. We learn for the first time that Jacob understood that his family's remaining in Egypt after the period of the famine will end up being to their detriment. He was unable to alter the divine plan, which was revealed to Abraham at the 'covenant between the pieces'. He was only able to leave a reminder for his offspring, to not become addicted to the exilic life and to not become assimilated there; but rather preserve their uniqueness and their connection to their promised land, in which their ancestors lived and were buried. This is the meaning of Jacob's instructions that they bury him with his ancestors. He tried to thereby confirm the fulfillment of the promise of the Land of Israel for his offspring.[318]

The second encounter between Jacob and Joseph occurred later, when Jacob weakened and was suffering from his final illness. Joseph – The viceroy, who is occupied with ruling Egypt – received a report that his father was ill and he immediately came with his two sons, Ephraim and Manasseh, to visit him. Jacob, whose vision was very weak, recognized Joseph and began to make what is ostensibly a very bizarre speech. He goes back in time and describes El Shaddai's having appeared to him at Luz, when he returned from Padan-aram. At that time, El Shaddai blessed him that he be fertile and numerous, and that he and his progeny acquire the Land of Israel as an eternal inheritance. Jacob went on to inform Joseph that he had decided to add Joseph's sons, Ephraim and Manasseh, to the number of his sons who will inherit the land: "Ephraim and Manasseh shall be mine no less than Reuben and Simeon" (48:5 – specifically Jacob's two oldest sons).

---

318. S. R. Hirsch, 47:29; *Meshekh Hokhma*, Lev. 26:44, N. Leibowitz, 536-537, Regarding the need to have Joseph swear, cf. Rav Abraham ben HaRambam, Nahmanides and Sforno, 47:31.

parashat Vayehi

In his conclusion, he said something which is ostensibly a total non-sequitur: When he was returning from Paddan, Rachel died on the road to Ephrath and he buried her there. Why did Jacob decide to add his grandsons through Joseph to the number of his children? Why did he mention the death of Rachel and her burial? This last question is addressed by a number of commentators. Some of them (following in the footsteps of the Midrash)[319] see these words of Jacob's as an apology for his not burying Joseph's mother in the family grave which is in the cave of the field of Machpelah, but rather in Bethlehem, while demanding that his son travel all the way from Egypt to bury him with his ancestors. This interpretation does not explain the relevance of this narrative in this context. If this is, in fact, an apology for his demand that he be buried in the cave of the field of Machpelah, why was it not said in the first encounter, when Jacob made Joseph swear that he would bury him there? Similarly, this interpretation does not explain Jacob's decision in terms of Joseph's sons.

Other commentators[320] try to explain the totality of Jacob's final words to Joseph. This interpretation rests on the recognition that in the narrative-historical portion of the Bible, such as this, there needs to be a flow, or connection, between adjacent narratives. This is in contrast to the halakhic sections of the Bible, where one cannot always see a connection between laws which are adjacent to each other. Therefore, the flow of the narratives which lead up to this one can shed light on this last one. I will therefore survey the flow of events which occurred to Jacob when he came from Padan

---

319. Targum Jonathan, Rashi, Rashbam, Nahmanides, Ibn Ezra, Kimhi, Hizkuni, 48:7, based on *Pesikta Rabbati* 3.

320. Saadia Gaon, (cf. Ibn Ezra, 48:4), Ibn Caspi *Mitzraph Lakeseph*, *Aqedat Yitzchak*, Sforno, Malbim, *Ohr Hahaim*, 48:3-7, Luzzatto, 35:11, 48:7, and S. R. Hirsch, 48:7.

parashat Vayehi

right after the incident concerning Dinah in Shechem, as they are recounted in Parashat Vayishlah:

1) God commands Jacob in Shechem to ascend to Bethel and build and altar there, as a sign of thanksgiving for his having been saved from Esau and returning in peace as God has promised him twenty years earlier, when he first appeared to him in Bethel.

2) God appeared to Jacob in Bethel and blessed him: "I am El Shaddai. Be fertile and increase; a nation, yea an assembly of nations, shall descend from you. Kings shall issue from your loins. The land that I assigned to Abraham and Isaac I assign to you; And to your offspring to come Will I assign the land." (35:11-12)

3) Rachel died at the crossroads giving birth to Benjamin.

4) Reuben sleeps with Rachel's maidservant, Bilhah, who was Jacob's concubine, and Jacob becomes aware of it.

5) The Torah enumerates the twelve sons of Jacob, organized by their mothers.

The commentators attempt to find a connection between these events, and through this connection – the explanation for the words of Jacob here. This explanation rests on the interpretation which Jacob gave to the promises which he received from God: Seeing them as global promises – applying to the nation which will come from him, and also as personal promises for himself. In order to clarify the matter, I will review how the matters evolved through the five points outlined above.

As was mentioned, in the dream of the ladder in Luz, God gave Jacob the blessing of Abraham: Inheritance of the Land of Israel and abundance of progeny, through whom the nations will be blessed. Jacob also received a **personal** assurance, that God would protect him on his journey, and return him to his home in peace. The

parashat Vayehi

promise was fulfilled, Jacob returned to the Land of Israel, went up the Bethel, where (as mentioned in points 1-2 above) God appeared to him again, blessed him that he be fertile and numerous, and promised him the Land of Israel. Jacob interpreted this as both as a blessing for the distant future, and as a **personal** blessing for him, in the present. Jacob already had eleven sons and one daughter, and his beloved wife was pregnant with an additional son. Jacob hoped, based on this blessing, that Rachel would have more sons, such that they would be at least as numerous as the sons of Leah. Now Rachel died and his hopes were dashed. The suddenness of her death and burden of the children and livestock did not allow for a funeral procession to Hebron, and Jacob was forced to bury Rachel on the way. He therefore wondered about the personal aspect of the blessing of fertility, and attempted to actualize it in a way that Rachel herself had initiated earlier, namely, to father children by means of her maidservant, Bilhah. However, Reuben overtook him and slept with Bilhah – in order to prevent Jacob from becoming estranged from Leah and having children by means of Rachel's maidservant. At the conclusion of the unfolding of these events, the Torah finally affirms that the number of sons, twelve, is finalized, and it enumerates them by name. Jacob's hope had ostensibly vanished and the personal blessing, which he understood that he had received, remained incomprehensible and unfulfilled.

The meaning of the blessing only became clear to Jacob on his death bed, in his second encounter with Joseph. It is possible that his awareness of the assimilation of Joseph's sons into Egyptian culture pushed Jacob to ensure that they join the family and not settle in Egypt. But beyond this, it seems that suddenly, in a flash of inspiration, he understood the personal aspect of the blessing which he received in Luz. It is also possible that the two sons of Joseph suddenly appeared in his mind's eye in place of the two

parashat Vayehi

sons of Reuben whose father offered to kill – and thereby to forgo the double inheritance, which he anticipated receiving as firstborn – if he did not bring Benjamin back home (42:37). With that offer, Reuben essentially forfeited the birthright. Jacob therefore made two determinations: Joseph will be the head of the family, the chosen firstborn (in place of Reuben, the biological firstborn), and Joseph's two sons will be counted among Jacob's sons. Each will receive an inheritance in the Land of Israel, and their two portions will constitute Joseph's double portion, the portion of the firstborn. As such, the primogeniture was actualized by the grandsons of Rachel, rather than by the two sons of Reuben, the grandsons of Leah; and it was they who balanced out the portion of Rachel in the Land of Israel relative to that of Leah,[321] to a certain degree. Jacob, therefore, told Joseph the story from the beginning, starting with the personal blessing "I will make you fertile and numerous, making of you a community of peoples" (48:4). He then informed Joseph "Now, your two sons, who were born to you in the land of Egypt before I came to you in Egypt, shall be mine" (48:5), and as a rationale for this decision – a rationale which I just explained – he noted Rachel's dying in her prime.

Jacob, having impaired vision, suddenly noticed two silhouettes dressed like Egyptians. Perhaps he heard additional voices, besides those of Joseph's, in the background, and wanted to know "who are these?" (48:8).[322] It is possible that he thought that they were Joseph's bodyguards, but why then did Joseph bring them into his room? When Joseph clarified that they were Ephraim and

---

321. Compare H. Y. Chamiel, *Limudim BeFarashat HaShavua*, Miketz 2, 64-66.

322. Rashbam, Kimhi, Hizkuni, Sforno, 48:8, Ibn Ezra, 48:10. E. Samet suggests that the verses 8 to 21 are actually the continuation of 41:31 when Jacob first reunited with Joseph.

parashat Vayehi

Manasseh, he wanted to bring them closer to him in order to bless them. Once they came closer, he kissed and hugged them. He addressed Joseph and said to him, very emotionally, that before his descent to Egypt, he did not expect to ever see his face, and now he had the opportunity to see both him and his sons. Jacob gave the primogeniture to Ephraim in place of Manasseh who was the firstborn. Joseph placed them before him such that Manasseh would be standing to Jacob's right, but Jacob put his hands together at an angle, one on top of the other,[323] and placed his right hand on the head of Ephraim, the younger brother.[324] He transposed his hands to avoid changing where his grandsons stood; in order to avoid slighting Manasseh too much.[325] Joseph, who was surprised, tried to 'correct' the error and to move his father's right hand from Ephraim's head to Manasseh's head; but, Jacob explained to him that he prefers Ephraim. True, both of them will grow gloriously, but Ephraim will become greater than Manasseh. The Torah once again emphasizes that biological primogeniture is not the true primogeniture, certainly not in a Jewish home: That is how it was in the case of Cain and Abel, Isaac and Ishmael, Jacob and Esau, Reuben and Joseph, and so too in the case of Manasseh and Ephraim.[326] Indeed, in the course of history, the tribe of Ephraim was greater in number than the tribe of Manasseh, and it was he who represented the sons of Rachel in their struggle with Judah over the rule among the Jewish nation, when the kingdom of Ephraim was established by Jeroboam.

---

323. Rabenu Hananel (explained by Rabbenu Bahyha), Rashbam, Bekhor Shor, Hizkuni, 48:14.

324. Saadia Gaon, Ibn Ezra, and the second explanation of Hizkuni, 48:14.

325. The first explanation of Hizkuni, ad loc.

326. *Kli Yakar* and S. R. Hirsch, 48:19. S. R. Hirsch adds Shem, Moses and David to this topic. Cf. H. Y. Chamiel, *Limudim BeFarashat HaShavua*, 74.

parashat Vayehi

Jacob, whose hands were resting in this fashion on the heads of Ephraim and Manasseh, blessed Joseph (48:15):[327] "**The God** [*Elokim*] in whose ways my fathers, Abraham and Isaac, walked, **The God** who has been my shepherd from my birth to this day – The Angel who has redeemed me from all harm – bless the lads. In them may my name be recalled, and the names of my fathers, Abraham and Isaac, and may they be teeming multitudes upon the earth" (48:15-16).[328] This is not Abraham's blessing, which was given using the name **Lord [*Hashem*]** and **El Shaddai**.[329] Rather, it is the blessing of success, like the blessing which Isaac intended for Esau ("and may **God** [*Elokim*] give you" 27:28). Its purpose this time is the unification of the family and the nation and their proliferation. The blessing of Abraham – inheritance of the Land of Israel and proliferation of progeny – is shared by all of Jacob's descendants, and is not the subject of conflict between them. The blessing which Joseph received was a dual one: First, that his sons would fully join the family – that they will be called by the names of the patriarchs, Abraham, Isaac and Israel the Hebrews (i.e. that the two of them would be recognizable as the offspring of the patriarchs)--despite the youths' detachment and their assimilation into Egypt culture until now. Secondly, that they be fertile and numerous.[330] Afterwards, Jacob blessed the youths directly – here too placing Ephraim before Manasseh – and this blessing turned

---

327. Rashbam and Ibn Caspi, 48:15.

328. The blessing was addressed to Joseph ('and he blessed Joseph') rather than to the sons; which is why Jacob said "the lads" and "by means of them" as opposed to "you" and "by means of you".

329. Cf. the discussion on this in *parashat Vaera*.

330. Cf. *Haketav Vehaqabbala*, 48:16, Yaakov Yehiel Weinberg, *Lifrakim*, (Jerusalem, 2002), 465, Samuel Huminer, *Sefer Eved Melekh*, Nosson Scherman, *Humash Artscroll*, 48:20, *Sefat Emet Vayehi*, 1901, The weekly *Parasha* sheet of Bar Ilan, 893, *Vayehi*, 2010, Benny Lau, *Etnahta*, 127-130.

them into role models: "By you shall Israel invoke blessings, saying: **God** make you like Ephraim and Manasseh" (48:20). This maxim became a standard formula, by which fathers bless their sons in many communities among the Jewish people.[331] In that very blessing, which Jacob used to unify his family, the hope can be heard that the sons follow in the path of their fathers, and that the parents will not be alienated from the son or daughter, even if they distance themselves. This blessing became part of the recitation of the Shema said when going to bed.

After this blessing, Jacob addressed Joseph, emphasizing to him the aspiration for the family's return to the Land of Israel: "I am about to die; but God will be with you and bring you back to the land of your fathers" (48:21). Jacob promised Joseph – because of his primogeniture – an additional portion in the Land of Israel, which will be conquered by his descendants by force of the sword and the bow.[332]

Jacob's Blessing to his Sons – Integration of Abilities

Jacob called all of his sons together for a final meeting before his death, in which he told them about the nature of the tribe which will arise from the progeny of each of them; and, therefore, about the portion each tribe would have in the building of the nation, along with the conquest of the Land of Israel, its division and its

---

331. Rashi, Rashbam, Kimhi, Nahmanides, 48:20.

332. Rashbam, Kimhi, Ibn Ezra, Nahmanides, Hizkuni, Luzzatto, 48:22. Bible criticism attributes this verse to ancient heroic myths preserved as fragments in a variety of locations in the Bible. Cf. A. Rofe, *Mavo Lesifrut Hamiqra,* 113, *Olam Hatanakh,* Genesis, 246. The general approach of Bible critics is that two traditions are contained within *Parashat Vayehi.* Joseph and Shechem are at the center of the more ancient tradition, and the later tradition is priestly, with all of the tribes, and Hebron, at the center. Cf. *Olam Hatanakh,* Genesis, 244.

parashat Vayehi

settlement.³³³ It was clear that none of the sons of Jacob would be disinherited from the blessing of Abraham, and that all of them would participate and contribute their abilities in order to strengthen and unify the collective; but he had to clarify who the leadership would be given to. Reuben is the symbol of initial boldness and good intentions, who bursts forth without calculation or discretion, a characteristic which was detrimental for him. Jacob does not have a blessing for Simeon and Levi, only anger and curses. Scattering them among the tribes will protect against invalid zealotry, which they demonstrated in the incident concerning Dinah,³³⁴ enabling intelligent and moderate use of zealotry and the existence of appropriate Jewish pride.³³⁵ Judah, strong and beloved by his brothers and their spokesman, one who takes responsibility both for the family and for himself – in correcting his mistakes – is destined for kingship and political power, and is compared to a lion, the king of the beasts, who rises above his prey. Zebulun is the merchant mariner, whose ships rule the sea. Issachar is the farmer. Dan – who is compared to a serpent – and Gad, are the daring and sophisticated warriors.³³⁶ Asher is the wealthy owner of property. Naphtali – who is compared to a swift hind – is the Torah scholar,

---

333. Ibn Caspi, *Mitzraph Lakeseph,* 49:8, Luzzatto, 49:1.

334. The commentators disagree regarding the meaning of Jacob's words, *"ubirtzonam iqru shor"*, 49:6. Rashi, following the *Targum Yerushalmi* suggests that it is referring to the sale of Joseph, who was referred to by Moses as *"bekhor Shoro"*, Deut. 33:17. However, Ibn Ezra, Kimhi, Bekhor Shor, Nahmanides, Hizkuni, Luzzatto, and S. R. Hirsch disagreed. They associated the statement with the walls of Shechem, which were destroyed by Simeon and Levi, or to its oxen which were hamstrung by them; or perhaps to the inhabitants of Shechem, who were circumcised at the demand of the brothers. This argument seems to be connected to the question of whether or not Jacob knew of the brothers' plot against Joseph. Cf. above nt. 305.

335. *Aqedat Yitzchak* and S. R. Hirsch, 49:7.

336. Rashbam, 49:18.

parashat Vayehi

whose speech is pleasant. Joseph, who was saved from all those seeking to harm him and who will be fertile and numerous, is the head of the family. He guards its unity, protects and supports; yet he cannot be king as he has not attained his brothers' approval. Benjamin – who is compared to a wolf – is the brave warrior who devours his enemies and divides his spoil with peers. The Bible teaches us about the importance of diversity of abilities and talents, working together toward a common goal: "All these were the tribes of Israel, twelve in number" (49:28). All of the qualities, talents and endeavors are equally important: The farmers, merchants, soldiers and officers are equal in stature to the scientists, intellectuals and Torah scholars. We learn from here about the value of unity and the value of each individual and of the group within this unity.[337] The Torah considers lording over another, exploiting him and denigrating him and his unique value, to be invalid. Even so every group of people requires leadership.[338] As was mentioned, Judah was appointed to lead the nation which would emerge from the sons of Jacob[339] and Joseph led the family for the time being. In the beginning of the discussion of Parashat Vayeshev, I discussed the consequences of the division of leadership between the 'household of Joseph' and that of 'the household of Judah'. When Jacob completed his blessing to his sons, he commanded them to bury him in the cave of the field of Machpelah, with his ancestors and with Leah, the mother of his older children. He then arranged himself on his bed and died. Joseph cried and kissed his dead father, and instructed the Egyptian physicians to embalm his father's body.

---

337. S. R. Hirsch, 48: 3-6.
338. Bekhor Shor, 49:4-7.
339. Bekhor Shor and S. R. Hirsch, 49:26. Regarding Jacob's blessings as bestowing the monarchy upon Judah, cf. Abravanel, ad loc.

parashat Vayehi

After Jacob's Death

At the conclusion of the seventy days of formal mourning which had been declared, including forty days of embalmment, while still in a state of mourning, Joseph transmitted Jacob's request that he be buried in Canaan to Pharaoh: "I am about to die. Be sure to bury me in the grave which I made ready for myself in the land of Canaan." (50:5) When Joseph addressed Pharaoh, he omitted Jacob's obvious unwillingness to be buried in Egypt, and emphasized his father's desire to be buried in the familial grave which had been prepared for him. Pharaoh understood this, as this was also customary for the Egyptian aristocracy.[340] He therefore authorized carrying out the command, and instructed that the body be brought for burial in Canaan by royal convoy, with an entourage, led by Joseph, which consisted of Pharaoh's slaves, Egyptian elders and officials, and all of Jacob's offspring. When they reached the southern border of Canaan, they conducted a large funeral for Jacob, and an additional formal mourning period of seven days. Afterwards, the funeral procession continued on to Hebron, carrying the deceased on his sons' shoulders, and they buried him in the familial grave which is in the cave.

When they returned to Egypt, it became clear that the brothers still did not trust Joseph. They were afraid that now that Jacob died, there is nothing to stop him from taking revenge on them. Their concern flowed from the fact that Joseph had never reproached them for their actions. Essentially, he had never clarified the matter of their plotting against him, and never 'closed the case'. They thought that his account against them remained open. They therefore fabricated an additional will of Jacob's, sending its contents to Joseph by means of messengers. According to what they claimed, Jacob found out before he died about their plotting against him,

---
340. N. Leibowitz, 530-532

parashat Vayehi

and he commanded Joseph to forgive his brothers' crime. Joseph discovered that his final goal had not been achieved. He wanted to prove to his brothers that his motives in putting them through the trials which he did were pure, but he failed to do so. He burst out crying, this time out of great disappointment and pain. He viewed this as a personal tragedy. The brothers, who heard of his reaction, came to him in person, fell to their knees before him, and declared that they were willing to be his slaves if he would forgive them. Joseph replied that he was well aware of the evil thoughts which they had concerning him, which led to their plotting against him, and he is not hiding it. However, only God can judge people for their thoughts. As far as he is concerned, God's will was expressed in the consequences of their actions: the survival of the family and its prosperity during the years of the famine (and perhaps he was also referring to the following stage in the divine plan: The family and nation spending four hundred years in Egypt): "Have no fear! Am I a substitute for God? Besides, although you intended me harm, God intended it for good, so as to bring about the present result—the survival of many people. And so, fear not. I will sustain you and your children. Thus he reassured them, speaking kindly to them." (50:19-21)[341]

Joseph fulfilled his promise and supported his extended family and even merited seeing grandchildren and great-grandchildren. Before his death, he transmitted to his brothers the lesson which he received from his father (48:21) and commanded them: "God will surely take notice of you and bring you up from this land to the land that He promised on oath to Abraham, to Isaac, and to Jacob" (50:24). They must not forget the Land of Israel. The promise made at the 'covenant of the pieces' will ultimately be kept, and then –

---

341. Rashi, 50: 16, 19, Luzzatto, 50: 17-19, according to *Bereshit Rabbah* 100:9, *Tanhuma Vayehi* 17, BT Yevamot 65b. Cf. also N. Leibowitz, ..568

parashat Vayehi

so Joseph made them swear – they are to bring his bones up to the Land of Israel. Joseph knew that his brothers would not be able to convince Pharaoh to allow his burial in Canaan. After his death at the age of 110, they embalmed his body and he was buried in Egypt, in a coffin, which could be taken with those leaving Egypt when the day arrived.[342]

---

342. Rashbam, Bekhor Shor, Hizkuni, Luzzatto, 50:26.

List of Commentators

Bible. *The English version of Biblical verses utilized the NJPS translation*

Abraham Ibn Ezra. *Peirush al Hatorah* (on Exodus- long and short versions). Torat Haim, Jerusalem, 1986-1993.

Abravanel, Isaac. *Peirush al Hatorah*. Warsaw, 1862; Jerusalem, 1960.

Abudraham, David. *Abudraham Hashalem*. Kroiser edition, Jerusalem, 1959.

Albo, Joseph. *Sefer Ikkarim*. Tel Aviv, 1951.

Alshikh, Moshe. *Torat Moshe*. (Commentary on the Torah). Warsaw, 1879.

Alter, Yehuda Aryeh Leib. *Sefat Emet*. Piotrkow, 1905.

Arama, Isaac. *Aqedat Yitzchak*. (Commentary on the Torah). Lwow, 1868.

Avot D'Rabbi Natan, Mishnayot, Shneur Zalman Schachter edition. Vienna, 1887.

Abraham ben HaRambam. *Peirush al Bereshit veShemot*. Sasson edition, London, 1958.

Babylonian Talmud, Vilna edition, 1880-1887.

Bahya ben Asher Ibn Halawa, *Peirush al Hatorah*. Ed. H. D. Chavel. Jerusalem, 1966-1968.

Bahya Ibn Pakudah. *Hovot Halevavot*. Warsaw, 1875.

Bar Shaul, Elimelekh, *Min Habe'er*. Tel Aviv, 1965.

Ben Nun, Yoel. *Megadim* 1 (1986), *Megadim* 13 (1991), *Teshura LeAmos,* 2007.

Berlin, Naphtali Zvi Yehuda (The Netziv). *Haamek Davar*, *Harhev Davar,* (Commentary on the Torah). Jerusalem, 1931.

List of Commentators

Breuer, Mordecai. *Pirkei Moadot*. Jerusalem, 1986.

Buber, Martin and Rozenzweig, Franz. German translation of the Torah, Berlin, 1925-1927.

Buber, Martin. *Darko Shel Miqra*, Jerusalem, 1978.

Buber, Martin. *Moses*, Jerusalem 1988.

Cassuto, Moshe David. *Peirush Al Sefer Shemot*, Jerusalem, 1952.

Cassuto, Moshe David. *MeAdam ad Noah*, Jerusalem, 1953.

Cassuto, Moshe David. *MeNoah ad Avraham*, Jerusalem, 1959.

Cassuto, Moshe David. *Sefer Bereshit Umivnehu*, Jerusalem, 1990.

Cassuto, Moshe David. *The Documentary Hypothesis and the Order of the Pentateuch,* Jerusalem, 1959.

Chamiel, Haim Yitzchak. *Limudim BeFarashat HaShavua*. Jerusalem, 2010.

Chamiel, Haim Yitzchak. *Maaynei Miqra Miqraei Kodesh*. Jerusalem, 1992.

Chamiel, Haim Yitzchak. *Maaynei Miqra*. Jerusalem, 1983.

Cohen, Hermann. *Dat Hatevunah Mimekorot Hayahadut*. trans. Zvi Wislevsky, Jerusalem, 1972.

Crescas, Hesdai. *Ohr Hashem*. Jerusalem, 1984.

Daat Miqra series. Yehuda Keel: *Bereshit*; Amos Hakham: *Shemot*; Menahem Bula: *Vayikra*; Yehiel Zvi Moshkovitz: *Bamidbar*; Aaron Mirsky: *Devarim*, Jerusalem, 1984-1997.

Ditrani, Isaiah. *Nimukei Humash*. ed. H.D. Chavel. Jerusalem, 2003.

Dubnow, Jacob. (The Maggid), Yaakov Kranz, Ohel Yaakov, Jerusalem, 1989.

Ehrlich, Arnold. *Miqra Kipeshuto*. Berlin, 1899.

Eilenburg, Issachar Ber. *Tzeida Laderekh*. (A Commentary on Rashi). Bnei Brak, 1998.

Epstein, Baruch. *Torah Temimah: Peirush al Derashot Hazal al Hatorah*. Vilna, 1904.

List of Commentators

Epstein, Baruch. *Tosefet Beracha al Hatorah*. Pinsk, 1937.

Flavius, Josephus. *Antiquities of the Jews,* Philadelphia 1854.

Goodman, Micah. *Maimonides and the Book That Changed Judaism: Secrets of "The Guide for the Perplexed"* Philadelphia, 2015. *Sodotav shel Moreh Hanevukhim,* Or Yehuda, 2009.

Haim Ibn Atar. Ohr Hahaim. (Commentary on the Torah). Zolkiev, 1799.

Halbertal, Moshe, *Mahapekhot Parshaniot Behithavutan,* Jerusalem, 1997.

Halbertal, Moshe, *Maimonides: Life and Thought,* Joel Linsider translator, Princeton and Woodstock, 2007.

Heschel, Abraham Joshua. *Heavenly Torah: As Refracted Through the Generations,* N.Y. and London, 2005. Torah min Hashamayim Beaspaklarya shel Hayahadut, London and N.Y., 1962-1965.

Heschel, Abraham Joshua. The Sabbath, N.Y. 1951, 1975, 1999. HaShabbat, A. Even Hen, Translator, Tel aviv, 2004.

Hirsch, Samson Raphael, *The Collected Writings*, vol. I-VIII, I. Grunfeld, J. Miller et al., translators. New York, 1997.

Hirsch, Samson Raphael, *The Hirsch Humash*, translated by Daniel Haberman. New York, 2002. 5 vols.

Hizkiya ben Manoah. *Hizkuni*. (Commentary on the Torah). Torat Haim, Jerusalem, 1986.

Hoffmann, David Zvi. *Sefer Bereshit* (Commentary on Genesis). trans. by Asher Wasserteil, Tel Aviv, 1969-1971.

Hoffmann, David Zvi. *Sefer Vayikra*. (Commentary on Leviticus). trans. by Zvi Har Sheffer and Aaron Lieberman, Jerusalem, 1853-1854.

Isserles, Moses (Rama). *Torat Haolah*. Prague, 1570.

Jacob ben Harosh (Rabbeinu Asher), *Baal Haturim*, Warsaw, 1885.

Jacob ben Harosh (Rabbeinu Asher). *Hatur Haarokh* (Commentary on the Torah). Jerusalem, 1861.

List of Commentators

Jacob, Benno. *Das erste Buch der Tora, Genesis. Übersetzt und erklärt von Benno Jacob* (Commentary on the Book of Genesis), Berlin, 1934; (Commentary on the Book of Exodus), Stuttgart, 1997.

Jonah Ibn Janah. *Sefer Hashorashim*, Berlin, 1896.

Joseph Bekhor Shor, (Rivash). *Peirush al Hatorah*. Yehoshaphat Nevo edition, Jerusalem, 2001.

Joseph Ibn Caspi, *Mitzraph Lakeseph al Hatorah*. Pressburg, 1905.

Joseph Ibn Caspi, *Tirat Keseph al Hatorah*. Pressburg, 1905.

Joseph Ibn Caspi. *Gevia Kesef*, ed. Basil Herring. New York, 1982.

Judah Halevi. *Sefer Kuzari*. Tel Aviv, 1973.

Judah Loew ben Bezalel (Maharal). *Gur Aryeh*. Warsaw 1862.

Judah Loew ben Bezalel (Maharal). *Tiferet Yisrael*. Hartman edition. Jerusalem, 2000.

Kagan, Yisrael Meir. (Hafetz Haim). *Hafetz Haim al Hatorah*. New York, 1943.

Kaufman, Yehezkel. *Mikivshonah shel Hayetzira Hamiqrait*. Tel Aviv, 1966.

Kaufman, Yehezkel. *Toldot Haemunah Hayisraelit*. vol. I. Tel Aviv, 1937.

Kimhi, David, (Radak). *Peirsuh al Hatorah*. Torat Haim, Jerusalem, 1986-1993.

Knohl, Yisrael. *Hashem*. Ohr Yehuda, 2012.

Knohl, Yisrael. *Meayin Banu*. Ohr Yehuda, 2008.

Kook, Avraham Yitzchak. *Eder Hayakar*. Beit El, 1993.

Kook, Avraham Yitzchak. *Ein Aya*. Jerusalem, 1995.

Kook, Avraham Yitzchak. *Hamisped BeYerushalayim*. Jerusalem, 1987.

Kook, Avraham Yitzchak. *Orot Hakodesh*. Jerusalem, 1985-1990.

Kook, Avraham Yitzchak. *Shabbat Haaretz*. Jerusalem, 1993.

Kook, Avraham Yitzchak. *Talelei Orot*. Har Brakha, 2011.

Lau, Binyamin. Etnachta. Tel Aviv, 2009.

List of Commentators

Leibowitz, Nechama. *Studies in the Books of the Pentateuch*, Jerusalem, 1972-1982.

Leibowitz, Yeshayahu. *Hearot Leparashiyot Hashavua*, Jerusalem, 1988.

Leibowitz, Yeshayahu. *Sheva Shanim shel Sihot al Parashat Hashavua*. Jerusalem, 2000.

Leibowitz, Yeshayahu. *Yahadut, Am Yehudi UMedinat Yisrael*. Tel Aviv, 1975.

Levi ben Gershom (Gersonides). *Milhamot Hashem*. Jerusalem, 1977.

Levi ben Gershom (Gersonides). *Peirsuh al Hatorah*. Jerusalem, 1993.

Luzzatto, Samuel David. "Torah Nidreshet," in *Mehqerei Hayahadut*, vol. 1, pt. 1, 49-109, first printed in *Kokhvei Yitzchak* 16-26 (5612-5621) [1852-1861].

Luzzatto, Samuel David. *Hamishtadel, al Hatorah,* Vienna, 1847.

Luzzatto, Samuel David. *Peirush 'Al Hamisha Humshei Torah*. Padua, 1871-1876; Tel Aviv, 1966; Jerusalem 2015.

Luzzatto, Samuel David. *Yesodei Hatorah* in *Al Hahemla Vehahashgakha*. Yonathan Bashy edition, Tel Aviv, 2008.

Maimonides, *Guide to the Perplexed*.

Maimonides, *Sefer Hamitzvot im Hassagot Haramban*. H. D. Chavel edition, Jerusalem, 1981.

Maimonides. *Sefer Mishneh Torah HaYad HaHazakah*. Mofet Yohai Makbili edition, Haifa, 2003.

Meir Leibush ben Yehiel (Malbim). *Hatorah Vehamitzvah*. Commentary on Genesis, Warsaw, 1876. Exodus Commentary on the *Mekhilta*, Vilna, 1913. Leviticus Commentary on *Torat Kohanim* (Sifra), Bucharest, 1860. Numbers Commentary on *Midrash Sifrei*, Vilna, 1913. Deuteronomy Commentary on *Midrash Sifrei*, Vilna, 1911.

List of Commentators

Meir Simha HaCohen of Dvinsk. *Meshekh Hokhma* (Commentary on the Torah). Riga, 1927.

Mecklenburg, Yaakov Zvi. *Haketav Vehaqabbala* (Commentary on the Torah). Kingsburg, 1837.

Mekhilta D'Rabbi Ishmael (Midrash on the Book of Exodus). Vilna, 1870.

Menahem ben Saruq. *Mahberet Menahem*. Jerusalem, 1987.

Mendelsohn, Moses (ed.) *Habeur: Netivot Hashalom* (Commentary on the Torah) Genesis: Shlomo Dubna; Exodus: Moses Mendelsohn; Leviticus: Naphtali Hertz Wessely; Numbers: Aaron Yaroslav; Deuteronomy: Naphtali Hertz Homburg. Berlin, 1780-1783.

Metzudat Zion, (Commentary on the Prophets and Writings). Miqraot Gedolot.

Midrash Hagadol. ed. David H'adani. Berlin, 1914.

Midrash Rabbah. Constantinople, 1412; Venice, 1567; New York, 1960.

Midrash Tehilim, (Shoher Tov). Vilna, 1891; Jerusalem, 2012.

Milonshitz, Shlomo Ephraim ben Aharon. *Kli Yakar*. (Commentary on the Torah). Lublin, 1602.

Mishna. Kahati Edition. Tel Aviv, 1966-1967.

Nachshoni, Yehuda. *Studies in the Weekly Parashah*, S. Himelstein, Translator, Jerusalem, Exodos 1988, Levitikus, 1989.

Mizrahi, Elijah. *Re'em*. (Commentary on Rashi). Philip edition. Petah Tikvah, 1992.

Nahmanides, *Torat Hashem Temimah, Drasha, Kitvei Haramban*, H. D. Chavel edition, Jerusalem, 1963-1964.

Nahmanides. *Peirush al Hatorah*. Torat Haim, Jerusalem, 1986-1993.

Nissim of Gerona (Ran). Feldman edition. Jerusalem, 1977.

Olam Hatanakh. (Commentary on the Pentateuch) ed. by Menahem Haran et al., Tel Aviv, 1993-1994.

List of Commentators

Onkelos. (Aramaic Translation of the Torah). Torat Haim, Jerusalem, 1986-1993.

Palestinian Talmud, Berlin, 1929.

Pesikta D'Rav Kahanah. (Midrash). Buber edition, Lick, 1868; New York, 1959.

Pesikta Rabbati (Midrash). Vienna, 1880.

Philo, *The Complete Writings.*

Pirkei D'Rabbi Eliezer (Midrash),Venice, 1544.

Reggio, Yitzchak Samuel. Sefer Torat Elohim. Vienna, 1821.

Rofe, Alexander. *Mavo Lesifrut Hamiqra.* Jerusalem, 2006.

Rofe, Eliezer Ashkenazi. *Maasei Hashem.* Warsaw, 1871-1933.

Rosenzweig, Franz. *Naharaim.* Jerusalem, 1978.

Saadia Gaon, *Tafsir.* (Arabic Translation of the Torah). Direnburg edition, Paris 1893; Hebrew translation by Yosef Kapah in Torat Haim, Jerusalem, 1986-1993.

Samet, Elhanan. *Iyunim BeFarshat HaShavua.* Jerusalem, 2008.

Sefer Hahinukh. (A Commentary on the 613 Mitzvot). H. D. Chavel edition, Jerusalem, 1952.

Sefer HaZohar. Reuven Margaliot edition, Jerusalem, 1984.

Segal, Moshe Zvi. *Mavo Hamiqra.* Jerusalem, 1946-1950.

Sforno, Obadiah ben Jacob. *Peirush al Hatorah.* Torat Haim, Jerusalem, 1986-1993.

Shapira, Yehuda Leib. *Harekhasim L'biqah*, , Altuna, 1915.

Shlomo ben Aderet. (Rashba). *She'elot Uteshuvot.* (Responsa). Bnei Brak, 1958-1971; Jerusalem, 1960.

Shlomo Yitzchaki (Rashi). *Peirush al Hatorah.* Torat Haim, Jerusalem, 1986-1993.

Shmuel ben Meir. (Rashbam). *Peirush al Hatorah.* Torat Haim, Jerusalem, 1986-1993.

Sifra (Torat Kohanim). (Midrash on Leviticus).

Sifrei (Midrash on Deuteronomy).

List of Commentators

Sifrei (Midrash on Numbers).

Simon, Uriel. *Bakesh Shalom Verodfehu*. Tel Aviv, 2002.

Sofer, Moshe (Hatam Sofer). *Torat Moshe* (Commentary on the Torah). Pressburg, 1879-1893.

Sofer, Simha Bunim. *Shaarei Simha*. Vienna, 1923.

Soloveitchik, Joseph B. *Halakhic Man*, Lawrence Kaplan Translator, Philadelphia, 1983.

Soloveitchik, Joseph B. *Kol Dodi Dofek: Listen, My Beloved Knocks*, N. Y. 2006.

Soloveitchik, Joseph B. *The Rav Speaks: Five Addresses on Israel History and the Jewish People*. Jerusalem 1967.

Soloveitchik, Joseph B. *Divrei Hagut Vehaarakha*, Jerusalem, 1981.

Soloveitchik, Joseph B. *Lonely Man of Faith*, Tradition, N.Y. 1965.

Soloveitchik, Joseph Dov. *Beit Halevi*. Vilna, 1911.

Sorotzkin, Zalman. *Oznayim LaTorah*. Jerusalem, 1957.

Tabory, Joseph. *Moadei Yisrael Bitkufat Hamishna V'Hatalmud*. Jerusalem, 2000.

Tanhuma. (Midrash on the Torah). Buber edition. New York, 1946.

Tanhuma. (Midrash on the Torah). Vilna, 1913.

Tanna D'Vei Eliyahu, Seder Eliyahu Zuta (Midrash). Warsaw, 1912.

Targum Pseudo-Jonathan (The Jerusalem translation of the Torah into Aramaic; mistakenly attributed to Johnathan ben Uziel). Ginzburger edition, Berlin, 1903.

Tedeski-Ashkenazi, Moshe Yitzchak. *Hoil Moshe*. Levorno, 1870.

Tishbi, Yeshayahu. *Mishnat HaZohar*. vol.1, 1949; vol.2, 1975.

Tosefta. Zuckermandel edition, Jerusalem, 1963.

Yalkut Shimoni. (Collected Midrashim on the Torah). Ed. Shimon Ashkenazi, Salonika, 1527.

parashat XXX

parashat XXX

parashat XXX

parashat XXX

Made in the USA
Monee, IL
23 July 2021